Perspectives on James's
The Portrait of A Lady

Other books edited by William T. Stafford:
Melville's Billy Budd and The Critics
James's Daisy Miller: The Story, The Play,
   The Critics
Twentieth Century American Writing

PERSPECTIVES ON JAMES'S
The Portrait of a Lady

A COLLECTION OF CRITICAL ESSAYS

EDITED WITH AN INTRODUCTION BY
William T. Stafford

New York • NEW YORK UNIVERSITY PRESS
London • UNIVERSITY OF LONDON PRESS LIMITED
1967

ACKNOWLEDGMENTS

MY APPRECIATION goes to those many authors and publishers who have permitted me to reprint their copyright works in this volume. The details of that acknowledgment appear on the first page of each essay used. It is also a pleasure to express my appreciation to Professor Oscar Cargill of New York University for first persuading me to compile this volume; to my colleagues in the English Department at Purdue University for various and numerous kindnesses; and to the Purdue Research Foundation for an XL Grant during July of 1965.

For Fran

For Ruth

The Portrait of a Lady, like all great novels, is ultimately impervious to criticism—even as it continuously invites it. Henry James's portrait of Isabel Archer *is* a great novel—by all of the "outward" standards we customarily use to designate great works of fiction as well as, I am convinced, by most "inward," that is, intrinsic, ones. The essays collected in this volume are eloquent testimony to both criteria. From the author himself, from the early reviewers of the novel, and from the literary historians and critics who have given it their attention unfolds this history of how one great example of the nineteenth-century creative imagination became a part of the literary consciousness of the Western world. From a conception that was operative even if changing while the novel was first being written (as recorded in James's own *Notebook* entries in late 1880 or early 1881) to whatever "place" it currently holds—in whatever current literary consciousness actually is—*The Portrait of a Lady* has been and is a viable literary fact.

It represents by intention, for example, a major effort on the part of a major novelist whose credentials have been satisfactorily established for a sufficient length of time. Enough generations have recognized and accepted this seriousness of intent to dispel effectively possible charges of mere topical vagaries of taste. Its appeal has been to general readers and critics alike for almost a century. Literary historians in both England and America have, without exception, awarded it a prominent position in the canon of its author. It is widely taught in schools, colleges, and universities for a variety of pedagogical purposes.¹ It has been translated into most modern European languages, transformed into a Braille edition, and read onto records for the blind.² In short, it is difficult to imagine any outward standard of literary excellence the novel has not met.

Its inward standards are another matter. Although it is easy enough simply to say that *The Portrait of a Lady* is a great novel because the mind that created it was a great mind, to do so is not enough. "That the deepest quality of a work of art will always be the quality of the mind that produced it" is what James himself, in another connection, called "a very obvious truth." It is a truth we should not forget, nonetheless, for the achievement of this particular novel is inextricably combined with the "quality" of James's mind. And the definable nature of that quality is of course precisely what the essays in this volume are all about.

The language, the characterization, the setting, the plot, and the form of this novel, as they do with any, collectively constitute its vision. And the best critics of James have been inevitably concerned with the ways parts of the novel define the whole. Just as inevitably, moreover, the best of these critics have also been concerned with the nature of the whole, that complex total vision which, for better or worse, is everything the novel finally is. These concerns, properly, I suppose, are the concerns of all critics for all important novels. But for the fiction of Henry James in general and for *The Portrait of a Lady* in particular there are additional critical problems, additional critical opportunities.

We do not have available for every novel, as we do for this one, for example, the author's own comment both before and after the fact in respectively James's *Notebooks* and his Prefaces. To be able to compare and contrast what a novelist apparently *intended* while writing the novel to what he himself viewed as its achievements and failures some two and a half decades later is a rare critical opportunity in itself. Nor do we often have the critical opportunity, as again we do have with this novel, of studying the revisions an author would make under that rare set of circumstances that would allow him (as the New York Edition did allow James) to rewrite a major novel some twenty-five years after its first publication.

The Portrait of a Lady is a special case in still other ways also. Much ink has been expended, for example, on the autobiographical element in the novel—especially as it relates to the part played by James's young cousin, Mary (Minny) Temple, to the conception of his "lady," Isabel Archer. Critics have also indulged in speculation about the relationship between James himself and his passive young protagonist, Ralph Touchett, or Gilbert Osmond and his relation to known acquaintances of James; but it is Isabel herself who most often has engaged the attention of the critic even as she has, of course, that of the general reader. Literary sources (in James's own earlier fiction as well as elsewhere) have been mined as thoroughly as autobiographical ones even when it was recognized that James's portrait of Isabel Archer was a unique one and that *his* canvas of her was ultimately the only source that mattered.

Yet, the proper gallery for that canvas is a relevant issue too. Leon Edel would place it in one that also contains "Anna Karenina . . . and . . . Emma Bovary and Becky Sharp, Camille and Nana and Elizabeth Bennet and Jane Eyre." And not far away, he continues, we might also find the portrait of another American woman "whom she [Isabel] in no way resembled"—that of Hester Prynne.[3] In so saying, Professor Edel suggests still another area that has much exercised the critics of this novel: its unique role in a national literature that had been spectacularly unable or unwilling, with the possible splendid exception of Hawthorne's great example, to create, before James, a believable American woman.

Literary historians who are also good critics have not found this problem easy to meet. The role of Isabel Archer in a developing conception, say, between Daisy Miller and Milly Theale *within* the James canon has a certain plausible intelligibility. The place, however, of the James canon itself—to which every important critic I know gives a prominent and often crucial position to *The Portrait of a Lady*—is perhaps still not satisfactorily answered. Yet this problem is never more often confronted than when this novel is under examination. Even to the partisan admirers of respectively the work of the early, middle, or late James, *The Portrait of a Lady* is likely to be seen as crucial: it is likely to be seen, for example, as some kind of prime fulfillment to admirers of the early years; as some kind of rich beginning to admirers of the middle years; or as some kind of sterling exception to admirers of the late years. It is, in short, of all of James's fiction, the one novel among the many that to most seems somehow to capture some of the best of all the rest.

These, then, are some of the problems—some of the opportunities—*The Portrait of a Lady* has presented to critics and literary historians who would go "outside" the novel—to the *Notebook* entries and Preface, to James's other work, to his life itself and those whom he knew, to its sources in the works of others, and to its place in the Anglo-American literary tradition out of which it came and of which it is still so viable a part. It is, on the other hand, meaningless to go down these outward paths until the reader has explored all of the wonders "within." *The Portrait of a Lady*, after all, is a thing in itself, a single work of fiction that ultimately constitutes its own excuse for being. And without wondrous wonders indeed *within* the novel, there would of course be no reason ever to go out at all.

The major wonder of *The Portrait of a Lady*, almost all critics agree, is the portrait itself—Isabel Archer. Always talented with titles, James was never happier than with this, for it precisely describes his method even as it presents his subject. Whatever else this novel is, it is first and foremost a picture— a picture, moreover, composed before our eyes and minds by the novel itself and completed only with the last period of the last sentence of the last page.

Everything of consequence in the novel *is* of consequence only as it relates to the total picture of Isabel. The settings in America (in Albany), in England (in Gardencourt), and in various locales in Italy are *in themselves* colorings whose hues are used to shadow or lighten our final look at the portrait before us. The same is true of the characters who surround our "subject." The suitors who woo Isabel are as much of their time and place, their setting, as they are lines of action shifting

our perspective of the figure always before us. Caspar Goodwood from America, Lord Warburton and Ralph Touchett
from England, and, of course, Gilbert Osmond from Italy are
never as important in themselves as they are as means defining
still more finely our sense of whatever we come to see Isabel to
be. And they too, like Isabel, are as much a part of where they
are most strongly tied—be it America, England, or Italy—as
they are by virtue of what they do or how they act. The major
women in the book, like Isabel's suitors, are always more as
lines to Isabel than they are as things in themselves, however
magnificently varied and intricate their own "lines" are. (Henrietta Stackpole and Serena Merle, for example, even when
distinctly seen as their unmistakably individual selves, are as
nothing in themselves in contrast to the ways they relate to
Isabel.) And they too "compose" her portrait—and with the
same tripartite balance we have already seen in setting and in
suitors. That is to say, they also "group": Henrietta, with
Caspar and America; Mrs. Touchett, with Ralph and Lord
Warburton and with England; Serena Merle, with Osmond
and with Italy. And that balance has still more intricate lines,
on the one end, as an extension of Osmond, through Pansy,
the Countess Gemini, and Ned Rosier; on the other, as an extension of Ralph, through his father and mother. Lord Warburton and Serena Merle are counterpointed against both ends
and serve the movement within even as they define the limits
without. But what they all serve and define—in the intricate
balance of these lines, these hues, these groups—is the central
figure herself, Isabel Archer.

Critics of the novel, often taking their cues from James's
own comments to himself, have most often questioned the
compositional effect as it relates to two particular parts. The
far more widely discussed one has been on the extent to which
the portrait by the end is indeed complete. James himself fore-
saw the criticism even as he rejected it. "The *whole* of anything," he wrote, "is never told; you can only take what groups
together." Readers have had sharply differing views about the
matter, and the issue continues to be hotly contested, as the
essays on the novel amply demonstrate. Perhaps not often
enough, however, is the question asked in terms of the com-

positional order of the narrative itself—the extent, that is, to which actions of others can continue to light for us what Isabel is. Is there, in short, more about her that we need to know? The other question is one of proportion, the possible "too great diffuseness," as James himself called it, of the earlier parts of the novel in contrast to the "crowded" action of the last. Critics have also often debated this issue, rarely, however, taking into account James's attendant remark that it was "a good defect" or specifying what particular "lights" are superfluous in the earlier parts or what "actions" need elongation or slower pacing in the latter.

All of this is *not* to suggest that critical attention to the over-all method of the novel has been in any way lacking. From Joseph Warren Beach's pioneering study of the novel (in *The Method of Henry James* in 1818) through Sister Corona Sharp's detailed examination of the function of Henrietta Stackpole and Madame Merle (in *The Confidante in Henry James* in 1963), critic after crtic has examined and re-examined the variety of ways that in whole and in part James reveals to the reader his total picture. It *is* to suggest, on the other hand, a possible deficiency of attention to the evaluative responsibility of the critic in terms demonstrably close to the original compositional "vision" of the author himself.

But what of Isabel Archer? One *might* have read into some of what has just been written an implication about James's central figure as some passive object without movement or life of her own, an object in existence only as she reflects the lights and responds to the actions of those around her. The very opposite, of course, is true, for Isabel is both the light and the life of this novel. If setting and character illuminate our developing awareness of all that she is, she more centrally illuminates our understanding of them, and a great deal more besides. If she is colored, and she is, by her American heritage, her move to England, her flights to and in Italy, they in turn are lighted by her. Isabel Archer affects all that her radiance reaches. And it has only to reach, to provoke.

In America, in the dimly lit study of her Albany home, Mrs. Touchett has only to see her to take her to Europe. In England, in the great houses and on the expansive lawns of

Gardencourt and Lockleigh, she is, in rapid succession, proposed to by Lord Warburton, followed to London and proposed to by Caspar Goodwood, and left a large fortune by Ralph Touchett and his father. In Italy, she also almost immediately provokes: Madame Merle cannot refuse to "manipulate" her; Gilbert Osmond "collects" her. The force of Isabel Archer's radiance, in short, is one major movement of the novel. *Her* moves constitute the other.

What Isabel Archer is, is no more important than what she represents. To look back again at the title, the portrait, we see, is not simply of Isabel Archer; it is the portrait of *a lady*. She is, moreover (we soon see), an American lady "affronting her destiny," to use James's own phrase that is quoted so often to describe Isabel's fate. What it is that we discover her destiny to be is prescribed and final in the novel itself, even if its meaning is not.

We can sense the great liberating opportunity inherent in her move to Europe. We can also see—and accept—her soon-to-follow concomitant rejections of both Lord Warburton and Goodwood as rejections of something, to use the famous words Fitzgerald was later to use about another American idealist, not "commensurate" to her "capacity for wonder." We can feel the throbbing possibilities for life made available to her by Ralph's inheritance no less than by her own lively and intelligent imagination. We can even understand her acceptance of Osmond as, in her eyes it first is, a possibility for a quality of experience not before open to her. And when we begin to see, with Isabel, in the famous scene before the fire in Chapter 42, what that possibility has in restrictive fact become—we begin also to see, as Isabel does not yet see, in Ralph Touchett's original magnanimous gesture to her, his "use" of her, and in Isabel's acceptance of Osmond, her use of him. When, therefore, we finally see, at the bedside of the dying Ralph and in the passionately live embrace of Caspar Goodwood at the end of the novel, that Isabel sees in them what she herself has been, we also finally see that she at last sees what she herself truly is. Only then is she invulnerable to Osmond, to whom she must return. Her *destiny* is complete.

What that destiny means is another matter—and precisely and appropriately *the* matter that the great bulk of the "inner" criticism of *The Portrait of a Lady* has devoted itself to.

That criticism rather than this Introduction is the place to examine the variety of things Henry James's *The Portrait of a Lady* has come and is continuing to come to mean. It is also the repository of a unique history—the critical history of a great book. It is thus, in addition, a kind of limited history of literary criticism over the more than eight decades since it was written. The course of that history, in one sense, is a wave of the course of the literary reputation of any great novel. In its most important sense, however, it is simply, yet significantly, the history of a single crucial novel by one of the most fertile and influential creative imaginations our culture has seen.

The "history" that is collected in this volume is consequently a representative one in a number of different directions. A rough chronological order is used, but a desired result is that the reader, like the best of the critics, will continually look back at the novel even as he explores new insights. And the last of the essays, that by Professor Oscar Cargill, not only looks back at the novel in a comprehensive way; it also looks back at its critical history, even as it looks forward to new critical problems.

But the history begins with the author himself. And we are fortunate indeed to have both the *Notebook* entry on the novel that the author wrote to himself while writing it and his own estimation, almost three decades later in its Preface, of its achievements and failures. Next are grouped two scholarly surveys: one from a study of James's contemporary reputation in American periodicals; the other from his contemporary reputation in British ones. Each of these in turn is followed by a representative review, one by W. C. Brownell from *The Nation* in America, one from *The Athenaeum* in England.

Each of the third group is a pioneer study of special problems in James's fiction. Joseph Warren Beach's *The Method of Henry James* appeared in 1918, only two years after the novelist's death, and it is still one of the basic examinations of James's technique. Cornelia P. Kelley's *The Early Development of Henry James* first appeared in 1930 and, like Beach's book, retains its usefulness as the earliest and still the most reliable survey of the literary sources of the early fiction. And F. O. Matthiessen's appended study of the novel in his *The Major Phase*, although it appeared somewhat later (1944), is nonetheless the first detailed analysis of the revisions in that novel—surely a result, at least in part, of the then exclusive availability of the *Notebooks* to him and Professor Murdock, who were at that time first editing them. That all three of these early scholars gave to *The Portrait of a Lady* a position of crucial importance in spite of their respectively wider concerns is, of course, of major significance in itself.

The next three essays are all from book-length studies of the English novel that appeared in the early 1950's. Arnold Kettle begins the second volume of his *An Introduction to the English Novel* with an analysis of *The Portrait of a Lady*, a novel, he says (after brief prefatory remarks), which makes all English novels which precede it, "except perhaps those of Jane Austen . . . , seem a trifle crude." Dorothy Van Ghent, in her *The English Novel: Form and Function*, moves from an analysis of Hardy's *Tess of the D'Urbervilles* to one of *The Portrait of a Lady* with the remark that the move is not only from "Stonehenge to St. Peter's," but it is also "from a frozen northern turnip field, eyed hungrily by polar birds, to the Cascine gardens where nightingales sing." And Walter Allen, in his *The English Novel: A Short Critical History*, begins his chapter on James with the observation that he remains "the greatest figure among the generation of novelists who came to maturity during the eighties—Stevenson, Gissing, and Moore . . ." Allen is later to describe *The Portrait* "as James's first great novel" and "still considered by some critics his best."

American affinities constitute the subject of the next group of essays, all of which appeared in the 1950's and 60's. The first, by Philip Rahv, is concerned with the "American-ness" of Henry James—a quality, for Rahv, best seen in his American heroines, for they are the ones who make "the most of his visions" and dominate "his drama of transatlantic relations." Each is "The Heiress of All the Ages"—and never more crucially so than when the Heiress is Isabel Archer. James, for Richard Chase (in his *The American Novel and Its Tradition*), is *the* American author with whom "we have to test the achievements of his compatriots." And in his "The Lesson of the Master," he says further, it is *The Portrait of a Lady* that "was the first novel by an American that made, within the limits of its subject, full use of the novel form. By comparison," he continues, "no previous American novel, even those of James, can claim to be fully 'done.' " For William Bysshe Stein, Isabel Archer is a "Victorian Griselda," embodying long before Henry Adams, "the problem of sexual inertia in *The Education*." And it is Stein's provocative contention, in his "*The Portrait of a Lady: Vis Inertiae*," that James's portrait of Isabel Archer, like Adams' *Education*, is a picture of how "the promiscuous charity of a rootless and sterile commercialism passes a sentence of doom upon the redemptive feminine in twentieth-century culture."

In Section Six I have grouped a representative sampling of special studies of special problems in the novel. Ernest Sandeen presents an extended, involved comparison of *The Portrait of a Lady* with *The Wings of the Dove*, the late great example of James's fiction that clearly has the closest ties with *The Portrait*, in the mutual affinities of Isabel Archer and Milly Theale with Minny Temple no less than in theme and attitude. William H. Gass's "The High Brutality of Good Intentions" provides a profound analysis of one way "the novels and stories of Henry James constitute the most searching criticism available of the pragmatic ideal of the proper treatment and ultimate worth of man." Sister M. Corona Sharp's book-length investigation, *The Confidante in Henry James*, gives over thirty of its remarkable pages to an examination of the ways Henrietta Stackpole and Madame Merle perform their technical functions in the novel of "highlight[ing] in different ways their young confider, who has come to Europe to see and to learn."

The last two essays are recent but contrasting over-all views of the novel. They both appeared in 1961. The late R. P. Blackmur's essay is a brief, perceptive, almost "poetic" view of what he describes as "the first of Henry James's books to sound with the ring of greatness." Professor Oscar Cargill's study is a long, meticulous survey of the major issues in the novel, the scholarship that has concerned itself with those is-

sues, and a "composite" reading of the novel itself. It rounds
off with beautiful symmetry this selected "history" of *The
Portrait of a Lady.*

It rounds it off, but it does not of course complete it. Nor,
in fact, does this history even deplete the existing criticism of
this novel, as the nearly one hundred items in the selected
bibliography at the end of this volume suggests. The essays
here collected nonetheless do represent a fair sampling, I feel,
of that criticism. I was denied permission to reproduce one or
two important studies—Leon Edel's fine "Introduction" to
The Portrait of a Lady, for example. And space itself is of
course another kind of limitation. Yet, we do have represented
here comments on the novel from as early as 1881 by an English reviewer and almost every decade since. Early, dedicated
"Jamesians" such as Joseph W. Beach, Cornelia P. Kelley,
F. O. Matthiessen, R. P. Blackmur, and Oscar Cargill are represented. Voices from England, early and late, are here. The
"controversial" are here—in Rahv, and Chase and Stein, for
example—as are those who view the portrait as flawed (Oscar
Cargill) *and* those who see it as flawless (William Gass). We
have narrow, technical analyses (as with Sister Sharp), comparative studies (as with Ernest Sandeen), and broad brilliant
sweeps at the whole (as with Dorothy Van Ghent). We have
the early reviews surveyed (by Foley and Murray) and ex-
emplified (by Brownell and the *Athenaeum* reviewer). In
short, the perspective is varied—in time, in approach, in distance.

I wrote at the beginning of this Introduction that all great
novels continuously invite criticism. Few other novels, I would
now say here, have had that invitation more variously and continuously "accepted" than has *The Portrait of a Lady.* Few,
moreover, would have revealed among its "lists" more variously
distinguished critics. Although the novel itself was last touched
with James's final revisions in the first decade of this century,
the widespread attention since given to it is not likely to abate.
Nor should it.

Notes

1 At the time of this writing, the latest *Paperbound Books in Print* (October, 1965) lists nine editions of the novel in print, including one "simplified and adapted" edition for, I suppose, elementary readers.

2 See sections "E" and "F" of Leon Edel and Dan H. Laurence's *A Bibliography of Henry James* (2d Ed., Rev.; New York: Oxford University Press, 1961).

3 See Professor Edel's Introduction, *The Portrait of a Lady* (Rev. ed.; Boston, 1963), p. v.

CONTENTS

INTRODUCTION   ix

I. The Author Speaks
    1. Before the Fact—from The
       Notebooks   1
       by Henry James
    2. After the Fact—The Preface   6
       by Henry James

II. The Reviews
    3. A Survey of Early Reviews—
       American   25
       by Richard N. Foley
    4. An American Review—James's
       The Portrait of a Lady   29
       by William C. Brownell
    5. A Survey of Early Reviews—
       English   35
       by Donald M. Murray
    6. An English Review—The Portrait
       of a Lady   39
       Anonymous

III. Special Problems
    7. From The Method of Henry
       James   45
       by Joseph Warren Beach

    8. From The Early Development of
       Henry James   51
       by Cornelia Pulsifer Kelley
    9. The Painter's Sponge and Varnish
       Bottle   63
       by F. O. Matthiessen

IV. In the Tradition of the English Novel
    10. From An Introduction to the
        English Novel   91
        by Arnold Kettle
    11. From The English Novel: Form
        and Function   113
        by Dorothy Van Ghent
    12. From The English Novel: A Short
        Critical History   132
        by Walter Allen

V. American Affinities
    13. From "The Heiress of All the
        Ages"   139
        by Philip Rahv
    14. The Lesson of the Master   148
        by Richard Chase
    15. The Portrait of a Lady: Vis
        Inertiae   166
        by William Bysshe Stein

VI. Methods Revealed
   16. The Wings of the Dove and The
       Portrait of a Lady: A Study of
       Henry James's Later Phase   187
       by Ernest Sandeen
   17. The High Brutality of Good
       Intentions   206
       by William H. Gass
   18. From The Confidante in Henry
       James   217
       by Sister M. Corona Sharp, O.S.U.

VII. The Total Novel
   19. The Portrait of a Lady   247
       by R. P. Blackmur
   20. The Portrait of a Lady   256
       by Oscar Cargill

Studies of *The Portrait of a Lady:* A Selected
Bibliography   297

I. The Author Speaks

Henry James

1·Before the Fact—from *The Notebooks*

P. OF A L. After Isabel's marriage there are *five* more instalments, and the success of the whole story greatly depends upon this portion being well conducted or not. Let me then make the most of it—let me imagine the best. There has been a want of action in the earlier part, and it may be made up here. The elements that remain are in themselves, I think, very interesting, and they only need to be strongly and happily combined. The weakness of the whole story is that it is too exclusively psychological —that it depends to[o] little on incident; but the complete unfolding of the situation that is established by Isabel's marriage may nonetheless be quite sufficiently dramatic. The idea of the whole thing is that the poor girl, who has dreamed of freedom and nobleness, who has done, as she believes, a generous, natural, clear-sighted thing, finds herself in reality ground in the very mill of the conventional. After a year or two of marriage the antagonism between her nature and Osmond's comes out—the open opposition of a noble character and a narrow one. There is a great deal to do here in a small compass; every word, therefore, must tell—every touch must count. If the last five parts of the story appear crowded, this will be rather a good defect in consideration of the perhaps too great diffuseness of the earlier portion. Isabel awakes from her sweet delusion—oh, the art required for making this delusion natural!—and finds herself

From *The Notebooks of Henry James*, ed. by F. O. Matthiessen and Kenneth B. Murdock (New York, 1947), pp. 15–18. Copyright 1947 by Oxford University Press, Inc. Reprinted by permission.

face to face with a husband who has ended by conceiving a
hatred for her own larger qualities. These facts, however, are
not in themselves sufficient; the situation must be marked by
important events. Such an event is the discovery of the relation
that has existed between Osmond and Madame Merle, the discovery that she has married Madame Merle's lover. Madame
Merle, in a word, is the mother of Pansy. Edward Rosier comes
to Rome, falls in love with Pansy and wants to marry her; but
Osmond opposes the marriage, on the ground of Rosier's insuffi-
cient means. Isabel favours Pansy—she sees that Rosier would
make her an excellent husband, be tenderly devoted and kind
to her—but Osmond absolutely forbids the idea. Lord Warburton comes to Rome, sees Isabel again and declares to her
that he is resigned, that he has succeeded in accepting the fact
of her marriage and that he is now disposed, himself, to marry.
He makes the acquaintance of Pansy, is charmed with her, and
at last tells Isabel that he should like to make her his wife.
Isabel is almost shocked, for she distrusts this sentiment of Lord
Warburton's; and the reader must feel that she mistrusts it
justly. This same sentiment is a very ticklish business. It is honest
up to a certain point; but at bottom, without knowing it, Lord
W.'s real motive is the desire to be near Isabel whom he sees,
now, to be a disappointed, and unhappy woman. This is what
Isabel has perceived; she feels that it would [be] cruel to Pansy,
dangerous to herself, to allow such a marriage—for which, however, there are such great material inducements that she cannot
well oppose it. Her position is a most difficult one, for by begging
Lord Warburton to desist she only betrays her apprehension of
him—which is precisely what she wishes not to do. Besides, she
is afraid of doing a wrong to Pansy. Madame Merle, meanwhile,
has caught a glimpse of Warburton's state of mind and eagerly
takes up the idea of his marrying the girl. Pansy is very much in
love with Rosier—she has no wish to marry Lord W. Isabel is
[so] convinced at last of this that she feels absolved from considering her prospects with Lord W. and treats the latter with
such coldness that he feels the vanity of hope and withdraws
from the field, having indeed not paid any direct attention to
Pansy, whom he cannot in the least be accused of jilting.
Madame Merle, very angry at his withdrawal, accuses Isabel of

having dissuaded him, out of jealousy, because of his having
been an old lover of hers and her wishing to keep him for herself;
and she still opposes the marriage with Rosier, because she has
been made to believe by Lord Warburton's attentions that Pansy
may do something much more brilliant. Isabel resents Madame
Merle's interference, demands of her what she has to do with
Pansy. Whereupon Madame Merle, in whose breast the suppressed feeling of maternity has long been rankling, and who is
passionately jealous of Isabel's influence over Pansy, breaks out
with the cry that she alone has a right—that Pansy is her daughter. (To be settled later whether this revelation is to be made by
Mme Merle herself, or by the Countess Gemini. Better on many
grounds that it should be the latter; and yet in that way I lose
the 'great scene' between Madame Merle and Isabel.) In any
event this whole matter of Mme Merle is (like Lord W.'s state
of mind about Pansy) a very ticklish one—very delicate and
difficult to handle. To make it natural that she should have
brought about Isabel's marriage to her old lover—this is in
itself a supreme difficulty. It is not, however, an impossibility,
for I honestly believe it rests upon nature. Her old interest in
Osmond remains in a modified form; she wishes to do something
for him, and she does it through another rather than by herself.
That, I think, is perfectly natural. As regards Pansy the strange-
ness of her conduct is greater; but we must remember that we
see only its surface—we don't see her reasoning. Isabel has
money, and Mme Merle has great confidence in her benevolence,
in her generosity; she has no fear that she will be a harsh stepmother, and she believes she will push the fortunes of the child
she herself is unable to avow and afraid openly to patronize. In
all this Osmond sinks a little into the background—but one
must get the sense of Isabel's exquisitely miserable revulsion.
Three years have passed—time enough for it to have taken place.
His worldliness, his deep snobbishness, his want of generosity,
etc.; his hatred of her when he finds that she judges him, that
she morally protests at so much that surrounds her. The uncleanness of the air; the Countess Gemini's lovers, etc. Caspar
Goodwood of course must reappear, and Ralph, and Henrietta;
Mrs. Touchett, too, for a moment. Ralph's helpless observation
of Isabel's deep misery; her determination to show him nothing,

and his inability to help her. This to be a strong feature in the situation. Pansy is sent back to the convent, to be kept from Rosier. Caspar Goodwood comes to Rome, because he has heard from Henrietta that Isabel is unhappy, and Isabel sends him away. She hears from Ralph at Gardencourt, that he is ill there (Ralph, himself), that indeed he is dying. (The letter to come from Mrs. Touchett who is with him; or even it would be well that it should be a telegram; it expresses Ralph's wish to see her.) Isabel tells Osmond she wishes to go; Osmond, jealously and nastily, forbids it; and Isabel, deeply distressed and embarrassed, hesitates. Then Madame Merle, who wishes her to make a *coup de tête*, to leave Osmond, so that she may be away from Pansy, reveals to her her belief that it was Ralph who induced her father to leave her the £70,000. Isabel, then, violently affected and overcome, starts directly for England. She reaches Ralph at Gardencourt, and finds Caspar Goodwood and Henrietta also there: i.e., in London. Ralph's death—Isabel's return to London, and interview with Caspar G.—His passionate outbreak; he beseeches her to return with him to America. She is greatly moved, she feels the full force of his devotion—to which she has never done justice; but she refuses. She starts again for Italy—and her departure is the climax and termination of the story.

x   x   x   x   x

With strong handling it seems to me that it may all be very true, very powerful, very touching. The obvious criticism of course will be that it is not finished—that I have not seen the heroine to the end of her situation—that I have left her *en l'air*. —This is both true and false. The *whole* of anything is never told; you can only take what groups together. What I have done has that unity—it groups together. It is complete in itself—and the rest may be taken up or not, later.

—I am not sure that it would not be best that the exposure of Mme Merle should never be complete, and above all that she should not denounce herself. This would injure very much the impression I have wished to give of her profundity, her self-control, her regard for appearances. It may be enough that

Isabel should believe the fact in question—in consequence of what the Countess Gemini has told her. Then, when Madame Merle tells her of what Ralph has done for her of old—tells it with the view I have mentioned of precipitating her defiance of Osmond—Isabel may charge her with the Countess G.'s secret. This Madame Merle will deny—but deny in such a way that Isabel knows she lies; and *then* Isabel may depart.—The last (October) instalment to take place wholly in England. At the very last Caspar Goodwood goes to Pratt's hotel, and is told that Mrs. Osmond has left it the night before. Later in the day he sees Henrietta who has the last word—utters the last line of the story: a characteristic characterization of Isabel.

2 · After the Fact—*The Preface*

"THE PORTRAIT OF A LADY" was, like "Roderick Hudson," begun in Florence, during three months spent there in the spring of 1879. Like "Roderick" and like "The American," it had been designed for publication in "The Atlantic Monthly," where it began to appear in 1880. It differed from its two predecessors, however, in finding a course also open to it, from month to month, in "Macmillan's Magazine"; which was to be for me one of the last occasions of simultaneous "serialisation" in the two countries that the changing conditions of literary intercourse between England and the United States had up to then left unaltered. It is a long novel, and I was long in writing it; I remember being again much occupied with it, the following year, during a stay of several weeks made in Venice. I had rooms on Riva Schiavoni, at the top of a house near the passage leading off to San Zaccaria; the waterside life, the wondrous lagoon spread before me, and the ceaseless human chatter of Venice came in at my windows, to which I seem to myself to have been constantly driven, in the fruitless fidget of composition, as if to see whether, out in the blue channel, the ship of some right suggestion, of some better phrase, of the next happy twist of my subject, the next true touch for my canvas, might n't come into sight. But I recall vividly enough that the response most elicited, in general, to these restless appeals was the rather

From "The Preface," *The Novels and Tales of Henry James* (New York, 1908), III. Reprinted with the permission of Charles Scribner's Sons from *The Novels and Tales of Henry James*, Volume III. Copyright 1908 Charles Scribner's Sons; renewal copyright 1936 by Henry James.

grim admonition that romantic and historic sites, such as the
land of Italy abounds in, offer the artist a questionable aid to
concentration when they themselves are not to be the subject
of it. They are too rich in their own life and too charged with
their own meanings merely to help him out with a lame phrase;
they draw him away from his small question to their own greater
ones; so that, after a little, he feels, while thus yearning toward
them in his difficulty, as if he were asking an army of glorious
veterans to help him to arrest a peddler who has given him the
wrong change.

There are pages of the book which, in the reading over,
have seemed to make me see again the bristling curve of the
wide Riva, the large colour-spots of the balconied houses and
the repeated undulation of the little hunchbacked bridges,
marked by the rise and drop again, with the wave, of fore-
shortened clicking pedestrians. The Venetian footfall and the
Venetian cry—all talk there, wherever uttered, having the pitch
of a call across the water—come in once more at the window,
renewing one's old impression of the delighted senses and the
divided, frustrated mind. How can places that speak *in general*
so to the imagination not give it, at the moment, the particular
thing it wants? I recollect again and again, in beautiful places,
dropping into that wonderment. The real truth is, I think, that
they express, under this appeal, only too much—more than, in
the given case, one has use for; so that one finds one's self working less congruously, after all, so far as the surrounding picture
is concerned, than in presence of the moderate and the neutral,
to which we may lend something of the light of our vision. Such
a place as Venice is too proud for such charities; Venice does n't
borrow, she but all magnificently gives. We profit by that enor-
mously, but to do so we must either be quite off duty or be on
it in her service alone. Such, and so rueful, are these reminis-
cences; though on the whole, no doubt, one's book, and one's
"literary effort" at large, were to be the better for them. Strangely
fertilising, in the long run, does a wasted effort of attention often
prove. It all depends on *how* the attention has been cheated, has
been squandered. There are high-handed insolent frauds, and
there are insidious sneaking ones. And there is, I fear, even on
the most designing artist's part, always witless enough good faith,

always anxious enough desire, to fail to guard him against their deceits.

Trying to recover here, for recognition, the germ of my idea, I see that it must have consisted not at all in any conceit of a "plot," nefarious name, in any flash, upon the fancy, of a set of relations, or in any one of those situations that, by a logic of their own, immediately fall, for the fabulist, into movement, into a march or a rush, a patter of quick steps; but altogether in the sense of a single character, the character and aspect of a particular engaging young woman, to which all the usual elements of a "subject," certainly of a setting, were to need to be super-added. Quite as interesting as the young woman herself, at her best, do I find, I must again repeat, this projection of memory upon the whole matter of the growth, in one's imagination, of some such apology for a motive. These are the fascinations of the fabulist's art, these lurking forces of expansion, these necessities of upspringing in the seed, these beautiful determinations, on the part of the idea entertained, to grow as tall as possible, to push into the light and the air and thickly flower there; and, quite as much, these fine possibilities of recovering, from some good standpoint on the ground gained, the intimate history of the business—of retracing and reconstructing its steps and stages. I have always fondly remembered a remark that I heard fall years ago from the lips of Ivan Turgénieff in regard to his own experience of the usual origin of the fictive picture. It began for him almost always with the vision of some person or persons, who hovered before him, soliciting him, as the active or passive figure, interesting him and appealing to him just as they were and by what they were. He saw them, in that fashion, as *disponibles*, saw them subject to the chances, the complications of existence, and saw them vividly, but then had to find for them the right relations, those that would most bring them out; to imagine, to invent and select and piece together the situations most useful and favourable to the sense of the creatures themselves, the complications they would be most likely to produce and to feel.

"To arrive at these things is to arrive at my 'story,'" he said, "and that's the way I look for it. The result is that I'm often accused of not having 'story' enough. I seem to myself to have as much as I need—to show my people, to exhibit their relations with each other; for that is all my measure. If I watch them long enough I see them come together, I see them *placed*, I see them engaged in this or that act and in this or that difficulty. How they look and move and speak and behave, always in the setting I have found for them, is my account of them—of which I dare say, alas, *que cela manque souvent d'architecture.* But I would rather, I think, have too little architecture than too much—when there's danger of its interfering with my measure of the truth. The French of course like more of it than I give—having by their own genius such a hand for it; and indeed one must give all one can. As for the origin of one's wind-blown germs themselves, who shall say, as you ask, where *they* come from? We have to go too far back, too far behind, to say. Isn't it all we can say that they come from every quarter of heaven, that they are *there* at almost any turn of the road? They accumulate, and we are always picking them over, selecting among them. They are the breath of life—by which I mean that life, in its own way, breathes them upon us. They are so, in a manner prescribed and imposed—floated into our minds by the current of life. That reduces to imbecility the vain critic's quarrel, so often, with one's subject, when he hasn't the wit to accept it. Will he point out then which other it should properly have been?—his office being, essentially *to* point out. *Il en serait bien embarrassé.* Ah, when he points out what I've done or failed to do with it, that's another matter: there he's on his ground. I give him up my 'architecture,' " my distinguished friend concluded, "as much as he will."

So "this beautiful genius," and I recall with comfort the gratitude I drew from his reference to the intensity of suggestion that may reside in the stray figure, the unattached character, the image *en disponibilité.* It gave me higher warrant than I seemed then to have met for just that blest habit of one's own imagination, the trick of investing some conceived or encountered individual, some brace or group of individuals, with the germinal property and authority. I was myself so much more antecedently conscious of my figures than of their setting—a too preliminary, a preferential interest in which struck me as in general such a putting of the cart before the horse. I might envy, though I couldn't emulate, the imaginative writer so constituted as to see his fable first and to make out its agents afterwards: I could think so little of any fable that it didn't need its agents positively to launch it; I could think so little of any situation that did n't depend for its interest on the nature of the persons situated, and thereby on their way of taking it. There are methods of so-called presentation, I believe—among novelists who have appeared to flourish—that offer the situation as indifferent to that support; but I have not lost the sense of the value for me, at the time, of the admirable Russian's testimony to my not needing, all superstitiously, to try and perform any such gymnastic. Other echoes from the same source linger with me, I confess, as unfadingly— if it be not all indeed one much-embracing echo. It was impossible after that not to read, for one's uses, high lucidity into the tormented and disfigured and bemuddled question of the objective value, and even quite into that of the critical appreciation, of "subject" in the novel.

One had had from an early time, for that matter, the instinct of the right estimate of such values and of its reducing to the inane the dull dispute over the "immoral" subject and the moral. Recognising so promptly the one measure of the worth of a given subject, the question about it that, rightly answered, disposes of all others—is it valid, in a word, is it genuine, is it sincere, the result of some direct impression or perception of life?—I had found small edification, mostly, in a critical pretension that had neglected from the first all delimitation of ground and all definition of terms. The air of my earlier time shows, to memory, as darkened, all round, with that vanity —unless the difference to-day be just in one's own final impatience, the lapse of one's attention. There is, I think, no more nutritive or suggestive truth in this connexion than that of the perfect dependence of the "moral" sense of a work of art on the amount of felt life concerned in producing it. The question comes back thus, obviously, to the kind and the degree of the artist's prime sensibility, which is the soil out of which his subject springs. The quality and capacity of that soil, its ability to "grow" with due freshness and straightness any vision of life, represents, strongly or weakly, the projected morality. That element is but another name for the more or less close connexion of the subject with some mark made on the intelligence, with some sincere experience. By which, at the same time, of course, one is far from contending that this enveloping air of the artist's humanity—which gives the last touch to the worth of the work— is not a widely and wondrously varying element; being on one occasion a rich and magnificent medium and on another a comparatively poor and ungenerous one. Here we get exactly the high price of the novel as a literary form—its power not only, while preserving that form with closeness, to range through all the differences of the individual relation to its general subject-matter, all the varieties of outlook on life, of disposition to reflect and project, created by conditions that are never the same from man to man (or, so far as that goes, from man to woman), but positively to appear more true to its character in proportion as it strains, or tends to burst, with a latent extravagance, its mould.

The house of fiction has in short not one window, but a million—a number of possible windows not to be reckoned, rather; every one of which has been pierced, or is still pierceable, in its vast front, by the need of the individual vision and by the pressure of the individual will. These apertures, of dissimilar shape and size, hang so, all together, over the human scene that we might have expected of them a greater sameness of report than we find. They are but windows at the best, mere holes in a dead wall, disconnected, perched aloft; they are not hinged doors opening straight upon life. But they have this mark of their own that at each of them stands a figure with a pair of eyes, or at least with a field-glass, which forms, again and again, for observation, a unique instrument, insuring to the person making use of it an impression distinct from every other. He and his neighbours are watching the same show, but one seeing more where the other sees less, one seeing black where the other sees white, one seeing big where the other sees small, one seeing coarse where the other sees fine. And so on, and so on; there is fortunately no saying on what, for the particular pair of eyes, the window may *not* open; "fortunately" by reason, precisely, of this incalculability of range. The spreading field, the human scene, is the "choice of subject"; the pierced aperture, either broad or balconied or slit-like and low-browed, is the "literary form"; but they are, singly or together, as nothing without the posted presence of the watcher—without, in other words, the consciousness of the artist. Tell me what the artist is, and I will tell you of what he has *been* conscious. Thereby I shall express to you at once his boundless freedom and his "moral" reference.

All this is a long way round, however, for my word about my dim first move toward "The Portrait," which was exactly my grasp of a single character—an acquisition I had made, moreover, after a fashion not here to be retraced. Enough that I was, as seemed to me, in complete possession of it, that I had been so for a long time, that this had made it familiar and yet had not blurred its charm, and that, all urgently, all tormentingly, I saw it in motion and, so to speak, in transit. This amounts to saying that I saw it as bent upon its fate—some fate or other; *which*, among the possibilities, being precisely the question. Thus I had my vivid individual—vivid, so strangely, in spite of being still at large, not confined by the conditions, not engaged in the tangle, to which we look for much of the impress that constitutes an identity. If the apparition was still all to be placed how came it to be vivid?—since we puzzle such quantities out, mostly, just by the business of placing them. One could answer such a question beautifully, doubtless, if one could do so subtle, if not so monstrous, a thing as to write the history of the growth of one's imagination. One would describe then what, at a given time, had extraordinarily happened to it, and one would so, for instance, be in a position to tell, with an approach to clearness, how, under favour of occasion, it had been able to take over (take over straight from life) such and such a constituted, animated figure or form. The figure has to that extent, as you see, *been* placed—placed in the imagination that detains it, preserves, protects, enjoys it, conscious of its presence in the dusky, crowded, heterogeneous back-shop of the mind very much as a wary dealer in precious odds and ends, competent to make an "advance" on rare objects confided to him, is conscious of the rare little "piece" left in deposit by the reduced, mysterious lady of title or the speculative amateur, and which is already there to disclose its merit afresh as soon as a key shall have clicked in a cupboard-door.

That may be, I recognise, a somewhat superfine analogy for the particular "value" I here speak of, of the image of the young feminine nature that I had had for so considerable a time all curiously at my disposal; but it appears to fond memory quite to fit the fact—with the recall, in addition, of my pious desire but to place my treasure right. I quite remind myself thus of the dealer resigned not to "realise," resigned to keeping the precious object locked up indefinitely rather than commit it, at no matter what price, to vulgar hands. For there *are* dealers in these forms and figures and treasures capable of that refinement. The point is, however, that this single small corner-stone, the conception of a certain young woman affronting her destiny, had begun with being all my outfit for the large building of "The Portrait of a Lady." It came to be a square and spacious house—or has at least seemed so to me in this going over it again; but, such as it is, it had to be put up round my young woman while she stood there in perfect isolation. That is to me, artistically speaking, the circumstance of interest; for I have lost myself once more, I confess, in the curiosity of analysing the structure. By what process of logical accretion was this slight "personality," the mere slim shade of an intelligent but presumptuous girl, to find itself endowed with the high attributes of a Subject?—and indeed by what thinness, at the best, would such a subject not be vitiated? Millions of presumptuous girls, intelligent or not intelligent, daily affront their destiny, and what is it open to their destiny to *be*, at the most, that we should make an ado about it? The novel is of its very nature an "ado," an ado about something, and the larger the form it takes the greater of course the ado. Therefore, consciously, that was what one was in for—for positively organising an ado about Isabel Archer.

One looked it well in the face, I seem to remember, this extravagance; and with the effect precisely of recognising the charm of the problem. Challenge any such problem with any intelligence, and you immediately see how full it is of substance; the wonder being, all the while, as we look at the world, how absolutely, how inordinately, the Isabel Archers, and even much smaller female fry, insist on mattering. George Eliot has admirably noted it—"In these frail vessels is borne onward through

the ages the treasure of human affection." In "Romeo and Juliet"
Juliet has to be important, just as, in "Adam Bede" and "The
Mill on the Floss" and "Middlemarch" and "Daniel Deronda,"
Hetty Sorrel and Maggie Tulliver and Rosamond Vincy and
Gwendolen Harleth have to be; with that much of firm ground,
that much of bracing air, at the disposal all the while of their
feet and their lungs. They are typical, none the less, of a class
difficult, in the individual case, to make a centre of interest; so
difficult in fact that many an expert painter, as for instance
Dickens and Walter Scott, as for instance even, in the main, so
subtle a hand as that of R. L. Stevenson, has preferred to leave
the task unattempted. There are in fact writers as to whom we
make out that their refuge from this is to assume it to be not
worth their attempting; by which pusillanimity in truth their
honour is scantly saved. It is never an attestation of a value, or
even of our imperfect sense of one, it is never a tribute to any
truth at all, that we shall represent that value badly. It never
makes up, artistically, for an artist's dim feeling about a thing
that he shall "do" the thing as ill as possible. There are better
ways than that, the best of all of which is to begin with less
stupidity.

It may be answered meanwhile, in regard to Shakespeare's
and to George Eliot's testimony, that their concession to the
"importance" of their Juliets and Cleopatras and Portias (even
with Portia as the very type and model of the young person intelligent and presumptuous) and to that of their Hettys and
Maggies and Rosamonds and Gwendolens, suffers the abate-
ment that these slimnesses are, when figuring as the main props
of the theme, never suffered to be sole ministers of its appeal,
but have their inadequacy eked out with comic relief and under-
plots, as the playwrights say, when not with murders and battles
and the great mutations of the world. If they are shown as
"mattering" as much as they could possibly pretend to, the
proof of it is in a hundred other persons, made of much stouter
stuff, and each involved moreover in a hundred relations which
matter to *them* concomitantly with that one. Cleopatra matters,
beyond bounds, to Antony, but his colleagues, his antagonists,
the state of Rome and the impending battle also prodigiously
matter; Portia matters to Antonio, and to Shylock, and to the

Prince of Morocco, to the fifty aspiring princes, but for these gentry there are other lively concerns; for Antonio, notably, there are Shylock and Bassanio and his lost ventures and the extremity of his predicament. This extremity indeed, by the same token, matters to Portia—though its doing so becomes of interest all by the fact that Portia matters to *us*. That she does so, at any rate, and that almost everything comes round to it again, supports my contention as to this fine example of the value recognised in the mere young thing. (I say "mere" young thing because I guess that even Shakespeare, preoccupied mainly though he may have been with the passions of princes, would scarce have pretended to found the best of his appeal for her on her high social position.) It is an example exactly of the deep difficulty braved—the difficulty of making George Eliot's "frail vessel," if not the all-in-all for our attention, at least the clearest of the call.

Now to see deep difficulty braved is at any time, for the really addicted artist, to feel almost even as a pang the beautiful incentive, and to feel it verily in such sort as to wish the danger intensified. The difficulty most worth tackling can only be for him, in these conditions, the greatest the case permits of. So I remember feeling here (in presence, always, that is, of the particular uncertainty of my ground), that there would be one way better than another—oh, ever so much better than any other!—of making it fight out its battle. The frail vessel, that charged with George Eliot's "treasure," and thereby of such importance to those who curiously approach it, has likewise possibilities of importance to itself, possibilities which permit of treatment and in fact peculiarly require it from the moment they are considered at all. There is always the escape from any close account of the weak agent of such spells by using as a bridge for evasion, for retreat and flight, the view of her relation to those surrounding her. Make it predominantly a view of *their* relation and the trick is played: you give the general sense of her effect, and you give it, so far as the raising on it of a superstructure goes, with the maximum of ease. Well, I recall perfectly how little, in my now quite established connexion, the maximum of ease appealed to me, and how I seemed to get rid of it by an honest transposition of the weights in the two scales.

"Place the centre of the subject in the young woman's own consciousness," I said to myself, "and you get as interesting and as beautiful a difficulty as you could wish. Stick to *that*—for the centre; put the heaviest weight into *that* scale, which will be so largely the scale of her relation to herself. Make her only interested enough, at the same time, in the things that are not herself, and this relation need n't fear to be too limited. Place meanwhile in the other scale the lighter weight (which is usually the one that tips the balance of interest): press least hard, in short, on the consciousness of your heroine's satellites, especially the male; make it an interest contributive only to the greater one. See, at all events, what can be done in this way. What better field could there be for a due ingenuity? The girl hovers, inextinguishable, as a charming creature, and the job will be to translate her into the highest terms of that formula, and as nearly as possible moreover into *all* of them. To depend upon her and her little concerns wholly to see you through will necessitate, remember, your really 'doing' her."

So far I reasoned, and it took nothing less than that technical rigour, I now easily see, to inspire me with the right confidence for erecting on such a plot of ground the neat and careful and proportioned pile of bricks that arches over it and that was thus to form, constructionally speaking, a literary monument. Such is the aspect that to-day "The Portrait" wears for me: a structure reared with an "architectural" competence, as Turgenieff would have said, that makes it, to the author's own sense, the most proportioned of his productions after "The Ambassadors"—which was to follow it so many years later and which has, no doubt, a superior roundness. On one thing I was determined; that, though I should clearly have to pile brick upon brick for the creation of an interest, I would leave no pretext for saying that anything is out of line, scale or perspective. I would build large—in fine embossed vaults and painted arches, as who should say, and yet never let it appear that the chequered pavement, the ground under the reader's feet, fails to stretch at every point to the base of the walls. That precautionary spirit, on re-perusal of the book, is the old note that most touches me: it testifies so, for my own ear, to the anxiety of my provision for the reader's amusement. I felt, in view of the possible limitations of my subject, that no such provision could be excessive, and the development of the latter was simply the general form of that earnest quest. And I find indeed that this is the only account I can give myself of the evolution of the fable: it is all under the head thus named that I conceive the needful accretion as having taken place, the right complications as having started. It was naturally of the essence that the young woman should be herself complex; that was rudimentary—or was at any rate the light in which Isabel Archer had originally dawned. It went, however, but a certain way, and other lights, contending, conflicting lights, and of as many different colours, if possible, as the rockets, the Roman candles and Catherine-wheels of a "pyrotechnic display," would be employable to attest that she was. I had, no doubt, a groping instinct for the right complications, since I am quite unable to track the footsteps of those that constitute, as the case stands, the general situation exhibited. They are there, for what they are worth, and as numerous as might be; but my memory, I confess, is a blank as to how and whence they came.

I seem to myself to have waked up one morning in possession of them—of Ralph Touchett and his parents, of Madame Merle, of Gilbert Osmond and his daughter and his sister, of Lord Warburton, Caspar Goodwood and Miss Stackpole, the definite array of contributions to Isabel Archer's history. I recognised them, I knew them, they were the numbered pieces of my puzzle, the concrete terms of my "plot." It was as if they had simply, by an impulse of their own, floated into my ken, and all in response to my primary question: "Well, what will she *do?*" Their answer seemed to be that if I would trust them they would show me; on which, with an urgent appeal to them to make it at least as interesting as they could, I trusted them. They were like the group of attendants and entertainers who come down by train when people in the country give a party; they represented the contract for carrying the party on. That was an excellent relation with them—a possible one even with so broken a reed (from her slightness of cohesion) as Henrietta Stackpole. It is a familiar truth to the novelist, at the strenuous hour, that, as certain elements in any work are of the essence, so others are only of the form; that as this or that character, this or that disposition of the material, belongs to the subject directly, so to speak, so this or that other belongs to it but indirectly—belongs intimately to the treatment. This is a truth, however, of which he rarely gets the benefit— since it could be assured to him, really, but by criticism based upon perception, criticism which is too little of this world. He must not think of benefits, moreover, I freely recognise, for that way dishonour lies: he has, that is, but one to think of— the benefit, whatever it may be, involved in his having cast a spell upon the simpler, the very simplest, forms of attention. This is all he is entitled to; he is entitled to nothing, he is bound to admit, that can come to him, from the reader, as a result on the latter's part of any act of reflexion or discrimination. He may *enjoy* this finer tribute—that is another affair, but on condition only of taking it as a gratuity "thrown in," a mere miraculous windfall, the fruit of a tree he may not pretend to have shaken. Against reflexion, against discrimination, in his interest, all earth and air conspire; wherefore it is that, as I say, he must in many a case have schooled himself, from the first, to work but for a "living wage." The living wage is the reader's grant of the least possible quantity of attention required for consciousness of a "spell." The occasional charming "tip" is an act of his intelligence over and beyond this, a golden apple, for the writer's lap, straight from the wind-stirred tree. The artist may of course, in wanton moods, dream of some Paradise (for art) where the direct appeal to the intelligence might be legalised; for to such extravagances as these his yearning mind can scarce hope ever completely to close itself. The most he can do is to remember they *are* extravagances.

All of which is perhaps but a gracefully devious way of saying that Henrietta Stackpole was a good example, in "The Portrait," of the truth to which I just adverted—as good an example as I could name were it not that Maria Gostrey, in "The Ambassadors," then in the bosom of time, may be mentioned as a better. Each of these persons is but wheels to the coach; neither belongs to the body of that vehicle, or is for a moment accommodated with a seat inside. There the subject alone is ensconced, in the form of its "hero and heroine," and of the privileged high officials, say, who ride with the king and queen.

There are reasons why one would have liked this to be felt, as in general one would like almost anything to be felt, in one's work, that one has one's self contributively felt. We have seen, however, how idle is that pretension, which I should be sorry to make too much of. Maria Gostrey and Miss Stackpole then are cases, each, of the light *ficelle*, not of the true agent; they may run beside the coach "for all they are worth," they may cling to it till they are out of breath (as poor Miss Stackpole all so vividly does), but neither, all the while, so much as gets her foot on the step, neither ceases for a moment to tread the dusty road. Put it even that they are like the fishwives who helped to bring back to Paris from Versailles, on that most ominous day of the first half of the French Revolution, the carriage of the royal family. The only thing is that I may well be asked, I acknowledge, why then, in the present fiction, I have suffered Henrietta (of whom we have indubitably too much) so officiously, so strangely, so almost inexplicably, to pervade. I will presently say what I can for that anomaly—and in the most conciliatory fashion.

A point I wish still more to make is that if my relation of confidence with the actors in my drama who *were*, unlike Miss Stackpole, true agents, was an excellent one to have arrived at, there still remained my relation with the reader, which was another affair altogether and as to which I felt no one to be trusted but myself. That solicitude was to be accordingly expressed in the artful patience with which, as I have said, I piled brick upon brick. The bricks, for the whole counting-over—putting for bricks little touches and inventions and enhancements by the way—affect me in truth as well-nigh innumerable and as ever so scrupulously fitted together and packed-in. It is an effect of detail, of the minutest; though, if one were in this connexion to say all, one would express the hope that the general, the ampler air of the modest monument still survives. I do at least seem to catch the key to a part of this abundance of small anxious, ingenious illustration as I recollect putting my finger, in my young woman's interest, on the most obvious of her predicates. "What will she 'do'? Why, the first thing she'll do will be to come to Europe; which in fact will form, and all inevitably, no small part of her principal adventure. Coming to Europe is even for the 'frail vessels,' in this wonderful age, a mild adventure; but what is truer than that on one side—the side of their independence of flood and field, of the moving accident, of battle and murder and sudden death—her adventures are to be mild? Without her sense of them, her sense *for* them, as one may say, they are next to nothing at all; but isn't the beauty and the difficulty just in showing their mystic conversion by that sense, conversion into the stuff of drama or, even more delightful word still, of 'story'?" It was all as clear, my contention, as a silver bell. Two very good instances, I think, of this effect of conversion, two cases of the rare chemistry, are the pages in which Isabel, coming into the drawing-room at Gardencourt, coming in from a wet walk or whatever, that rainy afternoon, finds Madame Merle in possession of the place, Madame Merle seated, all absorbed but all serene, at the piano, and deeply recognises, in the striking of such an hour, in the presence there, among the gathering shades, of this personage, of whom a moment before she had never so much as heard, a turning-point in her life. It is dreadful to have too much, for any artistic demonstration, to dot one's i's and insist on one's intentions, and I am not eager to do it now; but the question here was that of producing the maximum of intensity with the minimum of strain.

The interest was to be raised to its pitch and yet the elements to be kept in their key; so that, should the whole thing duly impress, I might show what an "exciting" inward life may do for the person leading it even while it remains perfectly normal. And I cannot think of a more consistent application of that ideal unless it be in the long statement, just beyond the middle of the book, of my young woman's extraordinary meditative vigil on the occasion that was to become for her such a landmark. Reduced to its essence, it is but the vigil of searching criticism; but it throws the action further forward than twenty "incidents" might have done. It was designed to have all the vivacity of incident and all the economy of picture. She sits up, by her dying fire, far into the night, under the spell of recognitions on which she finds the last sharpness suddenly wait. It is a representation simply of her motionlessly *seeing*, and an attempt withal to make the mere still lucidity of her act

as "interesting" as the surprise of a caravan or the identification
of a pirate. It represents, for that matter, one of the identifica-
tions dear to the novelist, and even indispensable to him; but it
all goes on without her being approached by another person and
without her leaving her chair. It is obviously the best thing in
the book, but it is only a supreme illustration of the general
plan. As to Henrietta, my apology for whom I just left incomplete, she exemplifies, I fear, in her superabundance, not an
element of my plan, but only an excess of my zeal. So early
was to begin my tendency to *overtreat*, rather than undertreat
(when there was choice or danger) my subject. (Many members
of my craft, I gather, are far from agreeing with me, but I have
always held overtreating the minor disservice.) "Treating" that
of "The Portrait" amounted to never forgetting, by any lapse,
that the thing was under a special obligation to be amusing.
There was the danger of the noted "thinness"—which was to
be averted, tooth and nail, by cultivation of the lively. That is
at least how I see it to-day. Henrietta must have been at that
time a part of my wonderful notion of the lively. And then
there was another matter. I had, within the few preceding years,
come to live in London, and the "international" light lay, in
those days, to my sense, thick and rich upon the scene. It was
the light in which so much of the picture hung. But that *is*
another matter. There is really too much to say.

II. The Reviews

3·A Survey of Early Reviews—American

THE PUBLICATION of *The Portrait of a Lady*, c. December, 1881, was an important literary event. The product of scrupulous workmanship, it was the longest and, in every way, the most important of his works up to 1881. Today it is considered one of his masterpieces. For one of James's novels it was also popular in its own day and provoked a considerable body of criticism, most of which, however, consisted of what had already been said.[1] The usual complaints about James's indifference toward, even intolerance of, his countrymen appeared.[2] There was also the expected dissatisfaction with the ending[3] and the characters;[4] however, there was praise for the character drawing.[5] Critics in the *Literary World*, the *Catholic World*, the *Independent*, and the *Churchman*—all religious periodicals—and Huntington, noticing the absence of any religious sentiments in the characters, declared that the novel mirrored a decadent sector of society of the time and that the undertones of cynicism and despair were alarming symptoms of an age marked by bareness and aridity of spiritual life. These reviewers were somewhat puzzled about the purpose of the novel. They supposed that it was a didactic novel because of the satire in it. The *Independent* summed up the opinion of the majority of reviewers—an opinion which had become conventional.

> The merely literary merits . . . are great and many, so many that we wonder at its unsatisfactory . . . impression. There is no

From *Criticism in American Periodicals of the Works of Henry James from 1866 to 1916* (Washington, D.C., 1944), pp. 26–30. Reprinted by permission of The Catholic University of America Press and the author.

heart in it; there is plenty of brightness, acuteness, wit and good writing; but not enough to redeem it from the effect of literary Pyrrhonism.

Several fresh observations on the development of James's technique were made. Pointing to the consistency in his work, Horace Scudder [6] stated that James had concentrated his attention upon the central figure, Isabel Archer. Unlike Thackeray or Eliot, Scudder pointed out, James as a rule indulged in few generalizations: when the characters in *The Portrait of a Lady* stopped acting or talking, it was to allow him, not to make general reflections on the rank and file of human beings, but to explain the motives behind the words and acts of the characters, particularly Isabel. This method, he thought, resulted in a singular consistency, but this consistency was restricted within the novel itself:

> Within the boundaries of the novel the logic of character and events is close and firm. . . . The characters, the situations, the incidents, all are true to the law of their own being, but that law runs parallel with the law which governs life, instead of being identical with it . . . these characters are not bodily shapes, for the most part, but embodied spirits, who enjoy their materialization for a time, and contribute to a play which goes on upon a stage just a little apart from that great stage where the world's play . . . is carried forward.

Morse and Brownell were of the opinion that this novel represented near-perfection of the development theory of novelwriting, for in it James had dispensed with all the ordinary machinery of a novelist except the study of subtle shades of character; he had been primarily interested in picturing the development of character, particularly, emphasized Brownell, the change of Isabel Archer of Albany, New York, into Mrs. Gilbert Osmond of Rome, Italy, effected in part by her natural disposition and in part by the influence of the people around her: "If George Eliot was the first to make of this important moral phenomenon a distinct study, Mr. James has here . . . quite surpassed her." They observed that since there was little action to move forward the story, this had to be done by development of character, characters which developed themselves through dialogue.[7] Morse, who considered the dialogue somewhat protracted and forced, accused all characters of speaking alike, but Brownell defended the elegance and precision of their speech. The secret of James's success, he declared, was the "imaginative treatment of reality": the substance of *The Portrait of a Lady* was thoroughly real but its presentation was imaginative, and as a novel it succeded in combining "scientific value with romantic interest and artistic merit."

Continuing his discussion of James's technique in an essay, "Henry James, Jr., and the Modern Novel," [8] Morse declared that James was the product of "modern or scientific methods of novel-writing" and that he almost represented a school of novel-writing by himself; that he was above all a realist, a materialist, opposed to all that was spiritual and imaginative, especially transcendental. Morse believed that to James human character was mechanical; its springs could be touched; and if there were any power behind it, he failed to see or believe in it. Admitting the author's realistic technique, displayed best in the portrait-painting, the critic, like so many of his colleagues, nevertheless disliked James's novels because they did not satisfy the heart, as did the novels of Dickens, Scott, and Thackeray.

The illuminating analysis in *Lippincott's* of James's development as a writer of fiction, from *Roderick Hudson* to his latest novel, was sufficiently different from prevailing criticism to be outstanding. The flattering reviewer considered *The Portrait of a Lady* James's masterpiece. He did not think that this novel exhibited any sudden development of power; on the contrary, it represented the climax of a slow, steady progression: elements developed nearly perfectly here were present in undeveloped or not so highly developed form in his earlier novels. James's early minor crudities had disappeared, his limitations remained, but he had adapted himself to them: "Continual practice has not exhausted but has enlarged his power." The critic went on to say that there had been a certain unfinished aspect, a bareness in James's early novels: "the characters were so simple, the accessories so few that one was haunted afterwards by a recollection of large spaces of blank wall"; but *The Portrait of a Lady* was at once finer and closer in workmanship: "The walls are no longer blank; they are covered with arabesques of ingenious and delicate pattern."

28   THE REVIEWS

Notes

1. W. C. Brownell, "James's *Portrait of a Lady*," Nation, xxxiv (Feb. 2, 1882), 102–3. (See Chapter 4 of this book.)

2. *Independent*, xxxiv (Jan. 19, 1882), 11; *Catholic World*, xxxiv (Feb., 1882), 716–7:

3. H. A. Huntington, *Dial*, ii (Jan., 1882), 214–5; *Lippincott's*, xxix (Feb., 1882), 213–5; *Penn Monthly*, xiii (March, 1882), 233–4.

4. J. H. Morse, the *Critic*, I (Dec. 3, 1881), 333–4, found few characters to grow enthusiastic about or get interested in. This was the first review of James to appear in this important organ of literary criticism, which was to remain faithful to him until it ceased publication in 1906. The *Literary World*, xii (Dec. 17, 1881), 473–4, found few characters fit to live; the *Californian*, v (Jan., 1882), 86–7, stated that they were a group of sickly, cowardly, wretched personages, types that Turgenev, but not James, might have succeeded with; the *Churchman*, xlv (Jan. 28, 1882), 97–8, likewise judged most of them repulsive; the *Penn Monthly* objected to the artificial heroine—not a real person but a clever automaton. Huntington thought that the weakest spot in the story was that a woman of Isabel's perception could have been taken in by so transparent a cheat and dilettante as Gilbert.

5. Brownell, *Nation*; *Lippincott's*; *Harper's*, lxiv (Feb., 1882), 474. Even the critics who did not like the characters were impressed with the skill with which they were drawn.

6. "The Portrait of a Lady and Dr. Breen's Practice," the *Atlantic*, xlix (Jan., 1882), 126–30. In this comparison of two novels of James and Howells, Scudder noted that they were alike in that both Isabel Archer and Grace Breen were reflections of modern womanly life. The difference was in the methods of the novelists: "The perfection of Mr. James's art is in its intellectual order. . . . The imagination which rules governs a somewhat cold world, and gives forth light rather than heat. The oppositeness of Mr. Howells's method intimates the more human power which he possesses."

7. Morse was of the opinion that James had no skill in making action tell the story; Brownell explained that James's omission of action might be due to the influence of Turgenev.

8. *Critic*, ii (Jan. 14, 1882), 1.

William C. Brownell

4 · An American Review—James's
The Portrait of a Lady

MR. JAMES's novel, which caused each number of the *Atlantic Monthly* to be awaited with impatience last year, gains in its complete presentation, and, like most novels of any pretensions, is most readable when read consecutively. Unlike most novels, however, whose fate (and the fortune of whose authors) it is to appear serially, the reason for this does not consist in the condensation which the reader is thus enabled to make in spite of the author, but in the fact that it is a work of art of which the whole is equal to no fewer than all of its parts, and of which there is a certain "tendency," to lose which is to miss one of the main features of the book. In other words, 'The Portrait of a Lady' is an important work, the most important Mr. James has thus far written, and worthy of far more than mere perusal—worthy of study, one is inclined to say. It is in fact a little too important—to express by a paradox the chief criticism to be made upon it—or, at all events, the only impression left by it which is not altogether agreeable. For the first two or three hundred pages one is beguiled by a kind of entertainment always of a high order—the dissection of an interesting character by a clever and scrupulous demonstrator. After that, though it would be misleading to say that the interest flags—the interest being throughout the book remarkable for its evenness—the feeling supervenes that to be still entertained argues a happy aptitude for most serious and "intellectual" delectation. Most persons

From "James's *The Portrait of a Lady*," *Nation*, XXXIV (Feb. 2, 1882), 102–103.

will recall some experience of the same sensation in first becoming acquainted with undisguisedly philosophical writings—
such as the writings of Emerson or Burke. To others it may be
indicated by saying that it is just the sensation Carlyle missed
in finding the works of George Eliot "dool—just dool." In
America, it is well known, we do not find George Eliot dull,
and it is upon our appetite for this sort of provender that Mr.
James doubtless relies, and undoubtedly does well to rely. Nevertheless, it is possible to feel what Carlyle meant without agreeing
with it; and though maintaining firmly the absorbing interest
of "The Portrait of a Lady," we are ready to admit that once
or twice we have laid aside the book for a season, with the
exhilaration which Mr. Howells has somewhere observed to be
coincident with giving up a difficult task. One of the happiest
of the many happy remarks made in "The Portrait of a Lady"
is in Miss Stackpole's characterization of her *fiancé*: "He's as
clear as glass; there's no mystery about him. He is not intellectual, but he appreciates intellect. On the other hand, he doesn't
exaggerate its claims. *I sometimes think we do in the United
States.*" The person of whom this is said naturally cuts a smaller
figure in the novel than the more complex organizations, in
dealing with which Mr. James is most at home; and it is the
inference from this circumstance that we have in mind. For
not only are the simpler though perennial elements of human
nature in general eschewed by Mr. James, but his true distinction—that is to say, his strength and weakness also—consists in
his attempt to dispense with all the ordinary machinery of the
novelist except the study of subtle shades of character. In other
words, his masterpiece, as "The Portrait of a Lady" must be
called, is not only outside of the category of the old romance
of which "Tom Jones," for example, may stand as the type, but
also dispenses with the dramatic movement and passionate interest upon which the later novelists, from Thackeray to Thomas
Hardy, have relied. In a sense, and to a certain extent, Turgeneff
may be said to be Mr. James's master, but even a sketch or a
study by Turgeneff is turbulence itself beside the elaborate
placidity of these 519 pages. This involves the necessity of the
utmost care in presenting the material, and accordingly we have
that squaring of the elbows and minute painstaking which not

only result inevitably in occasional lumbering movement, but which lend the work an air of seeming more important than any book whatever could possibly be; so that it is perhaps fortunate for its popularity (which, by the way, we believe is extraordinary) that we exaggerate the claims of intellect occasionally in the United States.

Even this measure of fault-finding, however, seems a little ungracious, not to say hypercritical, in view of the distinguished success of Mr. James's experiment in applying the development theory to novel-writing, so to speak. We have ourselves followed the succession of his stories since "Roderick Hudson" appeared with mingled interest and regret, because he has seemed to be getting further and further away from very safe ground, where he was very strong, and into the uncertainties of an unfamiliar region of which it was impossible to tell whether its novelty or its real merit gave it its interest. The elemental characters and dramatic situations of the novel just mentioned were strongly handled, and the work being, comparatively speaking, a youthful one, its promise seemed even greater than its actual qualities. But, almost as if he had been an amateur dipping into another branch of effort after having demonstrated his ability in one, Mr. James immediately abandoned the field of imaginative romance as it is generally understood. He at once made clear his faculty for his new choice, and the field he entered on with "The American," and continued with the shorter stories illustrative of American types, became immediately popular. "Daisy Miller" may almost be said to mark an era in the mental progress of many persons who exaggerate the claims of intellect occasionally; it is wearisome to recall the "discussions" it occasioned in drawing-rooms and in print. There was, to be sure, a Chauvinist view, so to speak, taken of this and its associated sketches, by persons who omitted to perceive that Mr. James had not only made the current mechanical speculations about "the coming American novel" an anachronism, but had also displayed his patriotism and the national genius by inventing a new variety of literature. But naturally Mr. James might be expected to heed rather those of his readers who appreciated and enjoyed his motives and rejoiced in his discovery of romantic sociology. And this seemed his real danger; for though to these readers this reading conveyed a peculiarly refined pleasure, on account both of its novelty and the cleverness of its execution, there was no certainty that this pleasure was not a rather temporary mood, and likely to pass away after the novelty had worn off. Instead, however, of avoiding this danger by a return to the perennially interesting material with which he first dealt, Mr. James has conquered it, *vi et armis*, by a persistence that at one time seemed a little wilful. No one can now pretend, whatever his own literary likes and dislikes may be, that romantic sociology, exploited as Mr. James has shown it capable of being, is not a thoroughly serious field of literature, whose interest is permanent and dignified.

"The Portrait of a Lady" is a modest title, though an apt one. The portrait of the lady in question is indeed the theme of the book, and it is elaborated with a minuteness so great that when finally one begins to find it confusing it becomes evident that the ordinary point of view must be changed, and the last detail awaited—as in a professedly scientific work—before the whole can appear. Miss Isabel Archer is an orphan to whom her aunt gives an opportunity of seeing the world, and to whom her aunt's husband leaves a large fortune, at the instance of his son, who is unselfishly and romantically interested to see what his cousin will make of her life when nothing prevents her from doing as she wishes. The reader at once assumes the position of this young man, and with more or less (less in our own case, we confess) sympathy, watches the progress of the drama which he has set going. At the climax the heroine discovers that she has wrecked her life most miserably. The spiritual transition from the Isabel Archer of Albany to the Mrs. Osmond of Rome is of course accomplished in part by natural disposition and in part by the influence of the numerous characters which surround her. The way in which this influence is exhibited is a marked feature of the book. If George Eliot was the first to make of this important moral phenomenon a distinct study, Mr. James has here, in our opinion, quite surpassed her. Any one can judge by comparing the reciprocal effect upon the development of each other's characters of the Lydgates in "Middlemarch" with that of the Osmonds here. The other characters are treated with a microscopy hardly inferior. Osmond himself is one of the most palpable of those figures in fiction which are to be called subtle. Madame Merle, his former mistress, mother of his child, who makes the marriage between him and his poverty and Isabel and her wealth, and who, up to the climax of the book, is Isabel's ideal, is, if anything, even better done. There is something almost uncanny in the perfection with which these secretive natures are turned inside out for the reader's inspection. As for the heroine, the American girl *par excellence*, it seems as if, scientifically speaking, Mr. James had said the last word on this subject; at any rate till the model herself is still further developed. For example (p. 344): "She never looked so charming as when, in the genial heat of discussion, she received a crushing blow full in the face and brushed it away as a feather." There are pages as good.

It has long been evident that Mr. James's powers of observation are not only remarkably keen, but sleepless as well. But "The Portrait of a Lady" would not be what it is if it did not possess a *fonds* of moral seriousness, in addition to and underlying its extraordinary interest of purely intellectual curiosity. There is a specific lesson for the American girl in the first place; there are others, more general, which accompany every imaginative work of large importance. That these are nowhere distinctly stated is now nothing new in fiction even of a distinctly moral purpose. But Mr. James has carried suggestiveness in this regard further than any rival novelist, and though, unless one has ears to hear, it is entirely possible to miss the undertone of his book, to an appreciative sense there is something exquisite in the refinement with which it is conveyed. Refinement in this respect cannot be carried too far. In strictly literary matters Mr. James's fastidiousness may be objected to, perhaps, if one chooses; he has carried the method of the essayist into the domain of romance: its light touch, its reliance on suggestiveness, its weakness for indirect statement, its flattering presupposition of the reader's perceptiveness, its low tones, its polish. Upon occasion, where the circumstances really seem to warrant a little fervor, you only get from the author of "The Portrait of a Lady" irreproachability. Objection to this may easily be carried too far, however; and those who do thus carry it too far, and argue that no people ever spoke and acted with the elegance and precision of the personages here portrayed, must of necessity pay the penalty of ultra-literalness and miss the secret of Mr. James's success. To characterize this secret with adequate fulness would require far more than the space at our disposal; but it may be sufficiently indicated by calling it the imaginative treatment of reality. In this unquestionably lies Mr. James's truly original excellence. "The Portrait of a Lady" is the most eminent example we have thus far had of realistic art in fiction *à outrance*, because its substance is thoroughly, and at times profoundly, real, and at the same time its presentation is imaginative. On the one hand, wilfulness and fantasticality are avoided, and on the other, prose and flatness. One may even go further, and say that the book succeeds in the difficult problem of combining a scientific value with romantic interest and artistic merit.

Donald M . Murry

5 · A Survey of Early Reviews—English

THIS NOVEL, which a recent critic has named as among James's greatest,[1] received in most of the reviews almost equal proportions of praise and blame. The *Academy* was typical.[2] James had a passion, the reviewer said, for "the technique of craftsmanship," but a disdain for that "popular" element of fiction, plot. This latter fault was shown in the ending of the novel, where James left all the threads of narrative "hanging loose." Counterbalancing this, however, was the "masterly painting of moral and intellectual atmosphere—the realisable rendering—not of character itself, but of those impalpable radiations of character from which we apprehend it long before we have *data* that enables us to fully comprehend it." This statement was the nearest, perhaps, that any of the reviewers came to an analysis of James's indirect method in *The Portrait of a Lady*. Though he did not describe the technique clearly, the reviewer apparently appreciated it. James's "effect," he went on, was achieved by "honest and direct workmanship" which combined "lightness and precision of touch in a way which is all but unique in English fiction." The heroine was thus a "masterly portrait," and her relation with Osmond was "full of psychological interest." Like most of the other reviewers, the writer for the *Academy* liked the minor characters Ralph Touchett and Henri-

From "The Critical Reception of Henry James in English Periodicals, 1875–1916" (Unpublished dissertation, New York University, 1951), pp. 45–49. Reprinted by permission of The Graduate School, New York University, and of the author.

etta Stackpole. The former was rendered with "genuine and
not too insistent pathos," and the latter with "high comedy
humour."

The *Spectator*, though it found the book "clever," differed
radically on the character of Isabel.[3] Her mind and motives never
became clear, the reviewer complained. Osmond and Ralph were
clear, however. Interesting was the *Spectator's* moralistic objection to the ending. Henrietta's parting injunction to Goodwood was to this reviewer a "cowardly" hint by James that the
heroine saw a straight path to a liaison with Goodwood.[4] Never
before had the "agnosticism" of James set up "so cynical a
signpost into the abyss." The reviewer followed this with some
general reflections on "agnostic art."

The *Athenaeum* too liked the minor characters but found
the portrait of Isabel cloudy.[5] The reviewer even suggested deliberate mystification on James's part. He then reiterated the
frequently-voiced complaints about lack of strong passion, and
evasion of emotional crises. Alone of the reviewers, he devoted
a good deal of space to small matters of diction. He objected,
for instance, to James's "modicity" for "moderate"; "superurban" for a hill above the city. His sharp eye even caught an
instance in which James, in the same sentence, repudiated one
Americanism with quotation marks while accepting another.

The *Saturday Review* [6] deplored what it saw as inadequate
treatment of "deeper motives" and strong passions, advising
James to use his "surface" art on shorter pieces, and predicting
that *The Portrait of a Lady* would not raise his reputation.
Blackwood's, like the *Spectator*, was shocked at what it felt to
be a "most equivocal if not debasing conclusion." [7] Like all the
rest, it praised the minor characters. As did the *British Quarterly
Review*,[8] it saw the similarity between the renunciation of Isabel
and that of Newman in *The American*. As to the plot, it objected that Isabel's fortune of sixty thousand pounds would
have been too little to warrant the elaborate preparations of a
man like Osmond to catch her; and, misunderstanding Isabel's
character, it found "inexplicable" the sudden rupture between
Isabel and Osmond immediately after the marriage.

The *British Quarterly Review* added little to the discussion
except the reflection that the novel represented faithfully "the

tone of good society." [9] The *Literary World* devoted over three pages to the book, but added no new ideas.[10] Its concluding sentence was typical of the rest of the review: "It is an unsatisfactory, unfinished, though in its way a very clever, entertaining book."

An amusing article which appeared in the *Contemporary Review* some time later, "The Americans as Painted by Themselves," is perhaps appropriately mentioned at this point, since it contained an attack on all James's heroines, and especially on Isabel Archer.[11] Written by an English noblewoman whose complacency rivaled that of James's Lady Barb, the article had as its thesis that American women, as revealed in the works of James and others, were so vulgar as to be beneath the contempt of well-bred folk and unworthy of the attention of artists. Prominent among the offenders was Isabel, who had allowed one man after another to propose to her; who had gone to the deathbed of one of her "lovers" in a way "not usual with well-conducted young brides"; and who, according to the insinuations at the end of the novel, was finally revealed as no "lady" at all. Henrietta, of course, was deplorable, "yet Mr. James is evidently much surprised that this Gorgon is not taken to the homes and hearts of the British aristocracy." In conclusion, the writer of the article judged that representation of such vulgar and "supremely uninteresting" human beings as American young ladies was a "misuse of talent."

In few of the reviews, then, was there any real criticism. Significant is the fact that all except the *Academy* were far from feeling that the "frail vessel of a girl" was the "all in all for our attention," as James had intended.[12] His "trick" of revealing her through her relation to those surrounding her had, as far as the reviewers were concerned, not come off. They saw only the minor characters. Also, what James thought to be excellence of unity and proportion ("architectural competence") did not reveal itself to them. They admired vignettes of characterization, and *Blackwood's*, for instance, seemed to feel that such "fine sketches" were completely detachable from the whole.

Notes

1. F. R. Leavis, *The Great Tradition* (New York, 1949), Chapter III.
2. xx (Nov. 26, 1881), 397–98.
3. LIV (Nov. 26, 1881), 1504–6.
4. It will be remembered that after Isabel has left for Rome, Henrietta says, "Look here Mr. Goodwood . . . just you wait!" New York Edition, III, 437. Two other critics interpreted the passage in this way. See *Blackwood's*, cited below, p. 47, and Lady F. P. Verney's article "The Americans as Painted by Themselves," *Contemporary Review*, XLVI (Oct., 1884), 549.
5. No. 2822 (Nov. 26, 1881), 699. (See Chapter 6 of this book.)
6. LII (Dec. 3, 1881), 703–4.
7. CXXXI (Mar., 1882), 381.
8. LXXV (Jan., 1882), 227–8.
9. *Ibid.*, p. 228.
10. XXVI (July 21, 1882), 40–43.
11. Lady F. P. Verney, *op. cit.*, see also H. Rider Haggard's "About Fiction," *Contemporary Review* (Feb., 1887), 172, for another attack upon James's heroines.
12. New York Edition, III, xv.

6 · An English Review—
The Portrait of a Lady

IT IS IMPOSSIBLE not to feel that Mr. James has at last contrived
to write a dull book. 'The Portrait of a Lady' is of enormous
length, being printed much more closely than is usual with
three-volume novels; and a large part of it is made up of page
after page of narrative and description, in which the author goes
on refining and distinguishing, as if unable to hit on the exact
terms necessary to produce the desired effect. There is, of course,
plenty of dialogue as well, but not very much of a kind to make
the reader wish, as he may have done in the case of some of
Mr. James's stories, that he had himself been a sharer in it.
Here and there a tiresome artifice is employed, that of indicating
a conversation by giving one person's remarks only, much as a
cross-examination is reported in the newspapers. The theme
is one which seems to possess an inexhaustible attraction for
the author. An American girl, brought up more or less uncon-
ventionally though among ordinary people, conceives high but
somewhat undefined notions of her duty, refuses some excellent
men on the ground that she does not want to marry anybody, and
in a few months is caught by the first æsthetic impostor whom
she comes across. After this the history becomes fragmentary;
but we find on our next meeting with the heroine that her husband, on perceiving that he has married a woman with views
of her own and disinclined to take her place among his *bibelots*,
has begun to hate her. Finally, a revelation is made to her about
some passages in his former life, and the reader fancies that

From "Novels of the Week," *The Athenaeum*, Nov. 26, 1881, p. 699.

Mr. James intends to bring about a crisis; yet the only result is to decide her to take a journey against her husband's wishes, and the story leaves her just started back to rejoin him. Nor is the least hint given to show in what way their subsequent relations are to be modified either by her knowledge of his past offences or by her disobedience to his orders. That is to say, this so-called "portrait of a lady" is left unfinished just at the point where some really decisive and enlightening strokes begin to be possible. It may, of course, be wrong to assume that the portrait to which the title refers is that of the heroine. There are other ladies in the story of whom we form a far clearer conception than of Isabel Osmond. For example, there is her friend Miss Stackpole, the lady-correspondent of the *New York Interviewer*, who is really an admirable representative of the literary lady—hard-headed and tender-hearted, shrewd and naïve, unconventional to the verge of scandal, yet as ignorant of evil as a child. There is Isabel's aunt, Mrs. Touchett, who "agrees to differ" from her husband, and lives, *more Americano*, in Italy when she is not at New York or on the way between the two, the husband being domiciled wholly in England. There are, indeed, portraits of ladies enough and clear enough; the only one who is not portrayed so as to make the reader understand her is the heroine. This may be a bit of mystification on Mr. James's part; if so, it can only be said that it is not a novelist's business to mystify his readers, certainly not at this length. That he has aimed at brevity may sometimes excuse an author for being obscure; but obscurity through three long volumes is unpardonable. Mr. James sins in a small matter of style. He has taken to coining and using some very awkward words. "Modicity" as the noun of *moderate*, "superurban" of a house on a hill above a town, "fine" in the sense of *clever* (French *fin*), are not desirable additions to the language. Nor does the epithet "weary" as applied to the brickwork of an old house add much to the picture. When we read of "doors perched upon little 'stoops' of red stone, which descended *sidewise* to the street," we are disposed to smile alike at the ingenuity with which the writer repudiates one term belonging to the English of the United States and the simplicity with which he adopts another. To revert once more to general criticism: there is no doubt that reticence is a virtue in a novelist, but it may be carried too far, and this Mr. James, from a feeling, probably, of repugnance for the gushing and sensational, seems to have done. He should remember that much of human life cannot be painted in "tertiary" tints, and that if he wishes to be a master in the art of portraying it he must furnish his box with some stronger colours, and lay them on boldly.

III. Special Problems

7·From *The Method of Henry James*

MOST JOYOUS of dates in all our chronicle is the year 1880. It is in contemplation of that year that the lover of James feels his blood run warmest. The footlights flash on, the fiddles begin, and faces brighten in anticipation of the three knocks and the parted curtain. It is not that *Scribner's* was concluding in January of that year the publication of *Confidence*, nor that *Harper's* from July to December was setting forth the charming study of *Washington Square*. It is that the *Atlantic* this side the water and *Macmillan's* in London were showing each month in successive tableaux the enthralling "Portrait of a Lady." This was the first masterpiece of Henry James.

He was still far from his technical goal. In mechanical ways the work is still very different from that, for example, of *The Golden Bowl*, to which it bears a considerable likeness in theme. *The Portrait* is a novel like other novels, taking us through successive stages in the history of its characters. It is the biography of Isabel Archer, and has the general character of a chronicle. It covers a number of years, and includes a number of substantial events. Nearly the whole first volume is taken up with material which would have been excluded from the more distinctive work of the later years. The episode of Lord Warburton and his proposal, the death of Mr. Touchett and his bequest to Isabel are two major blocks of material which would

From *The Method of Henry James* (New Haven, 1918), pp. 205–11. Reprinted by permission of Yale University Press. Copyright 1918 by Yale University Press.

45

have been treated briefly and referentially as a part of the antecedent facts of the story. *The Golden Bowl* begins at a point corresponding to a point somewhat beyond the opening of the second volume of the earlier novel—just before the marriage of the heroine, which ushers in (for Isabel as for Maggie) the main dramatic complication. Not merely does the author of *The Portrait* give a whole volume to Isabel's earlier history as a grown woman. When he has once got her launched in this earlier career, he stops for the length of more than two chapters to bring up to date her history as a girl and that of her cousin Ralph. And this is not done, as it would have been done after 1896, by reminiscence and dialogue as an integral part of the narrative of present experience.

Again the earlier technique appears in the large number of characters of considerable importance. As in "The Golden Bowl," there are but four major characters—Isabel, Osmond, Madame Merle and Warburton. But over against the chorus-figure of Mrs. Assingham stand, in *The Portrait*, Ralph Touchett and Goodwood, Henrietta Stackpole and Pansy, even if we leave out of account Mr. and Mrs. Touchett, Mr. Rosier and Mr. Bantling, and the Countess Gemini. And we can hardly leave even them out of account, considering how much attention is given to the character and personal history of each one of them.

Mrs. Assingham, it will be remembered, is given no personal history, and no character except that of a woman exceedingly ingenious in the interpretation of human nature. She is necessary for the dialogue. The minor characters of *The Portrait* have a similar function; but they do not fulfil it to anything like the same extent, since the dialogue has taken on very little of its later character. It serves chiefly to display the various breeding and humors of the persons taking part. The author has not yet so completely neutralized his characters as to social tone. They still exhibit some of the variety and picturesqueness proper to characters in a Victorian novel. Vividest in this respect is Henrietta Stackpole, with her militant Americanism, her militant independence, her journalistic preoccupations, and her intense earnestness. But even Madame Merle is occasionally given a touch that suggests Thackeray more than James. She is

perhaps the most perfect creation of the book, and her line is
by no means any sort of vividness. Her line is the most perfect
suavity of manner, the most impeccable of self-effacing good
taste. But there is at least one occasion on which she is treated
for a moment or two like a person in a novel (or comedy) of
"manners." Mrs. Touchett is discussing the comparatively
liberal treatment accorded her by her husband in his will.

> "He chose, I presume, to recognise the fact that though I
> lived much abroad and mingled—you may say freely—in for-
> eign life, I never exhibited the smallest preference for anyone
> else."
> "For anyone but yourself," Madame Merle mentally ob-
> served; but the reflection was perfectly inaudible.
> "I never sacrificed my husband to another," Mrs. Touchett
> continued with her stout curtness.
> "Oh, no," thought Madame Merle; "you never did any-
> thing for another!"[1]

The author now goes on to explain the "cynicism in these mute
comments." Madame Merle had not of course expected any
bequest to herself. But—

> The idea of a distribution of property—she would almost
> have said of spoils—just now pressed upon her senses and irri-
> tated her with a sense of exclusion. I am far from wishing to
> picture her as one of the hungry mouths or envious hearts of
> the general herd, but we have already learned of her having de-
> sires that had never been satisfied. If she had been questioned,
> she would of course have admitted—with a fine proud smile
> —that she had not the faintest claim to a share in Mr.
> Touchett's relics. "There was never anything in the world be-
> tween us," she would have said. "There was never that, poor
> man!"—with a fillip of her thumb and her third finger.[2]

Perhaps something of this kind is necessary at this point to give
the reader a bit of a "tip" on what lies below the surface of
Madame Merle's exquisite manner. But in the later work James
would have managed to convey a sense of these depths without
the false note of vulgarity. Or else, to the reader's confusion, he
would have left him to find out for himself without the aid of
tips.

But the early manner is found in points more technical and
superficial than essential and organic. Essentially *The Portrait*

is the development of an idea by the method of "revelation."
. . . The adventures of Isabel Archer are more spiritual than
material. The stages of her chronicle are the stages by which
the painter fills out her portrait. Even in the preliminary period
of her English sojourn, we are occupied with the discovery of
a woman intensely concerned to make her life fine, hoping "to
find herself in a difficult position, so that she should have the
pleasure of being as heroic as the occasion demanded." The
proposal of Lord Warburton is admitted merely in order that
she may assert in striking fashion her "enlightened prejudice in
favour of the free exploration of life." [3] It is not ease and security
that are desired by this adventurous American soul. She explains to her reproachful suitor that she cannot hope to escape
her fate, cannot avoid unhappiness by separating herself from
life—"from the usual chances and dangers, from what most
people know and suffer." [4]

With the entry of Madame Merle towards the end of the
first volume, the painter attacks the real background of his picture. A few chapters later his task begins in earnest with the
appearance of the Florentine gentleman who is to become the
most prominent feature in the heroine's experience. From this
point on, the work is a masterpiece of revelation; and if the
details brought out are chiefly details of "background"—having
to do with the characters of Osmond and Madame Merle—
that is essentially the case in the later books. The background
circumstances are revealed through the consciousness of the
heroine who is the foreground figure; and they tend to bring out
in brighter relief the beauty of this figure. Every trait of vanity
and selfishness in Osmond gives play to the corresponding traits
of generous largemindedness in Isabel, as well as giving her occasion for the display of resourcefulness in difficult social relations. The coldness of his nature serves as foil to the flame-like
warmth of hers. And the earlier stages of their acquaintance
bring out sufficiently the large ground of taste and sensibility
which they have in common. I must deny myself the agreeable
task of tracing from scene to scene the nicely graduated steps
by which this "sterile dilettante" is betrayed to us first and then
to Isabel, and the steps by which there dawn upon her consciousness the more and more bewildering, the more and more
heroic features of her great adventure.

Nowhere is the concern of the story more beautifully than in *The Portrait* the *quality* of experience. It is not the bare facts of Gilbert's relation to Madame Merle and Pansy, revealed at the climax of the story by the Countess Gemini, that are of importance. It is the values of life as conceived by Gilbert and by Madame Merle upon which these facts throw their final interpretative light. Nowhere is there a finer indication of those social and esthetic values to which all the leading characters of James are devoted than in the scenes of Isabel's growing admiration for Osmond. Nowhere short of *Poynton* and *The Golden Bowl* is there a finer display of the spiritual values that transcend the others than in the scenes of Isabel's growing horror of her husband. *The Portrait of a Lady* has thus the distinction of being the first novel in which the "figure in the carpet" stands out in distinct and glowing beauty.

But no mere indication of the order of this novel in the author's development will explain the many graces and charms it possesses in its own right. There is something about the personality and situation of Isabel that gives her a place unique in the whole gallery. It is a place no man can occupy. A man may have the advantage when it comes to the freedom of adventure of a Pendennis or a Tom Jones. But the very limitations upon her freedom, the delicacy of her position, give to the adventures of a brave woman an attaching pathos, and even a spiritual richness, which a man's can seldom have. The limits of her experience outwardly compel her to cultivate it intensively.

Of course it may be urged that Ralph Touchett shares this advantage in disadvantage. And I am willing to grant him a very large measure of the attractiveness of the generous fettered woman. He is a figure beautifully conceived and executed. And indeed there is no novel of James in which we find so many characters of a warm and simple humanity. Something of a like appeal is made by Mr. Touchett, by Pansy. We are fond even of Henrietta, and we have a measure of charity for Mrs. Touchett and the Countess Gemini.

In fineness of execution, Gilbert Osmond and Madame Merle take their place beside Isabel herself. Madame Merle is a figure of even rarer conception—having no counterpart, as Isabel may be thought to have, among the famous creations of Meredith and George Eliot. And she is herself so much of a victim, and a person of so much *savoir vivre* withal, and of so graceful and touching a manner of exit, that we cannot forbear to open our hearts even to her.

There is again a peculiar charm about the *mise en scène* of this drama. None of the English country-places that figure so largely in James is more lovely than that of the American banker on the Thames. Have we perhaps its model, by the way, in that other banker's home alluded to by Mr. James in his life of Story? Surely at least the golden air so often referred to in that reconstruction of the earlier time is what envelops the Florentine villa of Gilbert Osmond in the days before his true character has been revealed.

The lover of James will ever cherish this work as the prime example of his early manner. It has the open face of youth. There is a lightness and freshness of tone about it that never recurs in the more labored work of later years. It is the first of his compositions entirely free from crudity and the last to show the unalloyed charm of ingenuousness.

Notes

1. Henry James, *The Novels and Tales*, III (New York, 1907–09), pp. 295–96.
2. Pp. 296–97.
3. P. 155.
4. P. 187.

Cornelia Pulsifer Kelley

8 · From *The Early Development of Henry James*

THE BEGINNING of the 80's marked the end of James's early fictional development. There was the little masterpiece, *Washington Square*. There was also a large masterpiece, *The Portrait of a Lady*,[1] which, the preface written in 1907 states,[2] was started as early as the spring of 1879, designed from the first for serial publication in the *Atlantic Monthly* and *Macmillan's* where it began to appear in the fall of 1880. The commencement of its composition and appearance thus overlapped the ending of the writing and publication of *Washington Square*, but *The Portrait of a Lady* shows much more conclusively the ability of Henry James. It proves that he could do things on a large scale, deal with big effects, was a great humanist and a great artist as well. It is most interesting, too, for though it shows the imprint of Turgénieff and George Eliot upon James, it reveals also his individuality and independence. What we are to observe in this novel is not James slavishly working under the direction of the Russian or the English novelist, but James, having assimilated the lessons of both, treating a subject similar to one of George Eliot's with the skill which came from combining the best principles of each, supplementing them with his own theories, and emerging a novelist who was not only in possession of the secrets

From *The Early Development of Henry James*, University of Illinois Studies in Language and Literature, Vol. XV (1930), pp. 284, 291–300. Reprinted by permission of The University of Illinois Press and of the author. A paperback edition of this book was issued in 1965 with an introduction by Lyon N. Richardson (© 1965 by the Board of Trustees of the University of Illinois).

of his craft, but could do with them what he wished. *The Portrait of a Lady* shows that the days of hesitation and stumbling experiment were definitely ended.[3]

* * *

The outstanding characteristic of *The Portrait of a Lady* is its rich complexity—complexity of subject matter, plot, and treatment. Yet despite this, James placed his emphasis rightly, kept his material well in hand, and built up a story which, though complex, is so well made that it is quite as easy to follow as its simple predecessor. Never did the story or the characters get away from James; never did he go too far. His principle was not so much completeness of treatment, as it had been in *The American,* as adequacy of treatment, and he meant by this what the Greeks approved in their neither too much nor too little. He observed the mean, the just right, in every respect.

That he was able to do this was largely due to the way in which he approached and developed the story before he began to write it. The history of this he explained later to a certain extent in the preface which he wrote for the novel when he assembled the *Collected Edition.* He said here that he had begun *The Portrait* with the character of his heroine whom he had had in mind for a long time, but had refrained from treating because of a pious desire to place his treasure right.[4] To her, as she stood isolated, had been added the other characters and the setting, and these characters, who seemed just to have come to him, had suggested her story.

> I seem to myself to have waked up one morning in possession of them. . . . I recognized them, I knew them, they were the numbered pieces of my puzzle, the concrete terms of my "plot." It was as if they had simply, by an impulse of their own, walked into my ken, and all in response to my primary question: "What will she *do*?" Their answer seemed to be that if I would trust them, they would show me; on which, with an urgent appeal to them to make it at least as interesting as they could, I trusted them.[5]

In all this, he admitted, he had been proceeding as Turgénieff proceeded, and he had gained confidence because Turgénieff had assured him that this was a legitimate way to build up a novel.[6]

But there had been the question of unity and emphasis. He was using a "small" person, and he was in for organizing an "ado" about her. That it could be done, he had been certain, for Shakespeare and George Eliot had often done it—there were Juliet and Hetty and Maggie and Rosamond and Gwendolen—but George Eliot and Shakespeare always eked out such persons with subplots, never let them matter enough, as much as they might matter.[7] With a weak agent, such as he had in Isabel, there was the danger that the story would become that of someone else, of Ralph, or of Madame Merle, of Osmond, even possibly of Lord Warburton or of Caspar Goodwood, or of all of these people together. To get around this danger, he had wisely determined that he must make it a view not of Isabel's relation to them, but of theirs to her.

> There is always the escape from any close account of the weak agent of such spells by using as a bridge for evasion, for retreat and flight, the view of her relation to those surrounding her. Make it predominantly a view of *their* relation and the trick is played: you give the general sense of her effect, and you give it . . . . with the maximum of ease.[8]

While they were all interested in her, she must feel herself apart, think of herself as working out her destiny by herself. That had meant he would have to get into Isabel's mind, and this had suggested placing the *center* of the subject in Isabel's consciousness.

> "Place the center of the subject in the young woman's own consciousness," I said to myself, "and you get as interesting and as beautiful a difficulty as you wish. Stick to *that*—for the center; put the heaviest weight in *that* scale, which will be so largely the scale of her relation to herself. Make her only interested enough, at the same time, in the things that are not herself, and this relation needn't fear to be too limited. Place meanwhile in the other scale, the lighter weight . . . press less hard, in short, on the consciousness of your heroine's satellites, especially the male; make it an interest contributive only to the greater one."[9]

Thus James envisaged in 1907 the problem which had confronted him when he wrote *The Portrait of a Lady*, showing where Turgénieff had reassured him, George Eliot and Shakespeare had warned him, and he *himself* had solved his "deep

difficulty" by finding the most important way. But this is not all
of the story.

Where, the critic is led to ask because of the great fondness
of James for Isabel, had he obtained this "vivid individual?"
Was she someone he actually knew—one of his many cousins?
Had she grown out of the chance remark of a friend as Daisy
had? Had he seen her in a boarding house? Had she come from
his reading? The preface does not satisfy us on this point, and
yet it gives a broadly general hint in the enumeration of the
heroines of Shakespeare and George Eliot, who had been de-
frauded of mattering enough by their authors. And if one turns
back to the critical article which James wrote in 1876 when
Daniel Deronda completed its serial run,[10] the hint is confirmed.
From James's article more than from George Eliot's novel, it is
clear that Gwendolen Harleth was the prototype of Isabel
Archer, for the points which James noted about Gwendolen are
the points which a critic must note about his heroine.

Isabel is similar to Gwendolen in nature, in basic charac-
teristics:

> Gwendolen is a perfect picture of youthfulness—its eagerness,
> its presumption, its preoccupation with itself, its vanity and
> silliness, its sense of its own absoluteness. But she is extremely
> intelligent and clever, and therefore tragedy *can* have a hold
> upon her. Her conscience doesn't make the tragedy. . . . It is
> the tragedy which makes her conscience, which then reacts
> upon it.[11]

If there is any difference between the two heroines, it is that of
degree—an intensification in Isabel—and not of kind.

Isabel's story, broadly looked at, is the same as Gwendolen's:

> The universe, forcing itself with a slow, inexorable pres-
> sure into a narrow, complacent mind, and yet after all extremely
> sensitive mind, and making it ache with the pain of the process
> —that is Gwendolen's story. And it becomes completely char-
> acteristic in that her supreme perception of the fact that the
> world is whirling past her, is in the disappointment not of a
> base but of an exalted passion. The very chance to embrace
> what the author is so fond of calling a "larger life" seems re-
> fused to her. She is punished for being narrow, and she is not
> allowed a chance to expand.[12]

Of course in the particulars and details of plot there are differences, but in each novel, a young woman affronts her destiny.
In each case, her purpose is noble, exalted, and pursued with
passion, and *The Portrait* is, as James said of *Daniel Deronda*
as a whole, "the romance of a high moral tone."

Again Isabel and her story are presented in the same
manner:

> Gwendolen is a masterpiece. She is known, felt, and presented,
> psychologically, altogether in the grand manner.[13] . . . . Gwen-
> dolen's whole history is superbly told. And see how the girl is
> known, inside out, how thoroughly she is felt and understood.
> It is the most *intelligent* thing in all George Eliot's writing, and
> that is saying much. It is so deep, so true, so complete; it holds
> a wealth of psychological detail, it is more than masterly.[14]

Truer words cannot be found to describe the portrait of Isabel
and her history. Can it not be concluded that the desire, perhaps, too, the determination, to "do" thoroughly and completely, intelligently and feelingly, a similar heroine, had come
to James in 1876 as he read and reviewed *Daniel Deronda?*

And the desire had been cherished and fostered. For this,
James had experimented with American girls, trying out varia-
tions of the type, but hesitating to treat his "pious treasure" till
he was sure of himself. For this, he had experimented with
method, looking at his heroines through others, realizing that he
must get at them and their minds directly if he was to do them
justice, trying to on a small scale, but saving and storing up his
energy for the service of Isabel.[15] Thinking of this, he had probably tried to imagine other characters who might help him, and
one day these characters had suddenly stepped before him with
Isabel's story in their hands. Some of these, like Isabel, are like
people he had met in George Eliot—Osmond's refined and distilled brutality is like that of Grandcourt's; Ralph's helpless
devotion is related to that of Will Ladislaw's in *Middlemarch*.[16]
Others came from his own stories—Caspar is like Newman in
his persistency; Pansy is like Aurora but with more delicacy due
to her convent upbringing; Henrietta is related to Miranda
Hope. Not a little of the greatness of *The Portrait* is due to the
deep knowledge James had of all of his characters. He was
thoroughly acquainted with them.

When, three years after writing the review, he turned to work on the portrait of Isabel, he probably had no consciousness of having borrowed her or her attendants. She was then *his* creature; like Gwendolen, to be sure, but there were many such in this world, and he had as much right to do her as he had to do Catherine, who was like Eugénie Grandet. Consider the following sentence from the review: " 'Gwendolen's history is admirably typical—as most things are with George Eliot: it is the very stuff that human life is made of.' " [17] What happened to Gwendolen often happened. James saw that it happened to American girls as well as to English—especially when they came to Europe with the desire to meet life, and the idea of their own competence to deal with it; then the universe forced itself in with a slow, inexorable pressure. James not only felt free to take a similar heroine, he felt impelled to, for he had discovered long before from George Eliot and others,[18] that it was the duty of the novelist to deal with the "very stuff" of life, and he had been proceeding with gradually increasing success ever since. He had even once tried a similar heroine of his own accord in Madame de Mauves.[19] There were no basically new subjects, for human nature was as old as the hills. The American side of it, however, had not yet been adequately done. The same conclusions are to be applied in regard to the resemblance of Osmond to Grandcourt and of Ralph to Will. Such people existed; such "refined and distilled brutality," such handicapped and silent devotion were only too characteristic of life. If Isabel was to face life, she must meet and feel—ah, so emphatically feel—both.

Accordingly James sought a plot, or rather took the one his characters offered, where this would be possible in the highest degree. It was not thus possible in George Eliot's novel where not only Gwendolen's story was thrust behind Deronda's but Gwendolen's hands were tied by poverty. James decided to give his American girl the center of the stage, and then he contrived by the device of the inheritance, which Ralph's love and interest made possible, to make her rich, thus putting it into her power to be magnanimous, to marry a poor man in the wish to help him. He made her, in her own opinion a free agent, and the most bitter part of her tragedy occurs when she finds that she has not been free, only blind, and that others have "made" her life.

What was in *Washington Square* on a small scale, is in *The Portrait of a Lady* on an enlarged and heightened scale. Isabel is intelligent and clever, but she is surrounded by people, two in particular, who are not only clever but wicked, and hence her defeat at their hands. It must not be overlooked, however, that defeated though she is externally, Isabel achieves a moral victory for herself.[20] Catherine did not; she sank into passive existence. Isabel, thus, is like Newman in *The American*.[21] Behind it all is the influence of Turgénieff and his use of failure,[22] now thoroughly absorbed by James as a dominating principle. When James wrote *The Portrait of a Lady*, he did not think of himself as working *under* George Eliot and Turgénieff, but as working along *with* them, even, indeed, as the preface indicates, of working *above* them.

He treated his heroine not only intelligently and truly and feelingly, he treated her artistically. He let Isabel matter *enough*. He gave the whole novel to her. He not only placed her in the center, he placed the center in her consciousness, in her view of herself and of life. However, he did not stay in her mind all of the time, as he had stayed in Mallet's and Newman's, for Isabel, like Catherine, was not to see the conniving about her. But he looked at the others *only* as their plotting involved her, and except for Ralph, who was lovingly watching and seeing all, he stayed as much as possible out of the minds of those surrounding her. He kept everything focussed upon her; then he looked at everything as she saw it. The method which James used in *The Portrait of a Lady* was a combination of his method of using a mind as his glass and the direct approach which he used in *Washington Square*—it was his method made more flexible, adapted to his material, not ruthlessly applied despite the wisdom of the situation. James had control of it.

Then he put everything together, brought it out as he proceeded, built it up increasingly to a climax with an "architectural completeness" which only once again did he feel that he equalled.[23] In this regard, he mentioned in the preface one thing which he regretted and another thing of which he was most proud. He regretted that he had brought in Henrietta, that "light ficelle" who runs beside Isabel, listens to her ideas, and often takes her to task, but plays no essential part in the story.[24] He was pleased with the way in which he had converted Isabel's

sense of and for mild adventures into the very "stuff" of story.[25]
By giving Isabel a premonitory feeling when she first sees
Madame Merle that this grand lady is to play a part in her life,
he had been able to produce "the maximum of intensity with
the minimum of strain." He was proud, especially, of Isabel's
vigil with herself half way through the book, when she spends
the night viewing and reviewing the situation. That, brought
in where it is, picks up and moves forward the action, accomplishes vividly in one chapter an account of three years of Isabel's
life. "It was designed to have all the vivacity of incident and all
the economy of picture." [26] It *is* good, perhaps the best thing in
the book, where everything is well-nigh superlative. No wonder
James was proud.

There are details of treatment which James did not mention
in the preface but left to the reader to discern from the book.
The "architecture" which he was conscious of using enters on
the first page and supports the novel through to the last. James
set the stage for Isabel to appear—the spreading lawns at Gardencourt, the three men idly speculating—then brought her in,
plunging her into a new world, a new kind of existence. What
led to this, the antecedent action, he deferred for two chapters,
and then recounted it rapidly securing thus an advantage artistically over *Washington Square* where he had followed Balzac.
At the end, he left Isabel turning back to Rome to a scene which
will be more unpleasant than any in the book, and he gave
Henrietta the task of informing Caspar. Though it is stopped
short by the author, Isabel's story is by no means finished; she
must continue to live and suffer for many years, but there is no
need for her story to be finished completely as James had felt
compelled to finish the story of Catherine. The reader knows
how Isabel will now act and feel, with her eyes opened and
Ralph's love sustaining her and making life a bit more endur-
able. In the middle of the novel, James made everything lead to
something else, and not only this, but intentionally gave Isabel
premonitions of her unhappiness, vague foresight as to her
future. The use of the direct approach not only enabled him to
see the plotting of others, but it allowed him to look at Isabel
from the outside as well as from the inside. The advantage of
this he realized when he resumed Isabel's story after her mar-

riage and wisely revealed the state of her mind indirectly by
telling what others see and guess, before approaching it directly
in the midnight vigil. All this shows the hand of an artist and
a master as well, for though James trusted the stage to others
temporarily, the glance of author, characters, and reader is kept
focussed upon the mind of Isabel.

The finish of the novel is no less perfect than its architecture. It is narrative as James had never written it before—a
blending of incident, dialogue, description—one running into
the other so that the result is constant fluidity of motion.[27] The
portions of straight narrative—for want of a word one must so
distinguish what is not dialogue or description—run smoothly,
but because the nature of the story demands it, often slowly,
becoming quite analytical and expository in places. Still there
is always, even in the most expositional of the parts, movement
of a sort. James's concern was the *development* of a mind. The
narrative portions frequently melt into dialogue, which easily
assumes the burden of furthering the action, notably when
Isabel and Osmond are conversing, or of telling what has happened, as in Isabel's facing Caspar after she has accepted
Osmond. The dialogue operates still further in revealing character, both directly and indirectly. Much of the analysis of Isabel
comes from the mouth of Ralph or of Henrietta—who looked
at thus seems to have a function after all—as they talk with
Isabel, criticize her, and lead her to expose herself. Because of
this, little description of a pure, unmixed sort was needed, and
there are no sustained passages of description, no large blocks of
it such as James, following Balzac, had used in *Washington
Square*. It is wrought into the dialogue, into the incident. One
can say both that there is no description and that there is description on every page, achieved by a short remark, a phrase,
or even one word as it accompanies dialogue or is worked into
incident. The portrait of Isabel is the portrait of a mind rather
than that of a person with physical form and body, and it takes
the whole novel to give the complete portrait. The description
of place is likewise wrought into the story, and the mention of
place brings us to a discovery which is to be made in this novel
as to the changing trend in James's interests.

Of place, only Gardencourt, because it serves as an opening

setting, is done in any detail. Here the atmosphere is evoked by a short bit of pure description, and then by the attitude and talk of the three men over their tea, and then, most of all, by the effect of Gardencourt upon Isabel. When Isabel goes to Paris, to Florence, to Rome, however, except for Osmond's villa on the hill top, in which Osmond's personality expresses itself, James refrained from emphasizing in any way these cities which he had once thought it expedient to "do." He was now "doing" Isabel, and her story, after it gets started, is not of what place does to her but of what people do. It is above place. It is also above time to a certain extent. Though laid in the mid-nineteenth century when "frail vessels" were beginning to go to Europe as the first step into a larger life, it deals really with the revelation of permanent traits of human nature and not of transitory ones, and James did wisely not to emphasize place and time any more than was necessary for location of the action. *Washington Square* shows James still interested in history in the Balzacian sense—limited by time and place; *The Portrait of a Lady* shows him interested in it in the George Eliot sense—the history of human nature at large. Though he was to retain both interests for a time, the second was eventually to dominate.

THE CONCLUSION

In conclusion, it must be observed that *The Portrait of a Lady* has art as well as life. James proved to his own satisfaction that it was possible to have both in a novel. To this perfect reconciliation of the two he had advanced from small beginnings. In the early days he had striven for first one and then the other and often both at once with results that had made him dubious at times as to whether he could ever adjust the two into an even balance. In *Roderick Hudson*, he had almost hit the mark. In *The American*, he had shot past it. Shortly after that, under the negative influence of French writers who failed to have it and the positive influence of a Russian and an English novelist who did have it, he had declared that life at any rate was indispensable, and that art, though desirable, was not necessary. It was better not to have it than to abuse it by forcing it to serve in unclean causes. The love of art, however, was as strong within Henry James as the love of life. He had not been willing

to relinquish his dream of reconciling the two, and he had begun
all over again with a series of experimental studies in one phase
or another of life and art. And now at last in *The Portrait of a
Lady*, he had triumphed, writing a novel that has as much life
as those of George Eliot and Turgénieff and more art. For a
while he was to remain here, still claiming when he wrote of the
work of others or of the principles of fiction that if one had to
be sacrificed, it had better be art, but in his own novels balancing
the two. Gradually, by almost imperceptible degrees, the love
of art, as it became more and more an easy thing for him to
put into practice, was to encroach upon the love of life, and he
was in time to come to look upon art as the *summum bonum*.
Art then was to regulate life. This next and final development,
however, is material for another study. My dissertation must
end with James's first successful realization of his desire to write
novels which should have abundantly both art and life.

Notes

1. Appeared in *Macmillan's Magazine*, Oct., 1880 to Nov., 1881, and in
The Atlantic Monthly, Nov., 1880 to Dec., 1881.
2. Collected Edition, III, v.
3. They were to begin again, of course, in respect to the drama, and
James's attempts to become a dramatist, and he was to continue to experiment in the use of his method in his stories, but his experimentation there
was to be strong and confident; he knew how far he could go, what his
method was and was not suited for.
4. Collected Edition, III, xi, xii.
5. *Ibid.*, p. xvii.
6. The extent to which James was dependent upon Turgénieff in this
respect is to be seen also in the article written at the time of Turgéieff's
death; see Chapter xiv.
7. Collected Edition, III, xiii.
8. *Ibid*, p. xv.
9. *Ibid*, p. xv.
10. See Chapter xiv.
11. "Daniel Deronda: A Conversation," *The Atlantic Monthly*, Dec.,
1876, pp. 629.
12. *Ibid.*, p. 692.
13. *Ibid.*, p. 687.
14. *Ibid.*, p. 692.
15. In November, 1878, Henry James wrote to William that he had
been trying experiments in form using inferior subjects because he did not
wish to waste or to use gratuitously big situations, and that he had learned
to write and was coming to the big things. *Letters*, I, 66.

16. When *The Portrait* was published in book form, W. C. Brownell reviewed it and noted briefly the parallelism of James's novel with *Middlemarch* in respect to the Lydgates and the Osmonds. (*Nation*, Feb. 2, 1882, p. 103. (See Chapter 4 in this book.) This likeness exists just as *Daniel Deronda* shows resemblances to *Middlemarch*, but James's review of *Daniel Deronda* gives such definite clews that, lacking a review of *Middlemarch*, we must conclude that the later novel was the more active influence. Ralph, however, resembles Ladislaw more than he does Deronda.

17. *Atlantic Monthly*, Dec., 1876, p. 692.

18. See Chapters iv and v.

19. *Ibid.*, Chapter xi.

20. *Ibid.*, Chapter xii.

21. *Ibid.*, Chapter xv.

22. *Ibid.*, Chapter xii.

23. *I.e.*, in *The Ambassadors*. See *Collected Edition*, III, xvi.

24. *Ibid.*, pp. xviii f. Henrietta is so much of a "light ficelle" that in giving the synopsis, it was impossible to indicate how often she is on the stage.

25. *Ibid.*, p. xviii.

26. *Ibid.*, p. xx.

27. James's approval of such a blending is given in "The Art of Fiction," *Longman's Magazine*, Sept., 1884.

F. O. Matthiessen

9 · The Painter's Sponge and
Varnish Bottle

I

One sign of how little technical analysis James has received
is the virtual neglect of his revisions. Beyond Theodora Bosan-
quet's sensitive remarks in "Henry James at Work" and occasional citation to annotate the elaborations of his later manner,
they have been passed by. The only detailed exception is an
essay on *Roderick Hudson* wherein the writer held that James's
additions had largely served to spoil the clean outlines of its
style.[1] Yet James made these revisions at the plentitude of his
powers, and they constituted a *re-seeing* of the problems of his
craft. He knew that it would be folly to try to recast the structure
of any of his works. In the first preface that he wrote, that to
Roderick Hudson, he developed an analogy for his aims in the
way his fellow-craftsman on canvas went about to freshen his
surfaces, to restore faded values, to bring out "buried secrets."
He undertook, in particular, a minute verbal reconsideration of
the three early novels that he chose to republish.

My reason for singling out *The Portrait of a Lady* is that it
is a much richer book than either of the two others. *Roderick
Hudson* is full of interest for James's development, since the
two halves of his nature, the creator and the critic, are in a sense
projected in Roderick and Rowland. Moreover, he there first
tried out his device of having his narrative interpreted by the
detached observer. But the book as a whole remains apprentice

From *Henry James: The Major Phase* by F. O. Matthiessen (New
York, 1944), pp. 152–86. Copyright by Oxford University Press, Inc.
Reprinted by permission.

work. The revision of *The American*—the most extensive of all —might tell us, among other things, how James tried to repair what he had himself come to consider the falsely romantic aspects of his denouement. But *The Portrait of a Lady* is his first unquestioned masterpiece. By considering all the issues that the revisions raise, we may see it with renewed clarity.[2]

Larger changes are very few. A page of conversation between Ralph Touchett and Lord Warburton (at the very end of Chapter xxvii) was recast in a way that shows James's more mature sense of a dramatic scene. What had been two pages of psychological scrutiny of Osmond just before his proposal to Isabel (Chapter xxix) were felt by James to be otiose, and were cut to ten lines—an item of interest for the conventional view that the older James always worked the other way. But, with two important exceptions later to be looked into, we are to be concerned here with the tiniest brush strokes. What must be kept constantly in mind, therefore, is the design of the canvas as a whole. If that is done, we may have the intimate profit of watching the artist at his easel and of gaining insight into his principles of composition.

The writer's equivalent for the single flake of pigment is the individual word; and two words which James felt to be in need of consistent readjustment—"picturesque" and "romantic" —form in themselves an index to his aims. He had begun the book in Florence and had finished it in Venice. He had been at the time still strongly under the spell of Italian art, which, as he wrote William, had first taught him "what the picturesque is." He had consequently used the word freely as a kind of aesthetic catchall, too loosely as he came to feel, for he struck it out in almost every case. He had applied it to Gardencourt, to Isabel's grandmother's house in Albany, to Osmond's *objets d'art*; he changed it in the first case to "pictorial," in the others to "romantic." [3] Some of its many other occurrences must have made the later James wince, especially where he had said that Madame Merle had "a picturesque smile." That was altered to "amused." It is significant that when the word was retained, it was qualified by the speaker, by Isabel, who says that she would be a little on both sides of a revolution, that she would admire the Tories since they would have "a chance to behave so exquisitely. I mean so picturesquely." "So exquisitely" was added in the revision, and it is no accident that where, in the earlier version, Lord Warburton had remarked that Isabel found the British "picturesque," he was later made to say " 'quaint.' " That putting into quotation marks underscores Isabel's attitude, as, indeed, do several instances where James introduced "romantic" not merely as a substitute for "picturesque." Isabel's first judgment of Caspar as "not especially good looking" becomes "he was not romantically, rather obscurely handsome"; and her initial response to Warburton as "one of the most delectable persons she had met" is made much firmer—she judges him, "though quite without luridity—as a hero of romance." And when we find that she doesn't tell her sister about either his or Osmond's proposal, not simply because "it entertained her to say nothing" but because "it was more romantic," and she delighted in "drinking deep, in secret, of romance," we have the clue to what James is building up through his greatly increased use of this adjective and noun. He is bound to sharpen the reader's impression of how incorrigibly romantic Isabel's approach to life is, an important issue when we come to judge the effect of the book's conclusion.

Another word that shows the drift of James's later concern is "vulgar." One of James's most limiting weaknesses, characteristic of his whole phase of American culture, was dread of vulgarity, a dread that inhibited any free approach to natural human coarseness. But here the increased intrusion of the word does no great damage. When "the public at large" becomes "a vulgar world," or when Henrietta Stackpole asserts that our exaggerated American stress on brain power "isn't a vulgar fault" (she had originally pronounced it a "glorious" one), or when Isabel adds to her accruing reflections that Osmond had married her, "like a vulgar adventurer," for her money, we simply see more sharply the negative pole of James's vision.

His positive values come out in a whole cluster of words affecting the inner life of his characters, words in which we may read all the chief attributes of Jamesian sensibility. Ralph's "delights of observation" become "joys of contemplation." Warburton's sisters' "want of vivacity" is sharpened to "want of play of mind," just as Isabel's "fine freedom of composition" becomes "free play of intelligence." On the other hand, Warburton, in Ralph's description, is toned down from "a man of imagination" to "a man of a good deal of charming taste," in accordance with the high demands that James came to put upon the imagination as the discerner of truth. It is equally characteristic that Isabel's "feelings" become her "consciousness," and that her "absorbing happiness" in her first impressions of England becomes "her fine, full consciousness." She no longer feels that she is "being entertained" by Osmond's conversation; rather she has "what always gave her a very private thrill, the consciousness of a new relation." Relations, intelligence, contemplation, consciousness —we are accumulating the words that define the Jamesian drama. No wonder that James came to feel that it had been flat to say that Isabel was fond "of psychological problems." As he rewrote it, she became fond, as he was, "ever, of the question of character and quality, of sounding, as who should say, the deep personal mystery."

II

To progress from single words to questions of style, we note at once the pervasive colloquialization. The younger James had used the conventional forms, "cannot" and "she would"; in his revised conversation these always appear as "can't" and "she'd." Of more interest is his handling of the "he said—she said" problem, upon which the older James could well take pride for his ingenuity. Isabel "answered, smiling" becomes Isabel "smiled in return" or Isabel "gaily engaged." Osmond "hesitated a moment" becomes that Jamesian favorite, Osmond "just hung fire." And for one more out of a dozen other evasions of the obvious, the Countess Gemini no longer "cried . . . with a laugh"; her sound and manner are condensed into one word, "piped."

James's humor has often been lost sight of in discussion of the solemnities of his mandarin style. But he didn't lose it himself. His original thumb-nail characterization of Isabel's sister was descriptive: 'Lily knew nothing about Boston; her imagination was confined within the limits of Manhattan.' A graphic twist brings that to life with a laugh: "her imagination was all bounded on the east by Madison Avenue."

The later James was more concrete. He had also learned

what a source of life inheres in verbal movement. "Their multi-farious colloquies" is heavily abstract, whereas "their plunge . . . into the deeps of talk" takes us right into the action. So too with the diverse ways in which James launched his characters into motion, as when Henrietta "was very well dressed" became "she rustled, she shimmered"; or when the Countess, instead of entering the room "with a great deal of expression," did it "with a flutter through the air." Such movement means that James was envisaging his scenes more dramatically; and, in the passage where Isabel has just been introduced to Osmond, we can see how natural it had become for the novelist to heighten any theatrical detail. Where he had formerly written that Isabel sat listening to Osmond and Madame Merle "as an impartial auditor of their brilliant discourse," he now substituted "as if she had been at the play and had paid even a large sum for her place." And as this scene advances, instead of saying that Madame Merle "referred everything" to Isabel, James wrote that she "appealed to her as if she had been on the stage, but she could ignore any learnt cue without spoiling the scene."

Operating more pervasively, here as always, upon James's imagination, were analogies with pictures rather than with the stage. When he wanted to enrich his bare statement that the Countess "delivered herself of a hundred remarks from which I offer the reader but a brief selection," he said that she "began to talk very much as if, seated brush in hand before an easel, she were applying a series of considered touches to a composition of figures already sketched in." A phrase that shows us James's very process is when Isabel, instead of "examining the idea" (of Warburton's "being a personage"), is made to examine "the image so conveyed." The growth from ideas to images is what James had been fumbling for in his earlier preoccupation with the picturesque. The word might now embarrass him, but not the secret he had learned through it. He had originally opened the first of the chapters to be laid in Osmond's villa by remarking that "a picturesque little group" was gathered there. What he meant to imply was made much more explicit in the revision: "a small group that might have been described by a painter as composing well."

That concern with composition grew from the conviction

which he voiced in the preface to *Roderick Hudson*, that the novelist's subject, no less than the painter's, consisted ever in "the related state, to each other, of certain figures and things." And characters, he came to believe, could be best put into such relations when they were realized as visually, as lambently, as possible. This belief led him into one of his most recurrent types of revision, into endowing his *dramatis personae* with characterizing images. He had concluded his initial account of Ralph's ill health by remarking, "The truth was that he had simply accepted the situation." In place of that James was to introduce the poignancy that is Ralph's special note. "His serenity was but the array of wild flowers niched in his ruin." In comparable fashion, James added to his first description of Osmond, with no parallel in the original, an image that embodies the complex nature we are to find in him: "He suggested, fine gold coin as he was, no stamp nor emblem of the common mintage that provides for general circulation; he was the elegant complicated medal struck off for a special occasion."

Such elaborate images, more than any other aspect of James's later style, show his delight in virtuosity. Occasionally they seem to have been added purely because his eye fell on a dull patch of canvas, and he set out to brighten it up. Warburton's dim sisters don't contribute much in the original beyond "the kindest eyes in the world." But, in revising, James let himself go: their eyes are now "like the balanced basins, the circles of 'ornamental water,' set, in parterres, among the geraniums." In that image any functional intention may seem lost in the rococo flourish; but such was not usually the case. Take one very typical instance in the first detailed description of Caspar Goodwood—and it is significant of James's matured intentions that he introduced characterizing images of his chief figures at such important points. We are told in the first version that Caspar had undergone the usual gentleman athlete's education at Harvard, but that "later, he had become reconciled to culture." In the revision James conveyed much more of Caspar's energetic drive by means of a muscular image: "later on he had learned that the finer intelligence too could vault and pull and strain."

The full effect that James was trying for in such images

might be instanced by the chapter which introduces Henrietta.
Here we might follow James in the process of enlivening his
sketch by a dozen fresh touches. The most interesting of these
bring out Henrietta's character by the device of interrelating her
appearance with her career. He did not rest content with saying
that "she was scrupulously, fastidiously neat. From top to toe
she carried not an inkstain." He changed this into: "she was as
crisp and new and comprehensive as a first issue before the
folding. From top to toe she had probably no misprint." In
spite of the loudness of her voice (which caused James to alter
Henrietta "murmured" to Henrietta "rang out"), Ralph was
originally surprised to find that she was not "an abundant
talker." But in the revision the detailed glance at her profession
is sustained, and he finds her not "in the large type, the type of
horrid 'headlines.'" Yet she still remains fairly terrifying to
Ralph, and, a few pages farther on, James emphasized that by
another kind of image. To point up the fact that "she was
brave," he added, "she went into cages, she flourished lashes,
like a spangled lion-tamer." With that as a springboard James
could rise to the final sentence of this chapter. Originally Ralph
had concluded, "Henrietta, however, is fragrant—Henrietta is
decidedly fragrant!" But this became a punch line: "Henrietta,
however, does smell of the Future—it almost knocks one down!"

James remarked in his preface that he had given the
reader "indubitably too much" of Henrietta—a thing that could
be said of most of his *ficelles;* but in retouching he had at least
done what he could to brighten every inch. In relation to her
we may note another phase of his revision, his addition of
epithets to characterize the world of which she is part. In Rome
she is struck by the analogy between the ancient chariot ruts
and "the iron grooves which mark the course of the American
horse-car." These become more up to date: "the overjangled
iron grooves which express the intensity of American life."
Where James had written "the nineteenth century," he was
later to call it "the age of advertisement"; and glancing, not at
America but at Europe, he named it "an overcivilized age." But
it was Henrietta's realm he was thinking of again when, instead
of having Madame Merle remark that "it's scandalous, how
little I know about the land of my birth," he had her call it

rather, in his most revelatory addition of this type: "that splendid, dreadful, funny country—surely the greatest and drollest of them all."

III

So far I have avoided the question that is usually raised first about James's revisions: Didn't he sometimes overwrite to no purpose as a mere occupational disease? Occasionally, without doubt, it is the older James talking instead of a character, as when Pansy, instead of saying, "I have no voice—just a little thread," is made to transform this into ". . . just a small sound like the squeak of a slate-pencil making flourishes." But look at another sample where at first it would appear as though James had taken twice as many words to say the same thing, where "Marriage meant that a woman should abide with her husband" became "Marriage meant that a woman should cleave to the man with whom, uttering tremendous vows, she had stood at the altar." In its context we can at least see what James was after. This passage is part of Isabel's reflections, and both its fuller rhythm and density are meant to increase its *inner* relevance. The best way, therefore, to judge the final value of James's rewriting is to relate it in each case to the character involved, an obligatory proceeding in dealing with the writer who asked, in *The Art of Fiction:* "What is a picture or a novel that is *not* of character?"

The diverse types of revision demanded by the different characters may also remind us that we have in this book the most interestingly variegated group that James ever created. The center of attention is always Isabel, and the changes devoted to her may be read as a brief outline of the interpretation which James hoped we should give to his heroine. A few involve her looks. Whereas acquaintances of the Archer girls used to refer to her as "the thin one," James's tenderness for her was later to make this sound less invidious: "the willowy one." From his initial description of her in the house at Albany, he wanted to emphasize that she was less mistress of her fate than she fondly believed. He pointed this up by changing "young girl" to "creature of conditions." He also, as a past master of what could be gained by the specific notation, changed the conditioning of her taste from "a glimpse of contemporary aesthetics" to "the music of Gounod, the poetry of Browning, the prose of George Eliot" —a change which recalls that these were also Minny Temple's tastes.

But James's chief interest in his heroine is revealed through another type of change. Warburton's belief that she is "a thoroughly interesting woman" is made more intimate—"a really interesting little figure." And a few lines below, when Ralph concludes that a character like hers "is the finest thing in nature," he says more precisely what he means by adding, in the revision, that she is "a real little passionate force." James devoted many of his later brush strokes to bringing her out as exactly that. Instead of passively wanting "to be delighted," she now wants "to hurl herself into the fray." It is equally symptomatic of her conduct that she refuses Warburton, not because such a marriage fails "to correspond to any vision of happiness that she had hitherto entertained," but because it fails "to support any enlightened prejudice in favour of the free exploration of life." The Isabel whom the later James saw with so much lucidity is a daughter of the transcendental afterglow, far less concerned about happiness than about enlightenment and freedom.

Another addition indicates that what is most required to make her respond is "a bait to her imagination." That is exactly why she is caught by Osmond. Mrs. Touchett originally said that Isabel was capable of marrying him "for his opinions"; but she heightens this with more of the girl's romanticism in saying "for the beauty of his opinions or for his autograph of Michael Angelo." And that is how we see Isabel reacting to him. His "things of a deep interest" become "objects, subjects, contacts . . . of a rich association." She reads into them also, in a favorite phrase of the later James, "histories within histories." When she defends him to Ralph, the revision makes her grounds much more explicit by adding to her question, "What do you know against him?"—"What's the matter with Mr. Osmond's type, if it be one? His being so independent, so individual, is what I most see in him." And again, instead of saying "Mr. Osmond is simply a man—he is not a proprietor," she expands this with her feeling, "Mr. Osmond's simply a very lonely, a very cultivated and a very honest man—he's not a prodigious proprietor."

This is the Isabel of whom James felt it no longer adequate just to say, "she was an excitable creature, and now she was much excited." He transformed that into an image: "Vibration was easy to her, was in fact too constant with her, and she found herself now humming like a smitten harp." Such vibrations are intrinsic to the rhythm of her thought. She no longer reflects merely that "she had loved him," but extends that reflection with "she had so anxiously and yet so ardently given herself." It is not padding, therefore, when, upon discovering how wrong she has been about Osmond, she does not conclude, "There was only one way to repair it—to accept it," but adds ". . . just immensely (oh, with the highest grandeur!) to accept it."

The revisions affecting Osmond are of a very different sort. Far more of them relate to his appearance, to the polished, elegant and slightly ambiguous surface which James wants the reader to study more fully. His "sharply-cut face" becomes "extremely modelled and composed." James's description of his eyes is far more careful. They are no longer "luminous" and "intelligent" expressing "both softness and keenness," but "conscious, curious eyes . . . at once vague and penetrating, intelligent and hard." This is quite in keeping with his smile, which is now his "cool" smile, and with his voice, of which it is now said that, though fine, it "somehow wasn't sweet." He does not speak "with feeling" but "beautifully"; and his laugh, instead of being "not ill-natured," has now "a finer patience." James has done an expert job of heightening Osmond's thoroughly studied effect. He underscores the fact that Osmond's taste was his only law by saying, not that he lived "in a serene, impersonal way," but "in a sorted, sifted, arranged world," where his "superior qualities" become "standards and touchstones other than the vulgar."

Osmond is entirely devoted to forms, and to accent this trait, James introduces one of his most interesting later devices: he interrelates Osmond's character with his surroundings in a way that shows again how much the novelist had learned from the plastic arts.[4] On the first occasion that Osmond entertains Isabel, James wants her to be impressed with the rare distinction of the collector's villa. Osmond's footboy is now made deliberately picturesque: instead of remaining merely "the shabby footboy," he becomes "tarnished as to livery and quaint as to type," and, with a fine added flourish, James tells us that he might "have issued from some stray sketch of old-time manners, been 'put in' by the brush of a Longhi or a Goya." James also added in the revision that Osmond was marked for Isabel "as by one of those signs of the highly curious that he was showing her on the underside of old plates and in the corner of sixteenth-century drawings." As Isabel thinks over this visit afterwards, she reflects that his care for beauty "had been the main occupation of a lifetime of which the arid places were watered with the sweet sense of a quaint, half-anxious, half-helpless fatherhood." In the revision these thoughts rise from her impression of how she had seen him: his preoccupation with beauty made his life "stretch beneath it in the disposed vistas and with the ranges of steps and terraces and fountains of a formal Italian garden—allowing only for arid places freshened by the natural dews," and so on.

In building up the reasons why she took her romantic view of him, James also embarked on an extended flight:

> What continued to please this young lady was his extraordinary subtlety. There was such a fine intellectual intention in what he said, and the movement of his wit was like that of a quick-flashing blade.

> What continued to please this young woman was that while he talked so for amusement he didn't talk, as she had heard people, for "effect." He uttered his ideas as if, odd as they often appeared, he were used to them and had lived with them; old polished knobs and heads and handles, of precious substance, that could be fitted if necessary to new walking-sticks—not switches plucked in destitution from the common tree and then too elegantly waved about.

The new passage stresses, if in oblique ways and with some needless verbiage, Osmond's utter dependence on art rather than on nature. The "old polished knobs," like the "complicated medal" to which he is compared, make him indissever-able from his collector's items. It is not surprising that such a deliberately shaped work of art as he is "mystified" Isabel. (In the first version he had merely "puzzled" her.) It is fitting too that, as she comes under his fascination, she should feel not merely "a good deal older than she had done a year before," but also "as if she were 'worth more' for it, like some curious piece in an antiquary's collection." For, in ways that her inexperience cannot possibly fathom, that is precisely how Osmond proposes to treat her. She appeals to him, not for being "as bright and soft as an April cloud," but in one of James's most functional revisions, "as smooth to his general need of her as handled ivory to the palm."

The mystification is only Isabel's, the ambiguity is all in what Osmond concealed, not in any doubts that James entertained about him. The revision increases his "lost" quality. His "peculiarities" are called his "perversities," and where it was remarked that he consulted his taste alone, James now adds "as a sick man consciously incurable consults at last only his lawyer." The reader accepts entirely Ralph's judgment of Osmond as a sterile dilettante; but his quality is deepened when Ralph recognizes the futility of trying to persuade Isabel, not that the man is "a humbug," but rather that there is something "sordid or sinister" in him. With that deepening even Osmond becomes poignant: his "keen, expressive, emphatic" face becomes "firm, refined, slightly ravaged"—a far more telling portrait.

The character in this book around whom ambiguity gathers most is Madame Merle, since she has to play a double rôle throughout. James's changes involving her are chiefly of two sorts. He decided, for one thing, that her surface should be less transparent to Isabel. And so it is when Isabel asks her if she has not suffered that her "picturesque smile" is elaborated into "the amused smile of a person seated at a game of guesses." She is also called "smooth" instead of "plump." When Madame Merle introduced her to Osmond, Isabel wondered about "the nature of the tie that united them. She was inclined to imagine that Madame Merle's ties were peculiar." As James looked over that, it seemed to strike too close to the actual liaison, which he didn't want Isabel to suspect for a long time yet. So he toned it up to "the nature of the tie binding these superior spirits. She felt that Madame Merle's ties always somehow had histories."

But in the other type of change for Madame Merle, James

felt, as he did with Osmond, that he must make her character unmistakable to the reader. So he no longer endowed her with "a certain nobleness," but with "a certain courage"; not with "geniality" but with "grace." Even in changing the music that Isabel overheard her playing from "something of Beethoven's" to "something of Schubert's," James must have felt that he was bringing it more within Madame Merle's emotional compass. When Isabel finally comes to know her secret, the girl reflects, not just that her friend was "false," but "even deeply false . . . deeply, deeply, deeply." And Madame Merle's guilt is spoken of, not in terms "of vivid proof," but "of ugly evidence . . . of grim things produced in court."

Such details—of which there are many more—are important in allaying the usual suspicion that James's ambiguity is unintentional, the obscurantism of a man who couldn't make up his own mind. When the writing becomes denser, as it frequently does in the revision, this is owing rather to James's gradual development of one of his special gifts, the ability so to handle a conversation that he keeps in the air not merely what is said, but what isn't—the passage of thoughts without words. The situation here which challenged most this skill of the later James was when Warburton turned up again after Isabel's marriage. What she had to decide was whether, despite his honorable pretensions, he was still in love with her. Their interplay is made more subtle. To judge the value of this kind of rewriting you must follow the whole chapter, but one series of slight changes may show what James was about.

As they met again, in the first version, Isabel "hardly knew whether she were glad or not." Warburton, however, "was plainly very well pleased." In the revision his feelings are not given to us so explicitly: he "was plainly quite sure of his own sense of the matter." Only as the conversation advances do Isabel—and the reader—gain the evidence she is after. In a moment or two, he remarks how charming a place she has to live in. In the original he said this, "brightly, looking about him." But this became: "with a look, round him, at her established home, in which she might have caught the dim ghost of his old ruefulness." That reveals to Isabel nearly all she needs, and her impression is clinched, when, instead of turning upon her "an eye that gradually became more serious," he gives her, in addition, "the deeper, the deepest consciousness of his look." From that moment Isabel knows how unwise it would be for him to marry her stepdaughter Pansy, no matter how much Osmond wants the match.

If such a situation caused James thus to weave the texture of his style more complexly, the changes that relate to Pansy and to Ralph, though equally slight, may reveal another significant quality. In the scale of emotional vibrations James is more impressive in striking the note of tenderness than that of passion. We can observe this in the way he heightened some of his most moving passages. How utterly Pansy is at the mercy of her father's will is underlined by several details. Consider, for instance, her smile, in connection with which we can note again James's extraordinary care to bring out every revelatory phase of his characters' looks. At the moment of Pansy's first appearance in the narrative, James remarked that her "natural and usual expression seemed to be a smile of perfect sweetness." But the point about Pansy is that she has had so little chance to be natural or spontaneous, and so James revised this: her face was "painted with a fixed and intensely sweet smile." So too with the characterizing image that he created for her. Instead of saying that Pansy entertained Isabel "like a little lady," James wrote that she "rose to the occasion as the small, winged fairy in the pantomime soars by the aid of the dissimulated wire." Thus Pansy's trapped state is suggested to us from the outset, and on the occasion when Isabel tells her that she is going to marry her father, James made two additions that show how he had learned to handle irony. Originally Isabel had said, "My good little Pansy, I shall be very kind to you." But to that James added: "A vague, inconsequent vision of her coming in some odd way to need it had intervened with the effect of a chill." And when Pansy answered, "Very well then; I have nothing to fear," James no longer had her declare that "lightly," but "with her note of prepared promptitude." And he also added, as part of Isabel's reflection: "What teaching she had had, it seemed to suggest—or what penalties for non-performance she dreaded!"

We can read, in these extensions, the same thing that we

have observed in the major characters, James's deepening of emotional tones. The most affecting passage in the book is the death of Ralph, for there James is expressing the tenderness of pure devotion, disencumbered of any worldly aims. The characterizing image noted above was designed to increase our sense of Ralph's precarious holds on life. To increase also our sense of his devotion to Isabel, "his cousin" was twice changed to "the person in the world in whom he was most interested." The scene between these two, as he lies dying, is very short, and the only significant change is in Ralph's last speech. In the original this read: " 'And remember this,' he continued, 'that if you have been hated, you have also been loved.' " To that James added: " 'Ah, but, Isabel—*adored*' he just audibly and lingeringly breathed." There it may become a debatable matter of taste whether the simpler form is not more moving; but the later James felt impelled to a more high-keyed emotional register. Both Ralph and Isabel, instead of "murmuring" or "adding softly" are made to "wail."[5] It is difficult to keep such tones from becoming sentimental, but how little James was inclined to sentimentalize can be seen in his handling of Ralph's funeral. Originally James pronounced it "not a disagreeable one"; but he made his later statement stronger: it was "neither a harsh nor a heavy one."

IV

The two most extensive passages of rewriting are yet to be looked at. One relates to the Countess Gemini, and the other to Caspar Goodwood. Both can give us insight into how James conceived dramatic structure, and how he also felt that the climax of this book needed strengthening.

In comparing the two versions, it is notable that the sequence of chapters which James pronounced, in the preface, as being the best in the book—the sequence that extends from Isabel's glimpse of the two together, with Osmond seated while Madame Merle is standing, through the long vigil in which Isabel gradually pieces together her situation—that these three chapters (xl-xlii), with their important issues, were left substantially unchanged. So too with the fateful interview between Osmond and Isabel (Chapter xlvi) which shows how hopelessly far apart they have grown. But the scene with the Countess (Chapter LI), in which Isabel's suspicions are first given explicit names, was greatly recast. Some of the reasons for this are suggested by what James wrote in his notebook at the time when the novel had begun to appear in *The Atlantic* and he was trying to see his way clear to his conclusions:

> After Isabel's marriage there are five more instalments, and the success of the whole story greatly depends upon this portion being well conducted or not. Let me then make the most of it —let me imagine the best. There has been a want of action in the earlier part, and it may be made up here. The elements that remain are in themselves, I think, very interesting, and they are only to be strongly and happily combined. The weakness of the whole story is that it is too exclusively psychological—that it depends too little on incident; but the complete unfolding of the situation that is established by Isabel's marriage may nonetheless be quite sufficiently dramatic. The idea of the whole thing is that the poor girl, who has dreamed of freedom and nobleness, who has done, as she believes, a generous, natural, clear-sighted thing, finds herself in reality ground in the very mill of the conventional. After a year or two of marriage the antagonism between her nature and Osmond's comes out—the open opposition of a noble character and a narrow one. There is a great deal to do here in a small compass; every word, therefore, must tell—every touch must count. If the last five parts of the story appear crowded, this will be rather a good defect in consideration of the perhaps too great diffuseness of the earlier portion.

As James went on outlining his intentions, he was still undecided whether the revelation of Pansy's parentage should come through Madame Merle herself or through the Countess: "Better on many grounds that it should be the latter; and yet in that way I lose the 'great scene' between Madame Merle and Isabel." Twenty-five years later he was still bothered by what he had lost. In the passage of deadly quietness between Isabel and Osmond, and, subsequently, between Isabel and Madame Merle, he seems to have felt that his drama was too inward, that he needed a more emotional scene. And so he rewrote nearly all the lines in which the Countess told Isabel of the liaison.

He had already given considerable attention to making the Countess' character a more lively mixture. Ralph's first description of her was changed from "rather wicked" to "rather impossible"; and in her own disarming self-characterization, instead of saying, "I am only rather light," she pronounced herself "only rather an idiot and a bore." James had originally said that her expression was "by no means disagreeable"; but here he particularized: it was made up of "various intensities of emphasis and wonder, of horror and joy." Also, to a quite astonishing degree, by recurring to a bird-image for her, he sustained her in a whir. For example, in her first meeting with Isabel, she delivered her remarks "with a variety of little jerks and glances." But the bird-motif gave these the momentum of "little jerks and pecks, of roulades of shrillness," with the result that James was stimulated to a further flight of his own, and added that her accent was "as some fond recall of good English, or rather of good American, in adversity."

This kind of a character had dramatic possibilities, and, in his revision, James exploited them to the full. He did everything he could to make her revelations to Isabel into the "great scene" he had missed. Isabel is alone, thinking of what will happen if, in defiance of Osmond's wishes, she goes to England to see Ralph before he dies. Then, suddenly, the Countess "stood before her." Thus the original, but in the rewriting the Countess 'hovered before her.' And to give us an intimation that something is coming, James added that the Countess "lived assuredly, it might be said, at the window of her spirit, but now she was leaning far out." As Lawrence Leighton, who first drew my attention to the importance of this scene for James's structure, remarked, this is like "an extra blast from the trumpets" to announce the herald. It occurs to Isabel for the first time that her sister-in-law might say something, not "important," but "really human."

In what follows much subtle attention was paid to the Countess' diction. James endowed her with a more characteristic colloquial patter, with such epithets as "poverina" and "cara mia." Instead of saying that Madame Merle had wanted "to save her reputation," she says, "to save her skin"; and, in her view, Isabel has not merely "such a pure mind"—she calls it "beastly pure," as such a woman would. Her speeches are considerably increased in length, one of them by almost a page.

There is hardly any addition to her ideas, but as Mr. Leighton also observed, "James wanted a good harangue, the sort of speech an actress could get her teeth into." Her quality is melodramatic, but it is effectively more baleful than in the first version.

James has also built up the contrast between her and Isabel. The Countess expected—and hoped—that the girl would burst out with a denunciation of Osmond. But instead she is filled with pity for Madame Merle. She thinks even of Osmond's first wife, that "he must have been false" to her—"and so very soon!" That last phrase is an addition that emphasizes Isabel's incurable innocence, despite all the experience through which she is passing. It glances ironically also at her own situation. When she goes on to reflect that at least Osmond has been faithful to her, the Countess says it depends on what you call faithful: "When he married you he was no longer the lover of another woman—*such* a lover as he had been, *cara mia*, between their risks and their precautions, while the thing lasted!" Everything after the dash is added, and we can hear the Countess smacking her lips over such details, while Isabel recoils into herself. Where the first version had remarked that she "hesitated, though there was a question in her eyes," the utter cleavage between her and her gossipy interlocutress is now brought out: she "hesitated as if she had not heard; as if her question—though it was sufficiently there in her eyes—were all for herself." When, a moment or two later, Isabel wondered why Madame Merle never wanted to marry Osmond, the Countess had originally contented herself with saying that Madame Merle "had grown more ambitious." But to that James added: " 'Besides, she has never had, about him,' the Countess went on, leaving Isabel to wince for it so tragically afterwards—'she *had* never had, what you might call any illusions of *intelligence*.' " The Countess is happy to get in a dig at her brother, but for Isabel and for the reader there is the irony that Isabel herself had been fooled by just such illusions. That gives the final twist to the knife.

After this scene there remain only four chapters. There is the brief final encounter with Madame Merle, who sees in an instant that Isabel now knows everything. Isabel then says goodbye to Pansy, but promises that she won't desert her. The rest of the book is taken up with Isabel's trip to England, with her farewell to Ralph, and with Caspar's return to her. The last chapter is largely her struggle with him, and James's significant additions are led up to by the emphases that he has given to Caspar's character earlier in the book. He has introduced many details that sharpen the impression of Caspar's indomitable energy. When Isabel first compares him with Warburton, she feels that there is "something too forcible, something oppressive and restrictive" about him. But this was made more concrete: "a disagreeably strong push, a kind of hardness of presence." A revelatory image was introduced to contrast Isabel's feeling about Warburton: instead of refusing to "lend a receptive ear" to his suit, she now "resists conquest" at his "large quiet hands." But Caspar is "a kind of fate," now, indeed, "a kind of grim fate." He himself gives fuller expression to the tension between them when he has first pursued her to London. Instead of saying, "Apparently it was disagreeable to you even to write," he makes it "repugnant." And he remarks bitterly, not that his insistence on his suit "displeases" her, but that it "disgusts." As the best means of characterizing him, James developed a recurrent image of armor. In his first account he had merely remarked that Caspar was "the strongest man" Isabel had ever known; but to this he added: "she saw the different fitted parts of him as she had seen, in museums and portraits, the different fitted parts of armoured warriors—in plates of steel handsomely inlaid with gold." Later on, his eyes, instead of wearing "an expression of ardent remonstrance," seemed "to shine through the vizard of a helmet." And when Isabel tries to measure his possible suffering, she no longer reflects that "he had a sound constitution," but that "he was naturally plated and steeled, armed essentially for aggression."

He follows her to Italy to object strenuously to her engagement to Osmond: "Where does he come from? Where does he belong?" That second question was added in the revision, as was also Isabel's thought, "She had never been so little pleased with the way he said 'belawng.'" But, in spite of everything, Isabel cannot escape feeling Caspar's power; and in rewriting their final scene, James made an incisive analysis of his mixed repulsion and attraction for her. She is alone under the trees at Gardencourt, when Caspar suddenly appears—just as Warburton had surprised her there once before. In what follows we are made to feel her overpowering sensation of his physical presence, from the moment that James adds that he was "beside her on the bench and pressingly turned to her." As he insists that her husband is "the deadliest of fiends," and that he, Caspar, is determined to prevent her from the "horror" of returning to him (both "deadliest" and "horror" were additions), Isabel realizes that "she had never been loved before." To that realization the original had added: "It wrapped her about; it lifted her off her feet." But now James wrote: "She had believed it, but this was different; this was the hot wind of the desert, at the approach of which the others dropped dead, like mere sweet airs of the garden. It wrapped her about; it lifted her off her feet, while the very taste of it, as of something potent, acrid, and strange, forced open her set teeth."

That image takes her as far away from her surroundings and the gentlemanly devotion of a Warburton as it does from the decadent egotism of an Osmond. For a moment she is completely overpowered. Caspar's voice, saying, "Be mine, as I'm yours," comes to her, not merely "through a confusion of sound," but "harsh and terrible, through a confusion of vaguer sounds." He takes her in his arms, and, in the first version, the climax is reached with: "His kiss was like a flash of lightning; when it was dark again she was free." But now James felt it necessary to say far more: "His kiss was like white lightning, a flash that spread, and spread again, and stayed; and it was extraordinary as if, while she took it, she felt each thing in his hard manhood that had least pleased her, each aggressive fact of his face, his figure, his presence, justified of its intense identity and made one with this act of possession. So had she heard of those wrecked and under water following a train of images before they sink. But when darkness returned she was free."

That conveys James's awareness of how Isabel, in spite of her marriage, has remained essentially virginal, and of how her resistance and her flight from Caspar are partly fear of sexual possession. But the fierce attraction she also feels in this passage would inevitably operate likewise for a girl of her temperament, in making her do what she conceived to be her duty, and sending her back to her husband.

v

That brings us to the ending of the book, which has seldom been rightly interpreted. The difference between the two versions is one of the few of James's revisions that is generally known. Henrietta has told Caspar that Isabel has gone back to Rome:

> "Look here, Mr. Goodwood," she said; "just you wait." On which he looked up at her.

Thus the final lines in the original. But to these James added:

> —but only to guess, from her face, with a revulsion, that she simply meant he was young. She stood shining at him with that cheap comfort, and it added, on the spot, thirty years to his life. She walked him away with her, however, as if she had given him now the key to patience.

Many critics have held this difference to mean that James had changed his mind, that in the original he had given Caspar more hope. But he seems rather to have made unmistakably explicit what he had always intended to imply. He had said in his notebook outline that Isabel was to be greatly moved by Caspar's "passionate outbreak": "she feels the full force of his devotion—to which she has never done justice; but she refuses. She starts again for Italy—and her departure is the climax and termination of the story." James had also observed there that Henrietta was to have "the last word," to utter "a characteristic characterization of Isabel." But he must have felt in revising that he had been too brief, that he had failed to drive home to the reader that which was being expressed was no sure promise about Isabel, but rather Henrietta's optimism, which refuses to accept defeat.

The end of Isabel's career is not yet in sight. That fact raises a critical issue about James's way of rounding off his narratives. He was keenly aware of what his method involved. As he wrote in his notebook, upon concluding his detailed project:

> With strong handling it seems to me that it may all be very true, very powerful, very touching. The obvious criticism of course will be that it is not finished—that it has not seen the heroine to the end of her situation—that I have left her *en l'air*.

This is both true and false. The *whole* of anything is never told;
you can only take what groups together. What I have done has
that unity—it groups together. It is complete in itself—and the
rest may be taken up or not, later.

This throws a great deal of light—perhaps more than any
single passage of his published work—on how James conceived
of structure. He recounted in the preface to the *Portrait* how
Turgenieff had encouraged him in his belief that the important
thing to start with was not an air-tight plot, but rather a character or group of characters who are so living that the main
question becomes to "invent and select" the complications that
such characters "would be most likely to produce and to feel."

Years before the *Portrait*, William James had commented
on the effect of such a method, as it struck him in *A Most
Extraordinary Case* (1868), one of the first half dozen stories
that Henry had printed. William felt that here he understood
for the first time what Henry was aiming for: "to give an impression like that we often get of people in life: Their orbits
come out of space and lay themselves for a short time along
of ours, and then off they whirl again into the unknown, leaving
us with little more than an impression of their reality and a
feeling of baffled curiosity as to the mystery of the beginning and
the end of their being." William thought such a method difficult to make succeed, but "with a deep justification in nature."
He was to grow somewhat less sure of its efficacy, as can be read
in his tone about *The Tragic Muse*: 'the final winding up is, as
usual with you, rather a losing of the story in the sand, yet that
is the way in which things lose themselves in real life." Henry,
on the other hand, grew steadily to have more confidence in
what he was doing, until he declared, in the preface to *Roderick
Hudson*: "Really, universally, relations stop nowhere, and the
exquisite problem of the artist is eternally but to draw, by a
geometry of his own, the circle within which they shall happily
appear to do so." That gives his essential conception of the
kind of wholeness that form imposes.

He had been particularly concerned in the *Portrait* with
launching Isabel Archer into action, with presenting her so
vividly that his narrative would compose itself around the primary question, "Well, what will she *do*?" It has recently been as-

sumed that James believed entirely in the rightness of his heroine's conduct, and that since our age no longer feels as he—and
she—did about the strictness of the marriage vow, we can no
longer respond to the book except as to a period piece. But that
is to misread not merely the ending, but all of James's own
"characteristic characterization" of Isabel. He could hardly have
made a more lucid summary of the weaknesses that she exposed
to Europe: "her meagre knowledge, her inflated ideals, her confidence at once innocent and dogmatic, her temper at once
exacting and indulgent"—that whole passage of analysis on the
evening after her arrival at Gardencourt, a passage untouched
in the revision, is meant to have our closest scrutiny.

As Isabel embarks on her "free exploration" of life, Henrietta is outspoken in declaring that she is drifting rather to
"some great mistake," that she is not enough "in contact with
reality," with the "toiling, striving" world. Ralph tells her that
she has "too much conscience"—a peculiarly American complication in the romantic temperament. Although all her diverse
friends are united in their disapproval of Osmond, she proceeds
to do the wrong thing for the right reasons. She has a special
pride in marrying him, since she feels that she is not only
"taking," but also "giving"; she feels too the release of trans-
ferring some of the burden of her inheritance to another's conscience—James's way of commenting on how harm was done to
her by her money. But once she discerns what Osmond is really
like, and how he has trapped her, she is by no means supine
in his toils. She stands up to him with dignity, she even asks
Pansy, "Will you come away with me now?" Yet Isabel knows
that is impossible; she knows, even as she leaves, that she will
have to return to Rome for Pansy's sake.

But much more is involved than that—James's whole conception of the discipline of suffering. It is notable that his kin-
ship here to Hawthorne becomes far more palpable in the final
version. Take the instance when, at the time of Ralph's death,
Isabel realizes how Mrs. Touchett has missed the essence of life
by her inability to feel. It seemed to Isabel that Ralph's mother
"would find it a blessing today to be able to indulge a regret.
She wondered whether Mrs. Touchett were not trying, whether
she had not a desire for the recreation of grief." James made this

much fuller, particularly the latter portion. Isabel wondered if
Mrs. Touchett "were not even missing those enrichments of
consciousness and privately trying—reaching out for some after-
taste of life, dregs of the banquet; the testimony of pain or the
cold recreation of remorse." The view of suffering adumbrated
there, even the phrasing, recalls Hawthorne's *The Christmas
Banquet*, where the most miserable fate is that of the man whose
inability to feel bars him out even from the common bond
of woe.

The common bond of sin, so central to Hawthorne's
thought, was also accentuated through James's retouching. When
Madame Merle finally foresees what is ahead, she says to Osmond in the original, "How do bad people end? You have made
me bad." But James extended this with a new italicized emphasis, "How do bad people end?—*especially as to their common
crimes.* You have made me as bad as yourself." Isabel's link with
humanity, if not through sin—unless her willful spirit counts
as such—is through her acceptance of suffering. The inevitability of her lot is made more binding in the revision. Her reflection
that "she should not escape, she should last," becomes "she
should never escape, she should last to the end." She takes on
heightened stature when James no longer says that, while she
sat with Ralph, "her spirit rose," but that "her ache for herself
became somehow her ache for *him.*" The pathos of her situation
is also intensified in proportion to her greater knowledge of
what is involved. "She reflected that things change but little,
while people change so much" is far less affecting that "she envied the security of valuable 'pieces' which change by no hair's
breadth, only grow in value, while their owners lose inch by
inch, youth, happiness, beauty."

In both the original and the revision Isabel lays the most
scrupulous emphasis upon the sacredness of a promise. Despite
all her eagerness for culture, hers is no speculative spirit. Osmond
comes to despise her for having "the moral horizon" of a Unitarian minister—"poor Isabel, who had never been able to understand Unitarianism!" But whether she understands it or not,
she is a firm granddaughter of the Puritans, not in her thought
but in her moral integrity. In portraying her character and her
fate, James was also writing an essay on the interplay of free

will and determinism. Isabel's own view is that she was "perfectly free," that she married Osmond of her most deliberate choice, and that, however miserable one may be, one must accept the consequences of one's acts. James knew how little she was free, other than to follow to an impulsive extreme everything she had been made by her environment and background.

Thus he leaves her to confront her future, and is satisfied if he has endowed his characters with so much "felt life" that the reader must weigh for himself what is likely to lie ahead in her relation with Osmond. It may be that, as Isabel herself conjectures, he may finally "take her money and let her go." It may be that once she has found a husband for Pansy, she will feel that she no longer has to remain in Rome. James believed that the arbitrary circle of art should stimulate such speculations beyond its confines, and thus create also the illusion of wider life. He had about Isabel a tragic sense, but he did not write a tragedy, as he was to do in *The Wings of the Dove*, since this earlier drama was lacking in the finality of purgation and judgment. But this view of his material was not at all ambiguous. He knew how romantic Isabel was, how little experienced she was in mature social behavior. He had shown that she was completely mistaken in believing that "the world lay before her— she could do whatever she chose." But James also knew the meaning and the value of renunciation. The American life of his day, in its reckless plunge to outer expansiveness and inner defeat, had taught him that as his leading spiritual theme. Through Isabel Archer he gave one of his fullest and freshest expressions of inner reliance in the face of adversity. It is no wonder that, after enumerating her weaknesses, he had concluded: "she would be an easy victim of scientific criticism if she were not intended to awaken on the reader's part an impulse more tender. . . ."

Notes

1. Hélène Harvitt, "How Henry James Revised *Roderick Hudson*: A Study in Style," *PMLA* (March, 1924), 203–27.
2. James had developed early the habit of touching up his texts whenever possible; and he even made a few slight alterations in the *Portrait* between its appearance in *The Atlantic Monthly* (November 1880—December

1881) and in volume form. For instance, Madame Merle's first name was changed from Geraldine to Serena. But the changes that can instruct us in the evolution of his technique are naturally those he introduced when returning to the book after more than a quarter of a century.

James's copies of both *The American* and *The Portrait of a Lady*, containing his innumerable revisions in longhand on the margins and in inserted pages of typescript, are now in the Houghton Library at Harvard.

I want to thank the group of Harvard and Radcliffe students with whom I read through Henry James in the winter of 1943, since they did most of the spade work for this essay.

3. I have included all the detailed references to both editions in the version of this essay that appeared in *The American Bookman* (Winter 1944). To avoid spotting these pages with unnecessary footnotes, I refer to that periodical any reader who is interested in following out the comparison for himself.

4. I have given further instances from his earlier works in "Henry James and the Plastic Arts," *The Kenyon Review* (Autumn 1943).

5. This is also true in the other most directly emotional scene, the death of Ralph's father:

"My father died an hour ago."

"Ah, my poor Ralph!" the girl murmured, putting out her hand to him.

"My dear father died an hour ago."

"Ah, my poor Ralph!" she gently wailed, putting out her two hands to him.

IV. In the Tradition of the English Novel

III. In the Tradition of the English Novel

10 · From *An Introduction to the English Novel*

COMPARED WITH [*The Portrait of a Lady*] . . . the English novels which precede it, except perhaps those of Jane Austen, all seem a trifle crude. There is a habit of perfection here, a certainty and a poise, which is quite different from the merits and power of *Oliver Twist* or *Wuthering Heights* or even *Middlemarch.* The quality has something to do with the full consciousness of Henry James's art. Nothing in *The Portrait of a Lady* is unconscious, nothing there by chance, no ungathered wayward strands, no clumsiness. No novelist is so absorbed as James in what he himself might call his "game." But it is not an empty or superficial concern with "form" that gives *The Portrait of a Lady* its quality. James's manner, his obsession with style, his intricate and passionate concern with presentation, do not spring from a narrow "aesthetic" attitude to his art.

James had in his style and perhaps in his life which it reflected an idiosyncrasy so powerful, so overweening, that to many it seemed a stultifying vice, or at least an inexcusable heresy. . . . He enjoyed an excess of intelligence and he suffered, both in life and art, from an excessive effort to communicate it, to represent it in all its fullness. His style grew elaborate in the degree that he rendered shades and refinements of meaning and feeling not usually rendered at all. . . . His intention and all his labour was to represent dramatically intelligence at its most dif-

From "Henry James: *The Portrait of a Lady,*" *An Introduction to the English Novel,* II, (London, 1953), 13–34. Reprinted by permission of Hutchinson Publishing Group, Ltd., and of the author. Appreciation is also expressed to John Farquharson, on behalf of the estate of the late Henry James, for passages quoted herein from *The Portrait of a Lady.*

ficult, its most lucid, its most beautiful point. This is the sum of his idiosyncrasy.[1]

The Portrait of a Lady is not one of James's "difficult" novels; but Mr. Blackmur's remarks usefully remind us of the inadequacy of a merely formal approach to James's work. The extraordinary richness of texture of his novels makes such an approach tempting; but it will take us neither to James's triumphs nor to his failures.

The beauty of texture derives immediately from two qualities, which are ultimately inseparable. One is James's ability to make us know his characters more richly, though not necessarily more vividly, than we know the characters of other novelists; the other is the subtlety of his own standpoint. Without the latter quality the former would not, of course, be possible. You cannot control the responses of your reader unless you are in complete control of your material.

In *The Portrait of a Lady* there are—looking at the question from an analytical point of view—two kinds of characters: those whom we know from straightforward, though not unsubtle, description by the author and those who reveal themselves in the course of the book. The latter are, obviously, the important ones. The former—Mrs. Touchett, Henrietta Stackpole, the Countess Gemini, Pansy Osmond—are interesting primarily in their relationship to the chief characters, in their part in the pattern; we do not follow their existence out of their function in the book. But they are nevertheless not "flat" characters. They come alive not as "characters," not as personified "humours," but as complete people (Pansy, perhaps, is the exception, but then is not the intention that we should see her as scarcely an independent being at all?) and if we do not follow them out of the part of the plot which concerns them it is because our interests are more involved elsewhere, not because they do not have a full existence of their own.

The way Henry James introduces his characters to us depends entirely on the kind of function they are to have in his story. The main characters are never described as they *are* (i.e. as the author knows them to be) but—by and large—as Isabel Archer sees them. We know them at first only by the first im-

pression that they make. We get to know better what they are
like in the way that, in life, we get to know people better through
acquaintance. And just as in life we are seldom, if ever, quite
certain what another person is like, so in a Henry James novel
we are often pretty much at sea about particular characters for
considerable portions of the book. In *The Portrait of a Lady*
the person whom at first we inevitably know least about is
Madame Merle. Henry James lets us know right from the start
that there is something sinister about her; we are made quickly
to feel that Isabel's reaction to her is less than adequate, but
the precise nature of her character is not revealed until fairly
far into the book.

It is not quite true to say that everything in *The Portrait of
a Lady* is revealed through Isabel's consciousness. We know,
from the start, certain things that Isabel does not know. We
know, for instance—and twice Henry James explicitly reminds
us of it—more about Ralph Touchett's feeling for Isabel than
she herself perceives.

Indeed, there is a sense in which the novel is revealed to us
through Ralph's consciousness, for his is the "finest," the fullest
intelligence in the book and therefore he sees things—about
Madame Merle, about Osmond, about Isabel herself—which
Isabel does not see and inevitably such perceptions are trans-
mitted to the reader. Again, we are offered important scenes—
between Madame Merle and Osmond, between the Countess
and Madame Merle—which reveal to us not the whole truth
but enough of the truth about Madame Merle's stratagems to
put us at an advantage over Isabel.

The truth is that Henry James's purpose in this novel is
not to put Isabel between the reader and the situation (in the
way that Strether's consciousness is used in *The Ambassadors*)
but to reveal to the reader the full implications of Isabel's consciousness. For this to happen we must see Isabel not merely
from the inside (i.e. know how she feels) but from the outside
too. The method is, in fact, precisely the method of *Emma*,
except that Jane Austen is rather more scrupulously consistent
than Henry James. The scenes "outside" Emma herself (like
Jane Fairfax's visits to the post office) are brought to our knowledge by being related by a third party in the presence of Emma

herself. Our only "advantage" over Emma herself is provided by the words which Jane Austen uses to describe her. Henry James, as we have seen, takes greater liberties. Yet it is worth observing that the great scene at the centre of *The Portrait of a Lady* (Chapter XIII), in which Isabel takes stock of her situation, is of precisely the same *kind* as the scene in which (Vol. I, Chapter XVI) Emma takes stock of her dealings with Harriet.

Since James's purpose is to render the full implications of Isabel's situation it is necessary that we should know more than Isabel, should see her, that is to say, from the outside. The question remains: how *much* more should we know? And James's answer is: just as much as is necessary for a fully sympathetic understanding. Thus we are to know that Madame Merle has drawn Isabel into a trap, but we are not to know why. The full story is kept back, not because Henry James is interested in suspense in the melodramatic sense, but because if we were in on the secret the nature of Isabel's discovery of her situation could not be so effectively revealed. It is necessary to the novel that we should *share* Isabel's suspicions and her awakening. In order to give the precise weight (not just the logical weight but the intricate weight of feelings, standards, loyalties) to the issues involved in her final dilemma we must know not just what has happened to Isabel but the way it has happened.

It is from such a consideration that there will emerge one of Henry James's cardinal contributions to the art of the novel. With James the question "What happened?" carries the most subtle, the most exciting ramifications. To no previous novelist had the answer to such a question seemed so difficult, its implications so interminable. To a George Eliot the question is complicated enough: to understand what happened to Lydgate we must be made aware of innumerable issues, facets of character, moral choices, social pressures. And yet deep in George Eliot's novel is implicit the idea that if the reader only knows enough facts about the situation he will know the situation. It is the aim of Henry James to avoid the "about" or, at least, to alter its status, to transform quantity into quality. His is the poet's ambition: to create an object about which we say not "It means. . . ." but "It is. . . ." (In this he is with Emily Brontë.) We cannot *understand* Isabel Archer, he implies, unless we feel

as she feels. And it is, indeed, because he succeeds in this attempt that *The Portrait of a Lady* though not a greater novel
than *Middlemarch* is a more moving one.

As a rule when Henry James describes a character (as opposed to allowing the person to be revealed in action) the description is of the kind we have noticed in *Emma* or *Middlemarch*.

Mrs. Touchett was certainly a person of many oddities, of
which her behaviour on returning to her husband's house after
many months was a noticeable specimen. She had her own way
of doing all that she did, and this is the simplest description of
a character which, although by no means without liberal mo-
tions, rarely succeeded in giving an impression of suavity. Mrs.
Touchett might do a great deal of good, but she never pleased.
This way of her own, of which she was so fond, was not intrin-
sically offensive—it was just unmistakeably distinguished from
the way of others. The edges of her conduct were so very clear-
cut that for susceptible persons it sometimes had a knife-like
effect. That hard fineness came out in her deportment during
the first hours of her return from America, under circumstances
in which it might have seemed that her first act would have
been to exchange greetings with her husband and son. Mrs.
Touchett, for reasons which she deemed excellent, always re-
tired on such occasions into impenetrable seclusion, postponing
the more sentimental ceremony until she had repaired the dis-
order of dress with a completeness which had the less reason to
be of high importance as neither beauty nor vanity were concerned in it. She was a plain-faced old woman, without graces
and without any great elegance, but with an extreme respect
for her own motives. She was usually prepared to explain these
—when the explanation was asked as a favour; and in such a
case they proved totally different from those that had been attributed to her. She was virtually separated from her husband,
but she appeared to perceive nothing irregular in the situation.
It had become clear, at an early stage of their community, that
they should never desire the same thing at the same moment,
and this appearance had prompted her to rescue disagreement
from the vulgar realm of accident. She did what she could to
erect it into a law—a much more edifying aspect of it—by
going to live in Florence, where she bought a house and established herself; and by leaving her husband to take care of the
English branch of his bank. This arrangement greatly pleased
her; it was so felicitously definite. It struck her husband in the
same light, in a foggy square in London, where it was at times

the most definite fate he discerned; but he would have pre-ferred that such unnatural things should have a greater vague-ness. To agree to disagree had cost him an effort; he was ready to agree to almost anything but that, and saw no reason why either assent or dissent should be so terribly consistent.

Mrs. Touchett indulged in no regrets nor speculations, and usually came once a year to spend a month with her husband, a period during which she apparently took pains to convince him that she had adopted the right system. She was not fond of the English style of life, and had three or four reasons for it to which she currently alluded; they bore upon minor points of that ancient order, but for Mrs. Touchett they amply justified non-residence. She detested bread-sauce, which, as she said, looked like a poultice and tasted like soap; she objected to the consumption of beer by her maid-servants; and she affirmed that the British laundress (Mrs. Touchett was very particular about the appearance of her linen) was not a mistress of her art.[2]

Here the description depends for its effect entirely on the quality of the author's wit, his organized intellectual comment, and the wit is of the sort (a penetrating delicacy of observation within an accepted social group) achieved by Jane Austen or George Eliot.

But some of the described characters in *The Portrait of a Lady* come poetically to life. This is the description of Isabel's first meeting with the Countess Gemini.

The Countess Gemini simply nodded without getting up; Isabel could see she was a woman of high fashion. She was thin and dark and not at all pretty, having features that suggested some tropical bird—a long beak-like nose, small, quickly-moving eyes and a mouth and chin that receded extremely. Her expres-sion, however, thanks to various intensities of emphasis and wonder, of horror and joy, was not inhuman, and, as regards her appearance, it was plain she understood herself and made the most of her points. Her attire, voluminous and delicate, bristling with elegance, had the look of shimmering plumage, and her attitudes were as light and sudden as those of a creature who perched upon twigs. She had a great deal of manner; Isabel, who had never known anyone with so much manner, immediately classed her as the most affected of women. She re-membered that Ralph had not recommended her as an ac-quaintance; but she was ready to acknowledge that to a casual

view the Countess Gemini revealed no depths. Her demon-
strations suggested the violent wavings of some flag of general truce—white silk with fluttering streamers.[3]

We are never to get to know the Countess very well, but
already we see her with a peculiar vividness, the vividness evoked
by poetic imagery. The bird image has a visual force so intense
that it goes beyond surface illumination—"bristling with elegance" in its context contains a world of comment as well as
vividness. So does the image of the flag of truce.

Henry James's predominant interest is, however, by no
means in character. *The Portrait of a Lady*, he tells us in his
Preface, has its corner-stone "the conception of a certain young
woman affronting her destiny." The interest, it is already indicated, is not primarily a psychological one, not a matter of mere
personal analysis. And *The Portrait of a Lady* is indeed a novel
of the widest scope and relevance. Though it is in the line of
Jane Austen it has a quality which it is not misleading to call
symbolic (already we have hinted at a link with what would
appear at first to be a wholly different novel, *Wuthering
Heights*). *The Portrait of a Lady* is a novel about destiny. Or,
to use a concept rather more in tone with the language of the
book itself, it is a novel about freedom. It would not be out-
rageous, though it might be misleading, to call it a nineteenth-
century *Paradise Lost*.

Henry James is, of course, far too sophisticated an artist
to offer us the "subject" of his book on a platter. In his moral
interest he avoids like the plague anything approaching the
abstract.

> I might envy [he writes in his Preface], though I couldn't
> emulate, the imaginative writer so constituted as to see his fable
> first and to make out its agents afterwards: I could think so
> little of any fable that didn't need its agents positively to launch
> it; I could think so little of any situation that didn't depend for
> its interest on the nature of the person situated, and thereby on
> their way of taking it.

And again, a little later:

> There is, I think, no more nutritive or suggestive truth in
> this connexion than that of the perfect dependence of the

"moral" sense of a work of art on the amount of felt life concerned in producing it.*

James's novel is not a moral fable; but its moral interest is nevertheless central. Only the business of "launching," of presenting with all the necessary depth of "felt life," that "ado" which is the story of Isabel Archer, all this may easily distract our attention from the central theme. Indeed there was a time when James's novels apparently were regarded as "comedies of manners" (cf. Trollope) and even so superbly intelligent a reader as E. M. Forster seems to have missed the point of them almost completely.

The launching of *The Portrait of a Lady* is beautifully done. Gardencourt, the house in Albany, upper-class London: they are called up with magnificent certainty and solidity. So too are the people of the book: the Touchetts, Caspar Goodwood, Henrietta Stackpole, Lord Warburton, Isabel herself. If these characters are to contribute to a central pattern it will not be, it is clear, in the manner of anything approaching allegory. They are all too "round," too "free" to be felt, for even a moment, simply to be "standing for" anything. It is one of Henry James's achievements that he can convince us that his characters have a life outside the pages of his novel without ever leading us into the temptation of following them beyond his purpose. It is because everything in these early chapters of *The Portrait of a Lady* is realized with such fullness, such apparent lack of pointed emphasis, that we are slow to recognize the basic pattern of the novel, but it is also on this account that our imagination is so firmly engaged.

Before the end of the first chapter, however, a subsidiary theme has already been fairly fully stated and three of the main themes announced or, at any rate, indicated. The subsidiary theme is that generally referred to in Henry James's novels as the international situation—the relation of America to Europe. Graham Greene in a recent introduction to *The Portrait of a*

* I quote with some uneasiness from James's Preface (written, it will be recalled, some quarter of a century after the novel), not because I doubt the relevance or interest of his observations but because I am conscious of the difficulty of assimilating out of context sentences written in his most idiosyncratic, complex style.

Lady has tried to play down the importance of this theme. "It is true the innocent figure is nearly always American (Roderick Hudson, Newman, Isabel and Milly, Maggie Verver and her father), but the corrupted characters . . . are also American: Mme. Merle, Gilbert Osmond, Kate Croy, Merton Densher, Charlotte Stant. His characters are mainly American, simply because James himself was American." [4] In fact, of course, neither Kate Croy nor Densher is an American and one of the points about the other "corrupted" characters is that they are all expatriates, europeanized Americans, whom it is at least possible to see as corrupted by Europe.* The theme of the impact of European civilization on Americans—innocent or not— is not a main theme of *The Portrait of a Lady* but it is nevertheless there and we shall return to it later. And it is broached in the very first pages of the novel in the description of the Touchett *ménage* and in such details as the failure of Mr. Touchett to understand (or rather, his pretence at not understanding) Lord Warburton's jokes.

The main themes indicated in the first chapters are the importance of wealth, the difficulty of marriage and—fundamental to the other two—the problem of freedom or independence. In each case the theme appears to be merely a casual subject of conversation but in fact there is nothing casual there. The vital theme of freedom is introduced in the form of a joke —one of Mrs. Touchett's eccentric telegrams: " 'Changed hotel, very bad, impudent clerk, address here. Taken sister's girl, died last year, go to Europe, two sisters, quite independent'." The telegram is discussed by Mr. Touchett and Ralph.

"There's one thing very clear in it," said the old man; "she has given the hotel-clerk a dressing."
"I'm not sure even of that, since he has driven her from the field. We thought at first that the sister mentioned might be the sister of the clerk; but the subsequent mention of a niece seems to prove that the allusion is to one of my aunts. Then there was a question as to whose the two other sisters were; they are probably two of my late aunt's daughters. But who's 'quite independent,' and in what sense is the term used?—that point's not yet settled. Does the expression apply more particu-

* For a fuller discussion of this problem see *Henry James, the Major Phase* by F. O. Matthiessen and *Maule's Curse* by Yvor Winters.

larly to the young lady my mother has adopted, or does it characterize her sisters equally?—and is it used in a moral or in a financial sense? Does it mean that they've been left well off, or that they wish to be under no obligations?—or does it simply mean that they're fond of their own way?"[5]

Ralph's frivolous speculations do in fact state the basic problems to be dealt with in the novel. The point is indeed not yet settled: it will take the whole book to settle it. And, even then, "settle" is not the right word. One does not, Henry James would be quick to remind us, settle life.

The independence of Isabel is the quality about her most often emphasized. Mrs. Touchett has taken her up, but she is not, she assures Ralph "a candidate for adoption." " 'I'm very fond of my liberty'," [6] she adds. From the very first the ambiguous quality of this independence is stressed. Isabel is attractive, interesting, 'fine' ("she carried within her a great fund of life, and her deepest enjoyment was to feel the continuity between the movements of her own soul and the agitations of the world" [7]); but she is also in many respects inexperienced, naïve. " 'It occurred to me,' Mrs. Touchett says, 'that it would be a kindness to take her about and introduce her to the world. She thinks she knows a great deal of it—like most American girls; but like most American girls she's ridiculously mistaken'." [8] Henry James does not allow us, charming creature as she is, to idealize Isabel:

> "Altogether, with her meagre knowledge, her inflated ideals, her confidence at once innocent and dogmatic, her temper at once exacting and indulgent, her mixture of curiosity and fastidiousness, of vivacity and indifference, her desire to look very well and to be if possible even better, her determination to see, to try, to know, her combination of the delicate desultory flame-like spirit and the eager and personal creature of conditions: she would be an easy victim of scientific criticism: if she were not intended to awaken on the reader's part an impulse more tender and more purely expectant." [9]

The Portrait of a Lady is the revelation of the inadequacy of Isabel's view of freedom.

The revelation is so full, so concrete, that to abstract from it the main, insistent theme must inevitably weaken the impression of the book. But analysis involves such abstraction and we shall not respond fully to James's novel unless we are conscious of its theme. The theme in its earlier stages is fully expressed in the scene in which Caspar Goodwood for the second time asks Isabel to marry him (she has just refused Lord Warburton).

"I don't know," she answered rather grandly. "The world —with all these places so arranged and so touching each other —comes to strike one as rather small."

"It's a sight too big for me!" Caspar exclaimed with a simplicity our young lady might have found touching if her face had not been set against concessions.

This attitude was part of a system, a theory, that she had lately embraced, and to be thorough she said after a moment: "Don't think me unkind if I say it's just that—being out of your sight—that I like. If you were in the same place I should feel you were watching me, and I don't like that—I like my liberty too much. If there's a thing in the world I'm fond of," she went on with a slight recurrence of grandeur, "it's my personal independence." But whatever there might be of the too superior in this speech moved Caspar Goodwood's admiration; there was nothing he winced at in the large air of it. He had never supposed she hadn't wings and the need of beautiful free movements—he wasn't, with his own long arms and strides, afraid of any force in her. Isabel's words, if they had been meant to shock him, failed of the mark and only made him smile with the sense that here was common ground. "Who would wish less to curtail your liberty than I? What can give me greater pleasure than to see you perfectly independent—doing whatever you like? It's to make you independent that I want to marry you."

"That's a beautiful sophism," said the girl with a smile more beautiful still.

"An unmarried woman—a girl of your age—isn't independent. There are all sorts of things she can't do. She's hampered at every step."

"That's as she looks at the question," Isabel answered with much spirit. "I'm not in my first youth—I can do what I choose —I belong quite to the independent class. I've neither father nor mother; I'm poor and of a serious disposition; I'm not pretty. I therefore am not bound to be timid and conventional; indeed I can't afford such luxuries. Besides, I try to judge things for myself; to judge wrong, I think, is more honourable than not to judge at all. I don't wish to be a mere sheep in the flock; I wish to choose my fate and know something of human affairs beyond what other people think is compatible with propriety to tell me." She paused a moment, but not long enough for her companion to reply. He was apparently on the point of doing so when she went on: "Let me say this to you, Mr. Goodwood. You're so kind as to speak of being afraid of my marrying. If you should hear a rumour that I'm on the point of doing so— girls are liable to have such things said about them—remember what I have told you about my love of liberty and venture to doubt it."[10]

The Portrait of a Lady is far from allegory yet one is permitted to feel, in the symbolic quality of the novel, that the characters, though unmistakably individuals, are more than individuals. Thus, in her rejection of Caspar Goodwood, Isabel is rejecting America, or at least that part of America that Goodwood represents, young, strong, go-ahead, uninhibited, hard. For Goodwood (as for Henrietta, who essentially shares his quality) the problem of freedom is simple and might be expressed in the words of Mr. Archibald Macleish's American Dream:

> America is promises
> For those that take them.

Goodwood—and it would be wrong to see him as a wholly unsympathetic character—is prepared to take them with all that taking implies. To him and Henrietta (and they are, on one level, the most sensible, positive people in the book) Isabel's problem is not a problem at all. Freedom for them has the simple quality it possessed for the nineteenth-century liberal.

The rejection of Lord Warburton has, similarly, a symbolic quality—though, again, one must insist that this is not an allegory. Warburton is a liberal aristocrat. He embodies the aristocratic culture of Europe (that has so attracted Isabel at Gardencourt) and adds his own reforming ideas—a combination which Henry James, had he been the kind of aesthetic snob he is often held to be, might have found irresistible. Ralph Touchett sums up Warburton's social position magnificently:

> ". . . He says I don't understand my time, I understand it certainly better than he, who can neither abolish himself as a nuisance nor maintain himself as an institution."[11]

Isabel's rejection of Lord Warburton is not a light one. She feels very deeply the attraction of the aristocratic standards. But she feels also the limitations of Warburton and his sisters, the

Misses Molyneux (it is worth comparing them with another
"county" family—the Marchants—in the wonderful *Princess
Casamassima*; Henry James's attitude to the British aristocracy
is by no means uncritical).

> ". . . So long as I look at the Misses Molyneux they seem
> to me to answer a kind of ideal. Then Henrietta presents her-
> self, and I'm straightway convinced by *her*; not so much in re-
> spect to herself as in respect to what masses behind her."[12]

Ralph, too, (though he does not undervalue her) disposes of
Henrietta:

> "Henrietta . . . does smell of the Future—it almost knocks
> one down!"[13]

Goodwood and Warburton rejected (almost like two temptations), Isabel is now 'free' to affront her destiny. But she is not
free because she is poor. She has never, we are told early on,
known anything about money, and it is typical of this novel
that this fine, romantic indifference to wealth should be one
of the basic factors in Isabel's tragedy.

Henry James's characters always have to be rich and the
reason is not the obvious one. "I call people rich," says Ralph
Touchett, "when they're able to meet the requirements of their
imagination." [14] It is for this reason that he persuades his father
to leave Isabel a fortune. She must be rich in order to be free
of the material world. She must be free in order to "live."

It is Ralph's one supreme mistake in intelligence and it is
the mistake that ruins Isabel. For it is her wealth that arouses
Madame Merle's realization that she can use her and leads
directly to the disastrous, tragic marriage with Osmond. And in
the superb scene in which, sitting in the candlelight in the
elegant, spiritually empty house in Rome, Isabel takes stock of
her tragedy, she painfully reveals to herself the conclusion:

> But for her money, as she saw today, she would never have
> done it. And then her mind wandered off to poor Mr. Touchett,
> sleeping under English turf, the beneficent author of infinite
> woe! For this was the fantastic fact. At bottom her money had
> been a burden, had been on her mind, which was filled with the
> desire to transfer the weight of it to some other conscience, to
> some more prepared receptacle. What would lighten her own

conscience more effectually than to make it over to the man with the best taste in the world? Unless she should have given it to a hospital there would have been nothing better she could do with it; and there was no charitable institution in which she had been as much interested as in Gilbert Osmond. He would use her fortune in a way that would make her think better of it and rub off a certain grossness attaching to the good luck of an unexpected inheritance. There had been nothing very delicate in inheriting seventy thousand pounds; the delicacy had been all in Mr. Touchett's leaving them to her. But to marry Gilbert Osmond and bring him such a portion—in that there would be delicacy for her as well. There would be less for him—that was true; but that was his affair, and if he loved her he wouldn't object to her being rich. Had he not had the courage to say he was glad she was rich?"[15]

It is at the moment when Ralph is dying that the theme is finally stated in the form at once the most affecting and most morally profound.

She raised her head and her clasped hands; she seemed for a moment to pray for him. "Is it true—is it true?" she asked.

"True that you've been stupid? Oh no," said Ralph with a sensible intention of wit.

"That you made me rich—that all I have is yours?"

He turned away his head, and for some time said nothing. Then, at last: "Ah, don't speak of that—that was not happy." Slowly he moved his face toward her again, and they once more saw each other.

"But for that—but for that——!" And he paused. "I believe I ruined you," he wailed.

She was full of the sense that he was beyond the reach of pain; he seemed already so little of this world. But even if she had not had it she would still have spoken, for nothing mattered now but the only knowledge that was not pure anguish— the knowledge that they were looking at the truth together. "He married me for the money," she said. She wished to say everything; she was afraid he might die before she had done so.

He gazed at her a little, and for the first time his fixed eyes lowered their lids. But he raised them in a moment, and then, "He was greatly in love with you," he answered.

"Yes, he was in love with me. But he wouldn't have married me if I had been poor. I don't hurt you in saying that. How can I? I only want you to understand. I always tried to keep you from understanding; but that's all over."

"I always understood," said Ralph.

"I thought you did, and I didn't like it. But now I like it."
"You don't hurt me—you make me very happy." And as
Ralph said this there was an extraordinary gladness in his voice.
She bent her head again, and pressed her lips to the back of his
hand. "I always understood," he continued, "though it was so
strange—so pitiful. You wanted to look at life for yourself—
but you were not allowed; you were punished for your wish.
You were ground in the very mill of the conventional!"
"Oh yes, I've been punished," Isabel sobbed.[16]

The necessity here of stating in its dreadful simplicity the
agonizing truth so that the relationship of the two may be
purified and deepened shows an intuition the very opposite of
sentimental.

Isabel, then, imagining herself free, has in fact delivered
herself into bondage. And the bondage has come about not
casually but out of the very force and fortune of her own aspirations to freedom. She has sought life and because she has sought
it in this way she has found death.

Freedom, to Isabel and to Ralph (for he has been as much
concerned in the issue as she), has been an idealized freedom.
They have sought to be free not through a recognition of, but
by an escape from, necessity. And in so doing they have delivered
Isabel over to an exploitation as crude and more corrupting
than the exploitation that would have been her fate if Mrs.
Touchett has never visited Albany.

" 'Do you still like Serena Merle?' " is Mrs. Touchett's last
question of Isabel.

"Not as I once did. But it doesn't matter, for she's going
to America."
"To America? She must have done something very bad."
"Yes—very bad."
"May I ask what it is?"
"She made a convenience of me."
"Ah," cried Mrs. Touchett, "so she did of me! She does of
everyone."[17]

The Portrait of a Lady is one of the most profound expressions
in literature of the illusion that freedom is an abstract quality
inherent in the individual soul.

It is interesting to compare James's book with another great
novel written not very long before, *Madame Bovary*, the story

of another woman "ground in the very mill of the conventional."
It is true that Emma Bovary is, unlike Isabel Archer, not in the
least "fine," that she fails to escape from her petty-bourgeois
social *milieu* and that she is quite incapable of the exalted moral
discipline to which Isabel is dedicated, yet we will learn something of James's novel, I think, from a glance at Flaubert's.
What is shocking in *Madame Bovary* is the appalling passivity
of Flaubert's characters, their inability to fight in any effective
way the bourgeois world which Flaubert detests and which relentlessly warps and destroys all fineness in them. The strength
of the novel lies in the very ruthlessness of its exposure of romantic attitudes; but therein also lies its weakness, the sense
we get of something less than the human capacity for heroism,
the uneasy suspicions of a *roman à thèse. The Portrait of a
Lady* gives, as a matter of fact, no more positive response to its
revelation of bourgeois values than *Madame Bovary*, yet we do
experience a sense of human resilience and dignity. The interesting question is how far this sense—embodied in the "fineness" of Isabel herself—is merely romantic and illusory.

The issue can perhaps be put in this way: is not the accumulated effect of the novel to present human destiny as inexorably
one of suffering and despair? There are a number of tendencies
making for this effect. In the first place there is the insistent
use of dramatic irony in the construction of the book. Chapter
after chapter in the early reaches of the novel is designated to
emphasize the fatality facing Isabel's aspirations. The fifth
chapter tells us she has come to Europe to find happiness; the
sixth that she likes unexpectedness ("I shall not have success
(in Europe) if they're too stupidly conventional. I'm not in the
least stupidly conventional"). The seventh chapter ends with
the following exchange:

> "I always want to know the things one shouldn't do."
> "So as to do them?" asked her aunt.
> "So as to choose," said Isabel.

The eighth draws to a close with:

> "I shall never make anyone a martyr."
> "You'll never be one, I hope."
> "I hope not. . . ."

This is all, it may be argued, simply Henry James at work, extracting from every situation its maximum of point. But the art, it seems to me, is in a subtle sense self-betraying. What is achieved is a kind of inevitability, a sense of Isabel's never standing a chance, which amounts not to objective irony but to the creation of something like an external destiny. Is not martyrdom becoming, in a sense at once insidious and—with all the associations and overtones one may care to give the word—romantic? Is there not to be here a breath—a very sophisticated and infinitely worldly breath—of the emotional and moral inadequacy involved in George Eliot's vision of those latter-day Saint Theresas?

Our final judgment must depend on the climax—the famous ending—of the book. It is from this ultimate impression that we shall have to decide whether James indeed plays fair with Isabel and us, whether he reveals in full profundity and (in the least cold sense of the word) objectivity a tragic situation or whether there is a certain sleight of hand, the putting across not of life but of something which merely for the moment passes for life. But before we consider this final climax it is worth noting what would seem an odd weakness in the novel. Is it not a little strange that of all the essential parts of Isabel's story which are revealed to us the section of her life most pointedly avoided is that immediately before her decision to marry Osmond? She has met him, got to know him somewhat; she then goes away for a year, travelling in Europe and the Middle East with Madame Merle. When she comes back to Florence she has decided to marry Osmond. This is, from the novelist's point of view, the most difficult moment in the book. How to convince us that a young woman like Isabel would in fact marry a man like Osmond? And it is a moment which, despite the revealing conversation with Ralph (which does indeed tell us something) is, I suggest, not satisfactorily got over. And the point is that if Isabel's marriage to Osmond is in any sense a fraud perpetrated upon us for his own ends by the author, the book is greatly weakened.

At the end of the novel Isabel, after Ralph's death and another encounter with Caspar Goodwood, returns to Rome. Is her return to Osmond irrevocable, an acceptance now and for ever of her 'destiny,' or is it tentative, no ending, the situation unresolved? Mr. F. O. Matthiessen, arguing in the latter sense, has a most interesting observation:

> The end of Isabel's career is not yet in sight. That fact raises a critical issue about James's way of rounding off his narratives. He was keenly aware of what his method involved. As he wrote in his notebook, upon concluding his detailed project: "With strong handling it seems to me that it may all be very true, very powerful, very touching. The obvious criticism of course will be that it is not finished—that it has not seen the heroine to the end of her situation—that I have left her *en l'air*. This is both true and false. The *whole* of anything is never told; you can only take what groups together. What I have done has that unity—it groups together. It is complete in itself—and the rest may be taken up or not, later."[18]

James's own evidence is of course conclusive as to his intention, but it is not necessarily relevant as to what is in fact achieved; and it seems to me that, although the ending of *The Portrait of a Lady* does not completely and irrevocably round off the story—the possibility of Isabel's later reconsidering her decision is not excluded—yet the dominant impression is undoubtedly that of the deliberate rejection of "life" (as offered by Caspar Goodwood) in favour of death, as represented by the situation in Rome. The scene with Goodwood is indeed very remarkable with its candid, if tortured, facing of a sexual implication which James is apt to sheer off. On the whole the effect of this scene, though one understands completely the quality of Isabel's reaction, is further to weight the scales against a return to Rome. Even if Goodwood himself is impossible, the vitality that he conveys is a force to be reckoned with and Isabel's rejection of this vitality involves more clearly than ever the sense that she is turning her face to the wall.

Isabel's return to Rome is certainly not a mere surrender to the conventional force of the marriage vow. The issue as to whether or not she should leave her husband is twice quite frankly broached by Henrietta, as well as by Goodwood. Isabel's first reply to Henrietta is significant:

> "I don't know what great unhappiness might bring me to; but it seems to me I shall always be ashamed. One must accept

one's deeds. I married him before all the world; I was perfectly free; it was impossible to do anything more deliberate. One can't change that way," Isabel repeated.[19]

Later, when she discovers how little free she had in fact been, it is her obligation towards Pansy that becomes the most important factor. But always there is the sense of some deep inward consideration that makes the particular issues—the character of Osmond, her own mistakes, the needs of Pansy, the importunity of Goodwood—irrelevant. The recurring image in the last pages is of a sea or torrent in which Isabel is immersed. Goodwood becomes identified with the torrent. Her temptation is to give herself up to it.* When she breaks loose from him and the image she is once more "free," free and in darkness. The lights now are the lights of Gardencourt and now she knows where to turn. "There was a very straight path." [20]

It seems to me inescapable that what Isabel finally chooses is something represented by a high cold word like duty or resignation, the duty of an empty vow, the resignation of the defeated, and that in making her choice she is paying a final sacrificial tribute to her own ruined conception of freedom. For Henry James, though he sees the tragedy implicit in the Victorian ruling-class view of freedom, is himself so deeply involved in that illusion that he cannot escape from it. His books are tragedies precisely because their subject is the smashing of the bourgeois illusion of freedom in the consciousness of characters who are unable to conceive of freedom in any other way. His "innocent" persons have therefore always the characters of victims; they are at the mercy of the vulgar and the corrupt, and the more finely conscious they become of their situation the more unable are they to cope with it in positive terms. Hence the contradiction of a Fleda Vetch* whose superior consciousness (and conscience) leads her in effect to reject life in favour of death. This is a favourite, almost an archetypal situation, in James's novels. It achieves its most striking expression in *The Portrait of a Lady* and *The Wings of the Dove* in which an-

---

* It is at such a moment that one sees the force of Stephen Spender's linking of James with Conrad's "in the destructive element immerse" in an otherwise not very helpful book(*The Destructive Element*, 1937).

* In *The Spoils of Poynton*.

other rich American girl meets, even more powerfully and more exquisitely, the fate of Isabel Archer.

For James in his supreme concern for "living" (Milly Theale in *The Wings of the Dove*, Strether in *The Ambassadors* have, like Isabel, this immense, magnificent desire to "live") ultimately, in effect, turns his back on life. This is not unconnected, I think, with the fact that his characters never do anything like work. This description of Madame Merle is not untypical of a day in the life of a Henry James figure:

> When Madame Merle was neither writing, nor painting, nor touching the piano, she was usually employed upon wonderful tasks of rich embroidery, cushions, curtains, decorations for the chimney-piece; an art in which her bold, free invention was as noted as the agility of her needle. She was never idle, for when engaged in none of the ways I have mentioned she was either reading (she appeared to Isabel to read "everything important"), or walking out, or playing patience with the cards, or talking with her fellow inmates.[21]

The contemplation of such a way of life is likely, after all, to lead to idealism, for the necessities behind such an existence are by no means obvious. It is a superficial criticism to accuse James of snobbery or even of being limited by his social environment (what artist is not?). But there can be no doubt that what the bourgeois world did for James was to turn him into a moral idealist chasing a chimera of ideal conduct divorced from social reality.

It is not that his sense of social reality is in any way weak. On the contrary his picture of his world has, it has already been emphasized, a magnificent solidity, a concrete richness of the subtlest power. Nor is he in any easy, obvious sense taken in by that world (note his attitude to Warburton, his description of American-French society in Chapter XX and his total contempt for Osmond and his values); his picture of European bourgeois life is in its objective aspect as realistic as that of Balzac or Flaubert or Proust. No, if we are to isolate in James's novels the quality that is ultimately their limitation, it is to the core of his point of view, his philosophy, that we are led. The limiting factor in *The Portrait of a Lady* is the failure of James in the last analysis to dissociate himself from Isabel's errors of understanding.

One of the central recurring themes of James's novels is the desire to "live," to achieve a fullness of consciousness which permits the richest yet most exquisite response to the vibrations of life. And yet with this need to live is associated almost invariably the sense of death. Living, he seems to be saying again and again, involves martyrdom. The pleasure he finds in the contemplation and description of living at its most beautiful, most exalted point is subtly increased if the living creature is faced with death. Ralph Touchett is not alone among the dying swans of James's books: he is one of a line culminating in Strether (who discovers how to live too late) and in the fabulous Milly Theale. The attraction of this subject to James seems to me most significant. "Very true . . . very powerful . . . very touching . . ." one can almost hear him breathing out the words. It is a kind of apotheosis of his vision of life. And it is intimately, inextricably, linked up with his philosophic idealism. His "good" characters, in their unswerving effort to live finely, turn out to be in the full implication of the phrase, too good for this world. Their sensibility becomes an end in itself, not a response to the actual issues of life. The freedom they seek turns out to be an idealized freedom; it ends, therefore, can only end, in a desire not merely to be free *in* this world but to be free *of* this world.

The popularity of James's novels among our intelligentsia today is significant too. It includes, I feel certain, not merely a genuine admiration for his extraordinary qualities, but also a powerful element of self-indulgence. It is not only pleasanter but easier to involve oneself in an idealized sensibility, a conscience* removed into realms outside the common and often crude basis of actual living. Many besides Isabel Archer imagine that they can buy themselves out of the crudities through the means of a high-grade consciousness and a few thousand pounds. And Henry James, albeit unconsciously, offers a subtle encouragement. He expresses the fate of Isabel Archer but expresses it in a way that suggests that it has, if not inevitability, at least a kind of glory to it. So that when Isabel takes her decision to return to Rome the dominant sense is not of the waste and

* It is interesting to speculate whether Conrad, when he referred to James as "the historian of fine consciences" was using the word in its English sense or with the French implication of "consciousness."

degradation of a splendid spirit, but of a kind of inverted triumph. Better death than a surrender of the illusion which the novel has so richly and magnificently and tragically illuminated.

Notes

1. R. P. Blackmur, "Introduction to H. James," *The Art of the Novel* (New York, 1934), p. xii.
2. *The Portrait of a Lady*, Chap. iii.
3. *Ibid.*, Chap. xxiv.
4. *Ibid.*, "Introduction" (World Classics ed.), p. ix.
5. *Ibid.*, Chap. i.
6. *Ibid.*, Chap. ii.
7. *Ibid.*, Chap. iv.
8. *Ibid.*, Chap. v.
9. *Ibid.*, Chap. vi.
10. *Ibid.*, Chap. xvi.
11. *Ibid.*, Chap. viii.
12. *Ibid.*, Chap. x.
13. *Ibid.*, Chap. x.
14. *Ibid.*, Chap. xviii.
15. *Ibid.*, Chap. xlii.
16. *Ibid.*, Chap. liv.
17. *Ibid.*, Chap. liv.
18. Henry James, *The Major Phase* (New York, 1944), p. 151. (See Chapter 9 in this book.)
19. *The Portrait of a Lady*, Chap. xlvii.
20. *Ibid.*, Chap. lv.
21. *Ibid.*, Chap. xix.

Dorothy Van Ghent

11 · From *The English Novel: Form and Function*

TO GO from Hardy's *Tess* to James's *The Portrait of a Lady* is to go from Stonehenge to St. Peter's and from a frozen northern turnip field, eyed hungrily by polar birds, to the Cascine gardens where nightingales sing. Though both books concern the "campaign" of a young woman—a campaign that, expressed most simply, is a campaign *to live*—a greater difference of atmosphere could scarcely be imagined nor of articulation of what it means *to live*. The gaunt arctic birds in *Tess* have witnessed, with their "tragical eyes," cataclysms that no human eye might see, but of which they retain no memory. The birds offer a symbol of Tess's world: a world inimical to consciousness, where one should have no memory (Tess's fatal error is to remember her own past), where the eye of the mind should remain blank, where aesthetic and moral perceptivity is traumatic. The nightingales that sing to Isabel Archer and her lover in the "grey Italian shade" also offer a symbol of a world: they are the very voice of memory, of an imperishable consciousness at once recreating and transcending its ancient, all-human knowledge. It is to the tutelage of the European memory that Isabel Archer passionately surrenders herself in her campaign *to live*, that is, to become conscious; for, in James's world, the highest affirmation of life is the development of the subtlest and most various consciousness. In doing so, she must—like the girl in the barbarous legend

From *The English Novel: Form and Function* (New York, 1953), pp. 211–28. Copyright 1953 by Dorothy Van Ghent. Used by permission of Holt, Rinehart and Winston, Inc., publishers.

of the nightingale, who, likewise in a foreign land, read an obscene crime in the weaving of a tapestry—come into knowledge of an evil which, in its own civilized kind, is as corrupting and implacable as that in the old tale. But consciousness here, as an activity nourished by knowledge, transcends the knowledge which is its content: and this too is an analogy with the ancient symbolic tale, where knowledge of evil is transcended, in the very doom of its reiteration, by the bird's immortal song.

The Portrait is not, like Tess, a tragedy, but it is as deeply informed with the tragic view of life: that tragic view whose essence is contained in the words, "He who loses his life shall find it," and "Except a corn of wheat fall into the ground and die, it abideth alone: but if it die, it bringeth forth much fruit." We associate tragic seriousness of import in a character's destiny with tension between the power of willing (which is "free") and the power of circumstances ("necessity") binding and limiting the will; and if either term of the tension seems lacking, seriousness of import fails. Apparently no two authors could be at further antipodes than James and Hardy in the respective emphases they place on these terms. In Hardy, the protagonist's volition founders at every move on a universally mechanical, mysteriously hostile necessity; it is only in Tess's last acts, of blood sacrifice and renunciation of life, that her will appallingly asserts its freedom and that she gains her tragic greatness. In James's Portrait, and in his other novels as well, the protagonist appears to have an extraordinarily unhampered play of volition. This appearance of extraordinary freedom from the pressure of circumstances is largely due to the "immense deal of money" (the phrase is taken from an early page of The Portrait) with which James endows his world—for, in an acquisitive culture, money is the chief symbol of freedom. The vague rich gleams of money are on every cornice and sift through every vista of the world of The Portrait, like the muted gold backgrounds of old Persian illuminations; and the human correlative of the money is a type of character fully privileged with easy mobility upon the face of the earth and with magnificent opportunities for the cultivation of aesthetic and intellectual refinements. It is by visualizing with the greatest clarity the lustrously moneyed tones of the James universe that we make ourselves able to see the more clearly what grave, somber shapes of illusion and guilt he organizes in this novel. The tension between circumstances and volition, "necessity" and "freedom," is demonstrated at the uppermost levels of material opportunity where, presumably, there is most freedom and where therefore freedom becomes most threatening—and where necessity wears its most insidious disguise, the disguise of freedom.

In following the previous studies, the reader will perhaps have been impressed with the fact that the novel as a genre has shown, from *Don Quixote* on, a constant concern with the institutions created by the circulation of money and with the fantasies arising from the having of it, or, more especially, the not having it; a concern not always so direct as that of *Moll Flanders* and *Vanity Fair*, but almost inevitably implicit at least, expressed in indirect forms of aspiration and encitement to passion. As the definitively middle-class literary genre, the novel purchased its roots in a money-conscious social imagination. The wealth shining on the James world is a kind of apogee of the novel's historical concern with money, showing itself, in *The Portrait*, as a grandly sweeping postulate of possession: as if to say, "Here, now, is all the beautiful money, in the most liberating quantities: what ambition, what temptation, what errors of the will, what evil, what suffering, what salvation still denote the proclivities of the human even in a world so bountifully endowed?"

The "international myth" [1] that operates broadly in James's work, and that appears, in this novel, in the typical confrontation of American innocence and moral rigor with the tortuosities of an older civilization, gives its own and special dimension to the moneyed prospect. James came to maturity in a post-Civil War America euphoric with material achievement. In terms of the Jamesian "myth," American wealth is now able to buy up the whole museum of Europe, all its visible "point" of art objects and culture prestige, to take back home and set up in the front yard (we need look no further, for historical objectification of this aspect of the "myth," than to William Randolph Hearst's epic importation of various priceless chunks of Europe to California). If the shadows of the physically dispossessed—the sweat and the bone-weariness and the manifold anonymous deprivation in which this culture-buying power had its source—are excluded from James's money-gilded canvas, the shadow of spiritual dispossession is the somber shape under the money outline. We are now allowed to forget the aesthetic and moral impoverishment that spread its gross vacuum at the core of the American acquisitive dream—the greed, the obtuse or rapacious presumption, the disvaluation of values that kept pace to pace with material expansion. James's characteristic thematic contrasts, here as in other novels, are those of surface against depth, inspection against experience, buying power against living power, the American tourist's cultural balcony against the European abyss of history and memory and involved motive where he perilously or callously teeters. In *The Portrait*, the American heroine's pilgrimage in Europe becomes a fatally serious spiritual investment, an investment of the "free" self in and with the circumstantial and binding past, a discovery of the relations of the self with history, and a moral renovation of history in the freedom of the individual conscience. It is a growing of more delicate and deeper-reaching roots and a nourishment of a more complex, more troubled, more creative personal humanity. It is, in short, what is ideally meant by "civilization," as that word refers to a process that can take place in an individual.

The postulate of wealth and privilege is, in revised terms, that of the second chapter of Genesis (the story of Adam in the garden)—that of the optimum conditions which will leave the innocent soul at liberty to develop its potentialities—and, as in the archetype of the Fall of Man, the postulate is significant not as excluding knowledge of good and evil, but as presenting a rare opportunity for such knowledge. It is the bounty poured on Isabel Archer (significantly, the man who gives her the symbolical investiture of money is a man who is fatally ill; significantly, also, she is under an illusion as to the giver) that makes her "free" to determine her choice of action, and thus morally most responsible for her choice; but it is the very bounty of her fortune, also, that activates at once, as if chemically, the proclivity to evil in the world of privilege that her wealth allows her to enter—it is her money that draws Madame Merle and Osmond to her; so that her "freedom" is actualized as imprisonment, in a peculiarly ashen and claustral, because peculiarly refined, suburb of hell. Isabel's quest had, at the earliest, been a quest for happiness—the naïvely egoistic American quest; it converts into a problem of spiritual salvation, that is, into a quest of "life"; and again the Biblical archetype shadows forth the problem. After eating of the fruit of the tree of knowledge of good and evil, how is one to regain access to the tree of life?

The great fairy tales and saints' legends have identified life with knowledge. For the fairy-tale hero, the fruit of the tree of life that is the guerdon of kingdom is the golden fleece or the golden apples that his wicked stepmother or usurping uncle have sent him in quest of; and to achieve the guerdon he must go through all tormenting knowledge—of serpents, floods, fire, ogres, enchantment, and even of his own lusts and murderous capacities. The ordeal of the heroes of saints' legends is also an ordeal of knowledge of evil, and the guerdon is life. As do these ancient tales, *The Portrait* identifies life with the most probing, dangerous, responsible awareness—identifies, as it were, the two "trees," the tree of the Fall and the tree of the Resurrection. The heroine's voluntary search for fuller consciousness leads her, in an illusion of perfect freedom to choose only "the best" in experience, to choose an evil; but it is this that, by providing insight through suffering and guilt, provides also access to life —to the fructification of consciousness that is a knowledge of human bondedness. At the very end of the book, Caspar Goodwood gives passionate voice to the illusion of special privileges of choice and of a good to be had by exclusion and separateness: he says to Isabel,

> "It would be an insult to you to assume that you care for . . . the bottomless idiocy of the world. We've nothing to do with all that; we're quite out of it . . . We can do absolutely as we please; to whom under the sun do we owe anything? What is it that holds us, what is it that has the smallest right to inter- fere . . . ? The world's all before us—and the world's very big."

Isabel answers at random, "The world's very small." What atti- tude of mind takes her back to Rome, back to old evil and old servitude, is not described; we know only that she does go back. But it is evident that she does so because the "small" necessitous world has received an extension, not in the horizontal direction of imperial mobility that Caspar Goodwood suggests, but an invisible extension in depth, within her own mind—an extension into the freedom of personal renunciation and inexhaustible responsibility. The knowledge she has acquired has been tragic knowledge, but her story does not stop here, as it would if it were a tragedy—it goes on out of the pages of the book, to Rome, where we cannot follow it; for the knowledge has been the means to "life," and having learned to live, she must "live long," as she says. It is only the process of the learning that the portrait frame itself holds.

The title, *The Portrait*, asks the eye to see. And the handling of the book is in terms of seeing. The informing and strengthening of the eye of the mind is the theme—the ultimate knowledge, the thing finally "seen," having only the contingent importance of stimulating a more subtle and various activity of perception. The dramatization is deliberately "scenic," moving in a series of recognition scenes that are slight and low-keyed at first, or blurred and erroneous, in proportion both to the innocence of the heroine and others' skill in refined disguises and obliquities; then, toward the end, proceeding in swift and livid flashes. For in adopting as his compositional center the growth of a consciousness, James was able to use the bafflements and illusions of ignorance for his "complications," as he was able to use, more consistently than any other novelist, "recognitions" for his crises. Further, this action, moving through errors and illuminations of the inward eye, is set in a symbolic construct of things to be seen by the physical eye—paintings and sculptures, old coins and porcelain and lace and tapestries, most of all buildings: the aesthetic riches of Europe, pregnant with memory, with "histories within histories" of skills and motivations, temptations and suffering. The context of particulars offered to physical sight (and these may be settings, like English country houses or Roman ruins, or objects in the setting, like a porcelain cup or a piece of old lace draped on a mantel, or a person's face or a group of people—and the emphasis on the visual is most constant and notable not in these particulars, extensive as they are, but in the figurative language of the book, in metaphors using visual images as their vehicle) intensifies the meaning of "recognition" in those scenes where *sight* is *insight*, and provides a concrete embodiment of the ambiguities of "seeing."

In James's handling of the richly qualitative setting, it is characteristically significant that he suggests visual or scenic traits almost always in such a way that the emphasis is on *modulations of perception in the observer*. The "look" of things is a response of consciousness and varies with the observer; the "look" of things has thus the double duty of representing external stimuli, by indirection in their passage through consciousness, and of representing the observer himself. For instance, when Ralph takes Isabel through the picture gallery in the Touchett home, the "imperfect" but "genial" light of the bracketed lamps shows the pictures as "vague squares of rich colour," and the look of the pictures is Isabel's state at the moment—her eager and innately gifted is sensibility and her almost complete ignorance, her conscious orientation toward an unknown "rich" mode of being that is beautiful but indeterminate. Let us take another example from late in the book. Directly after that conversation with Madame Merle when Isabel learns, with the full force of evil revelation, Madame Merle's part in her marriage, she goes out for a drive alone.

> She had long before this taken old Rome into her confidence, for in a world of ruins the ruin of her happiness seemed a less unnatural catastrophe. She rested her weariness upon things that had crumbled for centuries and yet still were upright; she dropped her secret sadness into the silence of lonely places, where its very modern quality detached itself and grew objective, so that as she sat in a sun-warmed angle on a winter's day, or stood in a mouldy church to which no one came, she could almost smile at it and think of its smallness. Small it was, in the Roman record, and her haunting sense of the continuity of the human lot easily carried her from the less to the greater. She had become deeply, tenderly acquainted with Rome: it interfused and moderated her passion. But she had grown to think of it chiefly as the place where people had suffered. This was what came to her in the starved churches, where the marble columns, transferred from pagan ruins, seemed to offer her a companionship in endurance and the musty incense to be a compound of long-unanswered prayers.

Here the definition of visible setting—churches and marble columns and ruins, and comprehending all these, Rome—though it is full, is vague and diffuse, in the external sense of the "seen"; but in the sense that it is a setting evoked by Isabel's own deepened consciousness, it is exactly and clearly focused. It is Rome *felt,* felt as an immensity of human time, as a great human continuum of sadness and loneliness and passion and aspiration and patience; and it has this definition by virtue of Isabel's personal ordeal and her perception of its meaning. The "vague squares of rich colour" have become determinate.

The theme of "seeing" (the theme of the developing consciousness) is fertile with ironies and ambiguities that arise from the natural symbolism of the act of seeing, upon which so vastly many of human responses and decisions are dependent. The eye, as it registers surfaces, is an organ of aesthetic experience, in the etymological sense of the word "aesthetic," which is a word deriving from a Greek verb meaning "to perceive"—to perceive through the senses. James provides his world with innumerable fine surfaces for this kind of perception; it is a world endowed with the finest selective opportunities for the act of "seeing," for aesthetic cultivation. But our biological dependence upon the eye has made it a symbol of intellectual and moral and spiritual perception, forms of perception which are—by the makers of dictionaries—discriminated radically from aesthetic perception. Much of James's work is an exploration of the profound identity of the aesthetic and the moral. (In this he is at variance with the makers of dictionaries, but he has the companionship of Socrates' teacher Diotima, as her teaching is represented by Plato in the *Symposium.* Diotima taught that the way to spiritual good lay through the hierarchies of the "beautiful," that is, through graduations from one form of aesthetic experience to another.) Aesthetic experience proper, since it is acquired through the senses, is an experience of *feeling.* But so also moral experience, when it is not sheerly nominal and ritualistic, is an experience of *feeling.* Neither one has reality—has psychological depth—unless it is "felt" (hence James's so frequent use of phrases such as "felt life" and "the very *taste* of life," phrases that insist on the feeling-base of complete and integrated living). Furthermore, both aesthetic and moral experience are nonutilitarian. The first distinction that aestheticians usually make, in defining the aesthetic, is its distinction from the useful; when the aesthetic is converted to utility, it becomes something else, its value designation is different—as when a beautiful bowl becomes valuable not for its beauty but for its capacity to hold soup. So also the moral, when it is converted to utility, becomes something else than the moral—becomes even immoral, a parody of or a blasphemy against the moral life (in our richest cultural heritage, both Hellenic and Christian, the moral life is symbolically associated with utter loss of utility goods and even with loss of physical life—as in the Gospel passage, "Leave all that thou hast and follow me," or as in the career of Socrates, or as in Sophocles' *Antigone*). Moral and aesthetic experience have then in common their foundation in feeling and their distinction from the useful. The identity that James explores is their identity in the most capacious and most integrated—the most "civilized"—consciousness, whose sense relationships (aesthetic relationships) with the external world of scenes and objects have the same quality and the same spiritual determination as its relationships with people (moral relationships). But his exploration of that ideal identity involves cognizance of failed integration, cognizance of the many varieties of one-sidedness or one-eyedness or blindness that go by the name of the moral or the aesthetic, and of the destructive potentialities of the human consciousness when it is one-sided either way. His ironies revolve on the ideal concept of a spacious integrity of feeling: feeling, ideally, is *one*—and there is ironic situation when feeling is split into the "moral" and the "aesthetic," each denying the other and each posing as *all*.

There is comic irony in Henrietta Stackpole's moral busybodyness as she flutters and sputters through Europe obtaining feature materials for her home-town newspaper, "featuring" largely the morally culpable un-Americanism of Europeans to serve her readers as a flattering warning against indulgence in the aesthetic. Henrietta is a stock James comedy character, and she is essential. Without Henrietta's relative incapacity to "see" more than literal surfaces, the significant contrast between surface and depth, between outward and inward "seeing," between undeveloped and developed consciousness, would lose a needed demonstration. (But let us say for Henrietta that, like Horatio in *Hamlet*, she is employed by the dramatist for as many sorts of purposes as his scenes happen to demand; when a foil of obtuseness is wanted, Henrietta is there, and when a foil of good interpretive intelligence or plain charitable generosity is wanted, Henrietta is also there. She is the type of what James technically called the *ficelle*, a wholly subordinate character immensely useful to take in confidences from the principals and to serve other functions of "relief"—"relief" in that sense in which the lower level of a relievo provides perspective for the carved projections.) In Mrs. Touchett, what appears at first as the comic irony of absolute aesthetic insensitivity accompanied by a rugged moral dogmatism ("she had a little moral account-book—with columns unerringly ruled and a sharp steel clasp—which she kept with exemplary neatness") becomes at the end of the book, with her son's death, the tragic irony of that kind of ambiguous misery which is an inability to acknowledge or realize one's own suffering, when suffering is real but the channels of feeling have become nearly atrophied by lack of use. At the midday meal, when Isabel and Mrs. Touchett come together after the night of Ralph's death,

> Isabel saw her aunt not to be so dry as she appeared, and her old pity for the poor woman's inexpressiveness, her want of regret, of disappointment, came back to her. Unmistakably she would have found it a blessing to-day to be able to feel a defeat, a mistake, even a shame or two. [Isabel] wondered if [her aunt] were not even missing those enrichments of consciousness and privately trying—reaching out for some aftertaste of life, dregs of the banquet; the testimony of pain or the old recreation of remorse. On the other hand perhaps she was afraid; if she should begin to know remorse at all it might take her too far. Isabel could perceive, however, how it had come over her dimly that she had failed of something, that she saw herself in the future as an old woman without memories. Her little sharp face looked tragical.

Mrs. Touchett's habitual moralistic denial of feeling as an aesthetic indulgence has left her deserted even by herself, even by her love of her son, even by memory, even by suffering. She is stranded in a morality that is tragically without meaning.

In Madame Merle and Osmond the ironies intrinsic to James's theme receive another turn. Madame Merle first appeals to Isabel's admiration by her capacity for "feeling"—for that kind of feeling to which the term "aesthetic" has been specially adapted in common modern use: feeling for the arts, the sen-

suous perceptivity underlying the arts, and, by extension, feeling
for the finer conventions of manners as "arts of living." (Madame
Merle "knew how to feel. . . . This was indeed Madame Merle's
great talent, her most perfect gift.") At Gardencourt, when she
is not engaged in writing letters, she paints (she "made no more
of brushing in a sketch than of pulling off her gloves") or she
plays the piano (she "was a brave musician") or she is "employed
upon wonderful tasks of rich embroidery." (The presentation is
just a bit insidious, not only because of Madame Merle's so very
great plasticity in going from one art to another, but also in the
style of the phrases: the suggestion of conventional fluidity in
the comparison of her ease in painting with the ease of "pulling
off her gloves," the word "brave"—an honorific word in certain
places, but carrying here the faintest note of bravado—and the
word "employed," suggesting, as it reverberates, Madame Merle's
not disinterested professional aestheticism.) Her senses are active
and acute: walking in the English rain, she says,

> "It never wets you and it always smells good." She declared that
> in England the pleasures of smell were great . . . and she used
> to lift the sleeve of her British overcoat and bury her nose in it,
> inhaling the clear, fine scent of the wool.

Just how acute her perceptions are is shown never more clearly
than in that scene in which she learns of the distribution of
property after Mr. Touchett's death, occurring in Chapter 20
of Volume I. Mrs. Touchett has just told her that Ralph, because of the state of his health, had hurried away from England
before the reading of the will, in which Isabel had been left half
of the fortune accruing to him. With this news, Madame Merle
"remained thoughtful a moment, her eyes bent on the floor,"
and when Isabel enters the room, Madame Merle kisses her—
this being "the only allusion the visitor, in her great good taste,
made . . . to her young friend's inheritance." There are no other
signs than these (and the episode is typical of James's minor
"recognition scenes") of just how quickly and acutely Madame
Merle's senses—her perception, her intuition—have functioned
in apprising her of the possibilities of exploitation now opened,
and in apprising her also of the fact that Ralph is the real donor
of Isabel's fortune, a fact of which Isabel herself remains ignorant

until Madame Merle viciously informs her. Madame Merle's feeling for situation is so subtly educated that she needs but the slightest of tokens in order to respond. And yet, with a sensitivity educated so exquisitely and working at such high tension she is morally insensible—or almost so; not quite—for, unlike Osmond, whose damnation is in ice where the moral faculty is quite frozen, she still has the spiritual capacity of those whose damnation is in fire, the capacity to know that she is damned.

Madame Merle and Osmond use their cultivated aestheticism for utility purposes—Madame Merle, to further her ambition for place and power; Osmond, to make himself separate and envied. Their debasement of the meaning of the aesthetic becomes symbolically vicious when it shows itself in their relationships with people—with Isabel, for instance, who is for them an object of virtu that differs from other objects of virtu in that it bestows money rather than costs it. This is the evil referred to by Kant in his second Categorical Imperative: the use of persons as means—an evil to which perhaps all evil in human relationships reduces. In the case of Madame Merle and Osmond, it has a peculiar and blasphemous ugliness, inasmuch as the atmosphere of beauty in which they live—beauty of surroundings and of manners—represents the finest, freest product of civilization and is such, ideally, as to induce the most reverential feeling for people as well as for things. Isabel first appeals to Osmond as being "as smooth to his general need of her as handled ivory to the palm": it is an "aesthetic" image suggesting his fastidiousness but, ironically, suggesting at the same time his coarseness —for while ivory, like pearls, may be the more beautiful for handling, "handled ivory" might also be the head of a walking stick, and it is in some sort as a walking stick that he uses Isabel. An extension of the same figure, without the aesthetic and with only the utilitarian connotation, indicates Osmond's real degeneracy: Isabel finally realizes that she has been for him "an applied handled hung-up tool, as senseless and convenient as mere wood and iron." But the evil is not one that can be isolated or confined; it is automatically proliferative. Morally dead himself, incapable of reverence for the human quality in others, Osmond necessarily tries to duplicate his death in them, for it is by killing their volition that he can make them useful; dead, they are alone "beautiful." He urges upon Isabel the obscene suggestion that she, in turn, "use" Lord Warburton by exploiting Warburton's old love for herself in order to get him to marry Pansy; and Osmond can find no excuse for her refusal except that she has her private designs for "using" the Englishman. But it is in Osmond's use of Pansy, his daughter, that he is most subtly and horribly effective. He has made her into a work of art, the modeling materials being the least artful of childish qualities—her innocence and gentleness; and he has almost succeeded in reducing her will to an echo of his own. The quaint figure of Pansy, always only on the edge of scenes, is of great structural importance in the latter half of the book; for she shows the full measure of the abuse that Isabel resists, and it is to nourish in her whatever small germ of creative volition may remain—to salvage, really, a life—that Isabel returns to Rome and to Osmond's paralyzing ambiance.

The moral question that is raised by every character in the book is a question of the "amount of felt life" that each is able to experience, a question of how many and how various are the relationships each can, with integrity, enter into. Or, to put the matter in its basic metaphor, it is a question of how much each person is able to "see," and not only to see but to compose into creative order. The moral question, since it involves vision, feeling, and composition, is an aesthetic one as well. Madame Merle and Osmond are blind to certain relations: "I don't pretend to know what people are meant for," Madame Merle says, ". . . I know only what I can do with them." Mrs. Touchett is blind to certain others. Let us stop for a moment with Henrietta Stackpole's comic crudity of vision, for the "eye" is all-important, and the ranges of vision really begin with an eye like that of Henrietta. It is "a peculiarly open, surprised-looking eye." "The most striking point in her appearance was the remarkable fixedness of this organ."

> She fixed her eyes on [Ralph], and there was something in their character that reminded him of large polished buttons—buttons that might have fixed the elastic loops of some tense receptacle: he seemed to see the reflection of surrounding objects on the pupil. The expression of a button is not usually deemed human, but there was something in Miss Stackpole's gaze that made

him, a very modest man, feel vaguely embarrassed—less invio-
late, more dishonoured, than he liked.

Henrietta, with her gregariously refractive button-sight, has also
"clear-cut views on most subjects . . . she knew perfectly in advance what her opinions would be." Henrietta's is the made-up
consciousness, the pseudo consciousness, that is not a process
but a content hopelessly once and for all given, able to refract
light but not to take it in. (We can understand Henrietta's importance, caricatural as she is, by the fact that she is the primitive form of the pseudo consciousness which Madame Merle and
Osmond, in their so much more sophisticated ways, exhibit:
theirs too is the made-up consciousness, a rigidified content, impervious and uncreative.) The Misses Molyneux, Lord Warburton's sisters, have "eyes like the balanced basins, the circles of
'ornamental water,' set, in parterres, among the geraniums." Let
us note that the figure is drawn from an "aesthetic" arrangement, that of formal gardens—and in this sense has directly opposite associations to those of Henrietta's buttons (presumably
very American, very *useful* buttons). The Misses Molyneux's
eyes, like Henrietta's, also merely reflect surrounding objects, and
reflect more limitedly, far less mobilely; but the image is significant of certain kinds of feeling, of "seeing," that Henrietta
is incapable of, and that have derived from ancient disciplines
in human relationships—contemplative feeling, reverence, feeling for privacy and for grace. Extremely minor figures such as
these, of the buttons and the basins, are pregnant with the extraordinarily rich, extraordinarily subtle potentialities of the
theme of "seeing" as an infinitely graduated cognizance of relations between self and world.

In this book, the great range of structural significance
through figurative language is due to the fact that whatever
image vehicle a figure may have—even when the image is not
itself a visual one—the general context is so deeply and consistently characterized by acts of "seeing" that every metaphor
has this other implied extension of meaning. For example, a
very intricate and extensive symbolic construct is built on a
metaphor of opening doors. Henrietta, Ralph says, "walks in
without knocking at the door." "She's too personal," he adds.
As her eyes indiscriminately take in everything that is literally

to be seen, so she walks in without knocking at the door of personality: "she thinks one's door should stand ajar." The correspondence of eyes and doors lies in the publicity Henrietta assumes (she is a journalist): her eye is public like a button, and responds as if everything else were public, as if there were no doors, as if there were nothing to be seen but what the public (the American newspaper public) might see without effort and without discomfort. In James's thematic system of surfaces and depths, "sight" is something achieved and not given, achieved in the loneliness of the individual soul and in the lucidity of darkness suffered; privacy is its necessary stamp, and it cannot be loaned or broadcast any more than can the loneliness or the suffering. "I keep a band of music in my ante-room," Ralph tells Isabel.

> "It has orders to play without stopping; it renders me two excellent services. It keeps the sounds of the world from reaching the private apartments, and it makes the world think that dancing's going on within."

The notation has its pathos through Ralph's illness. Isabel "would have liked to pass through the ante-room . . . and enter the private apartments." It is only at the end, through her own revelations of remorse and loss, that those doors open to her.

The ironic force of the metaphor of doors, as it combines with the metaphor of "seeing," has a different direction in the crucial scene in Chapter 51 of the second volume—one of the major "recognition scenes" in the book, where Isabel sees Osmond's full malignancy, a malignancy the more blighting as it takes, and sincerely takes, the form of honor, and where Osmond sees unequivocally the vivid, mysterious resistance of a life that he has not been able to convert into a tool. Isabel comes to tell him that Ralph is dying and that she must go to England. She opens the door of her husband's study without knocking.

> "Excuse me for disturbing you," she said.
> "When I come to your room I always knock," he answered, going on with his work.
> "I forgot; I had something else to think of. My cousin's dying."
> "Ah, I don't believe that," said Osmond, looking at his drawing through a magnifying glass. "He was dying when we married; he'll outlive us all."

Osmond is here engaged in an activity representative of a man of taste and a "collector"—he is making traced copies of ancient coins (the fact that it is an act of tracing, of copying, has its own significance, as has the object of his attention: coins). What he "sees" in the situation that Isabel describes to him is quite exactly what he sees in the fact that she has opened the door without knocking: a transgression of convention; and what he does not see is the right of another human being to feel, to love, to will individually. Further, what he appallingly does not see is his dependence, for the fortune Isabel has brought him, on the selfless imagination of the dying man, Ralph; or, even more appallingly (for one can scarcely suppose that Madame Merle had left him ignorant of the source of Isabel's wealth), what he does not see is any reason for the moral responsibility implied by "gratitude," a defect of vision that gives a special and hideous bleakness to his use of the word "grateful," when he tells Isabel that she has not been "grateful" for his tolerance of her esteem for Ralph. The metaphor of the "doors" thus goes through its changes, each associated with a depth or shallowness, a straightness or obliquity of vision, from Henrietta's aggressive myopia, to Ralph's reticence and insight, to Osmond's refined conventionalism and moral astigmatism.

Let us consider in certain other examples this reciprocity between theme and metaphor, insight and sight, image and eye. Isabel's native choice is creativity, a "free exploration of life," but exploration is conducted constantly—vision is amplified constantly—at the cost of renunciations. It is in the "grey depths" of the eyes of the elder Miss Molyneux, those eyes like the balanced basins of water set in parterres, that Isabel recognizes what she has had to reject in rejecting Lord Warburton: "the peace, the kindness, the honour, the possessions, a deep security and a great exclusion." Caspar Goodwood has eyes that "seemed to shine through the vizard of a helmet." He appears always as an armor-man: "she saw the different fitted parts of him as she had seen, in museums and portraits, the different fitted parts of armoured warriors—in plates of steel handsomely inlaid with gold." "He might have ridden, on a plunging steed, the whirlwind of a great war." The image is one of virility, but of passion without relation, aggressive energy without responsibility. The

exclusions implied by Caspar's steel-plated embrace are as great
as those implied by the honor and the peace that Lord Warburton offers; and yet Isabel's final refusal of Caspar and of
sexual possession is tragic, for it is to a sterile marriage that she
returns.

Architectural images, and metaphors whose vehicle (like
doors and windows) is associated with architecture, subtend the
most various and complex of the book's meanings; and the reason for their particular richness of significance seems to be that,
of all forms that are offered to sight and interpretation, buildings
are the most natural symbols of civilized life, the most diverse
also as to what their fronts and interiors can imply of man's
relations with himself and with the outer world. Osmond's
house in Florence has an "imposing front" of a "somewhat in-
communicative character."

> It was the mask, not the face of the house. It had heavy lids,
> but no eyes; the house in reality looked another way—looked
> off behind . . . . The windows of the ground-floor, as you saw
> them from the piazza, were, in their noble proportions, ex-
> tremely architectural; but their function seemed less to offer
> communication with the world than to defy the world to look
> in . . .

(One notes again here the characteristic insistence on *eyes* and
looking.) The description, perfectly fitting an old and noble
Florentine villa, exactly equates with Osmond himself, and not
only Isabel's first illusional impression of him—when it is his
renunciatory reserve that attracts her, an appearance suggesting
those "deeper rhythms of life" that she seeks—but also her later
painful knowledge of the face behind the mask, which, like the
house, is affected with an obliquity of vision, "looked another
way—looked off behind." The interior is full of artful images;
the group of people gathered there "might have been described
by a painter as composing well"; even the footboy "might, tarnished as to livery and quaint as to type, have issued from some
stray sketch of old-time manners, been 'put in' by the brush of a
Longhi or a Goya"; the face of little Pansy is "painted" with a
"fixed and intensely sweet smile." Osmond's world, contained
within his eyeless house, is "sorted, sifted, arranged" for the
eye; even his daughter is one of his arrangements. It is a world

bred of ancient disciplines modulating through time, selection and composition, to the purest aesthetic form.

> [Isabel] carried away an image from her visit to his hill-top . . . which put on for her a particular harmony with other supposed and divined things, histories within histories. . . . It spoke of the kind of personal issue that touched her most nearly; of the choice between objects, subjects, contacts—what might she call them?—of a thin and those of a rich association . . . of a care for beauty and perfection so natural and so cultivated together that the career appeared to stretch beneath it in the disposed vistas and with the ranges of steps and terraces and fountains of a formal Italian garden . . .

The illusion is one of a depth and spaciousness and delicacy of relationships, an illusion of the civilized consciousness.

But while Osmond's world suggests depth, it is, ironically, a world of surfaces only, for Osmond has merely borrowed it. The architectural metaphor shifts significantly in the passage (Chapter 42 of Volume II) in which Isabel takes the full measure of her dwelling. "It was the house of darkness, the house of dumbness, the house of suffocation."

> She had taken all the first steps in the purest confidence, and then she had suddenly found the infinite vista of a multiplied life to be a dark, narrow alley with a dead wall at the end. Instead of leading to the high places of happiness . . . it led rather downward and earthward, into realms of restriction and depression where the sound of other lives, easier and freer, was heard as from above . . .

"When she saw this rigid system close about her, draped though it was in pictured tapestries . . . she seemed shut up with an odour of mould and decay." Again the architectural image changes its shape in that passage (quoted earlier in this essay) where Isabel takes her knowledge and her sorrow into Rome, a Rome of architectural ruins. Here also are depth of human times, "histories within histories," aesthetic form, but not "arranged," not borrowable, not to be "collected"—only to be *lived* in the creative recognitions brought to them by a soul itself alive. The image that accompanies Ralph through the book— "his serenity was but the array of wild flowers niched in his ruin" —gains meaning from the architectural images so frequent in the Roman scenes (as, for instance, from this:

[Isabel] had often ascended to those desolate ledges from which the Roman crowd used to bellow applause and where now the wild flowers . . . bloom in the deep crevices . . .)

Whereas Osmond's forced "arrangements" of history and art and people are without racination, blighting and lifeless, Ralph's "array of wild flowers" is rooted, even if precariously rooted in a ruin; it is a life *grown*, grown in history, fertilized in the crevices of a difficult experience. The metaphor is another version of St. John's "Except a corn of wheat fall into the ground and die, it abideth alone; but if it die, it bringeth forth much fruit." Isabel, still seeking that freedom which is growth, goes back to Osmond's claustral house, for it is there, in the ruin where Pansy has been left, that she has placed roots, found a crevice in which to grow straightly and freshly, found a feltilizing, civilizing relationship between consciousness and circumstances.

Notes

1. Discussion of James's "international myth" will be found in *The Question of Henry James*, edited by F. W. Dupee (New York: Henry Holt & Company, Inc., 1945), and Philip Rahv's *Image and idea* (New York: New Directions, 1949). See Chapter 13 in this book for part of Rahv's essay.

Walter Allen

12 · From *The English Novel:*
A Short Critical History

The Portrait of a Lady (1881), James's first great novel, is still
considered by some critics his best. "The idea of the whole
thing," he wrote in his Notebooks while at work on the novel,
"is that the poor girl, who had dreamed of freedom and nobleness, who has done, as she believes, a generous, natural, clear-
sighted thing, finds herself in reality ground in the very mill
of the conventional." Most of James's novels and stories had
their germ in a situation presented to him in conversation or
picked up in the course of his reading; they existed in the beginning in the form of a tiny, often fragmentary anecdote. In his
Notebook entry for Christmas Eve, 1893, he sets down a "little
history" "related to me last night at dinner at Lady Lindsay's,
by Mrs. Anstruther-Thompson. It is a small and ugly matter
—but there is distinctly in it, I should judge, the subject of a
little tale—a little social and psychological picture." As we read
on we realize we have the genesis of *The Spoils of Poynton*
(1897). *The Portrait of a Lady* began in a different way. The
germ consisted, he tells us in the preface, "altogether in the
sense of a single character, the character and aspect of a particular engaging young woman, to which all the usual elements
of a 'subject,' certainly of a setting, were to need to be super-
added . . . the conception of a certain young woman affronting

From *The English Novel: A Short Critical History* (New York, 1957),
pp. 314–18. Copyright, 1954, by Walter Allen. Reprinted by permission
of the author, E. P. Dutton & Co., Inc. (New York), and Phoenix House,
Ltd. (London).

her destiny." For the particular young woman he almost certainly went back to the memories of his adored cousin, Minny Temple, who died at the age of twenty-four.

The figure of Minny Temple was a most potent symbol in James's life, the symbol of youth and of all that was fine and candid, all that responded most ardently and generously to the promise of life and measured its own demands from life according to its own capacity for experience and greatly doing. Above all, perhaps, it was the symbol of something essentially American. This may not be easy to understand now; as we meet Isabel Archer, the Minny Temple figure of *The Portrait of a Lady*, she falls naturally into the same company of young women in fiction as Jane Austen's Elizabeth Bennet and Emma Woodhouse, George Eliot's Gwendolen Harleth, and Meredith's Clara Middleton, and those names define her quality, her sense of the value of herself. But wherein is the Americanness? It can be most easily realized by thinking of Trollope's representations of American women, of Mrs. Hurtle, for example, in *The Way We Live Now*. For Trollope, Mrs. Hurtle is frightening in the freedom she claims for herself: "she had shot a man through the head somewhere in Oregon." One doesn't quite see Henry James's heroines doing that, but they are free spirits in a way that more or less contemporary English heroines are not; freedom is something they are born to, a condition of their being, as it is not, for instance, of Clara Middleton's, to say nothing of Trollope's young women. They are the product of an attitude towards woman different from the English Victorians'.

When Isabel Archer is brought to England by her Aunt Touchett, she has already refused the rich American businessman Caspar Goodwood, and this itself is a sign that she is a free spirit; poor, she has rejected a fortune, and Goodwood loves her and is a good man. But it is not in her nature to play for safety. "She spent half her time thinking of beauty and bravery and magnanimity; she had a fixed determination to regard the world as a place of brightness, of free expansion, of irresistible action . . . She had an infinite hope that she would never do anything wrong." At the country house of the Touchetts, American bankers long resident in England but still consciously American, she meets Lord Warburton, who falls in love with her.

Warburton is presented as an admirable figure, the English aristocrat at his best, a Radical in politics through sheer *noblesse oblige*. He proposes, and Isabel refuses him; why she scarcely knows; but she knows she must find her own place in the world and Warburton's is not hers. To Mrs. Touchett, her refusal of Warburton is freakish, but Mr. Touchett and his son Ralph understand. Isabel delights them, and it is Ralph who persuades his father to leave her a fortune. "I call people rich," he says, "when they're able to meet the requirements of their imagination." It seems to him a moral duty to enable Isabel to meet hers.

Actually, it is Isabel's undoing. James sees her as clearly as Jane Austen does Emma Woodhouse, though he does not see her satirically:

> Altogether, with her meagre knowledge, her inflated ideals, her confidence at once innocent and dogmatic, her temper at once exacting and indulgent, her mixture of curiosity and fastidiousness, of vivacity and indifference, her desire to look very well and to be if possible even better, her determination to see, to try, to know, her combination of the delicate desultory flame-like spirit and the eager and personal creature of conditions: she would be an easy victim of scientific criticism: if she were not intended to awaken on the reader's part an impulse more tender and more purely expectant.

Her very qualities of ardor of spirit and innocence of the world make her a born victim. She meets Mme. Merle, a woman of the world, and Gilbert Osmond, an expatriate American living in Florence in pursuit of the beautiful. She is captivated by Osmond's life of apparent disinterestedness, of seeming dedication to art. She marries him, but the hideous irony is that Osmond has married her only to get her fortune, to provide Pansy, his daughter by Mme. Merle, with a dowry. They live in Rome, in a palace, and as Isabel reflects one night:

> It was the house of darkness, the house of dumbness, the house of suffocation. Osmond's beautiful mind gave it neither light nor air; Osmond's beautiful mind indeed seemed to peep down from a small high window and mock at her. Of course it had not been physical suffering; for physical suffering there might have been a remedy. She could come and go; she had her liberty; her husband was perfectly polite. He took himself so seriously; it was something appalling. Under all his culture, all

his cleverness, his amenity, under his good-nature, his facility, his knowledge of life, his egoism lay hidden like a serpent in a bank of flowers.

She saves Pansy from an unhappy marriage which is being thrust upon her and returns to England to nurse Ralph Touchett in his last illness. There she meets Caspar Goodwood again. He is still in love with her and pleads with her to leave Osmond for him. "We can do absolutely as we please," he says; "the world's all before us—and the world's very big." "The world's very small," she answers, and returns to Osmond. Happiness and love are consciously rejected.

This ending has been criticized. Given James's conception of his heroine, it seems inevitable, and to fail to see it as such is tantamount to misunderstanding the conception, an integral part of which is the notion of honor. Isabel had "an infinite hope that she would never do anything wrong." Right and wrong are not simple matters for James's great heroes and heroines; they are related to what may be called their life style. At the moment of choice they feel a categorical imperative to behave according to their deepest idea of themselves and of what they owe to self-respect, regardless of comfort or personal happiness. Isabel returns to Osmond because no other course would be fitting to her own conception of herself, just as Fleda Vetch, in *The Spoils of Poynton*, renounces Owen and Poynton, since not to do so, however much it might further her own happiness and her material comfort, would be to compromise her moral sense. Honor, in fact, is at stake.

When James wrote *The Portrait of a Lady* a whole range of possibilities of development lay before him. In *The Great Tradition* F. R. Leavis has examined the parallels between *The Portrait of a Lady* and *Daniel Deronda* and assessed the influence of George Eliot upon him. But there was another influence as potent, Balzac's, and the two novels that follow *The Portrait*, *The Bostonians* and *The Princess Casamassima*, both of which appeared in 1886, follow Balzac in that the notion of the novelist lying behind them is that of the novelist as the historian of his own time.

V. American Affinities

13·From "The Heiress of All the Ages"

HENRY JAMES is not fully represented in his novels by any one
single character, but of his principal heroine it can be said that
she makes the most of his vision and dominates his drama of
transatlantic relations. This young woman is his favorite American type, appearing in his work time and again under various
names and in various situations that can be taken as so many
stages in her career. Hence it is in the line of her development
that we must study her. Her case involves a principle of growth
which is not to be completely grasped until she has assumed
her final shape.

This heroine, too, is cast in the role, so generic to James,
of the "passionate pilgrim," whose ordinary features are those
of the "good American bewildered in the presence of the European order." But bewilderment is not a lasting motive in this
heroine's conduct; unlike most of her fellow-pilgrims in James's
novels, she soon learns how to adjust European attitudes to the
needs of her personality. Where she excels is in her capacity to
plunge into experience without paying the usual Jamesian penalty for such daring—the penalty being either the loss of one's
moral balance or the recoil into a state of aggrieved innocence.
She responds "magnificently" to the beauty of the old-world
scene even while keeping a tight hold on her native virtue: the
ethical stamina, good will, and inwardness of her own provincial

From *Image and Idea* (Norfolk, Conn., 1957), pp. 51–52, 62–70.
Copyright 1949, 1952, © 1957 by Philip Rahv. Reprinted by permission
of New Directions and of the author.

background. And thus living up to her author's idea both of Europe and America, she is able to mediate, if not wholly to resolve, the conflict between the two cultures, between innocence and experience, between the sectarian code of the fathers and the more "civilized" though also more devious and dangerous code of the lovers. No wonder James commends her in terms that fairly bristle with heroic intentions and that in the preface to *The Wings of the Dove* he goes so far as to credit her with the great historic boon of being "that certain sort of young American," exceptionally endowed with "liberty of action, of choice, of appreciation, of contact . . . who is more the 'heir of all the ages' than any other young person whatsoever."

If James's relation to his native land is in question, then more is to be learned from this young woman's career than from any number of discursive statements quoted from his letters, essays, and autobiographies. "It's a complete fate being an American," he wrote. Yes, but what does this fate actually come to in his work? The answer, it seems to me, is mostly given in his serial narrative of the heiress of all the ages.

*   *   *

As the 1870's come to a close, James is done with the preliminary studies of his heroine. Now he undertakes to place her in a longer narrative—*The Portrait of a Lady*—the setting and action of which are at last commensurate with the "mysterious purposes" and "vast designs" of her character. In the preface to the New York edition (written nearly a quarter of a century later) he recalls that the conception of a "certain young woman affronting her destiny had begun with being all my outfit for the large building of the novel"; and he reports that in its composition he was faced with only one leading question: "What will she 'do'?" But this is mainly a rhetorical question, for naturally "the first thing she'll do will be to come to Europe— which in fact will form, and all inevitably, no small part of her principal adventure." *The Portrait* is by far the best novel of James's early prime, bringing to an end his literary apprenticeship and establishing the norms of his world. Its author has not yet entirely divorced himself from Victorian models in point of structure, and as a stylist he is still mindful of the reader's more obvious pleasure, managing his prose with an eye to outward as well as inward effects. It is a lucid prose, conventional yet free, marked by aphoristic turns of phrase and by a kind of intellectual gaiety in the formulation of ideas. There are few signs as yet of that well-nigh metaphysical elaboration of the sensibility by which he is to become known as one of the foremost innovators in modern writing.

Isabel Archer is a young lady of an Emersonian cast of mind, but her affinity as a fictional character is rather with those heroines of Turgenev in whose nature an extreme tenderness is conjoined with unusual strength of purpose.* No sooner does Isabel arrive at the country-house of her uncle Mr. Touchett, an American banker residing in England, than everyone recognizes her for what she is—"a delicate piece of human machinery." Her cousin Ralph questions his mother: "Who is this rare creature, and what is she? Where did you find her?" "I found her," she replies, "in an old house at Albany, sitting in a dreary room on a rainy day. . . . She didn't know she was bored, but when I told her she seemed grateful for the hint. . . . I thought she was meant for something better. It occurred to me it would be a kindness to take her about and introduce her to the world." The American Cinderella thus precipitated from the town of Albany into the "great world" knows exactly what she must look forward to. "To be as happy as possible," she confides in Ralph, "that's what I came to Europe for." It is by no means a simple answer. On a later and more splendid occasion it is to be repeated by Maggie Verver, who proclaims her faith, even as the golden bowl crashes to the ground, in a "happiness without a hole in it . . . the golden bowl as it *was* to have been . . . the bowl with all our happiness in it, the bowl without a crack in it." This is the crowning illusion and pathos, too, of the heiress, that she believes such happiness to be attainable, that money can buy it and her mere good faith can sustain it. And even when eventually her European entanglements open her eyes to the fact that

* The influence may well be conscious in this case, though in the preface to the novel James admits to being influenced by the Russian novelist only on the technical plane, with respect to the manner of placing characters in fiction. James's critical essays abound with favorable references to Turgenev, whose friendship he cultivated in Paris and of whom he invariably spoke with enthusiasm.

virtue and experience are not so charmingly compatible after all, that the Old World has a fierce energy of its own and that its "tone of time" is often pitched in a sinister key, she still persists in her belief that this same world will yield her a richly personal happiness, proof against the evil spawned by others less fortunate than herself; and this belief is all the more expressive because it is wholly of a piece with the psychology of the heiress as a national type. The ardor of Americans in pursuing happiness as a personal goal is equalled by no other people, and when it eludes them none are so hurt, none so shamed. Happiness, one might say, is really their private equivalent of such ideals as progress and universal justice. They take for granted, with a faith at once deeply innocent and deeply presumptuous, that they deserve nothing less and that to miss it is to miss life itself.

The heiress is not to be humbled by the tests to which life in Europe exposes her. The severer the test the more intense the glow of her spirit. Is she not the child, as Isabel proudly declares, of that "great country which stretches beyond the rivers and across the prairies, blooming and smiling and spreading, till it stops at the blue Pacific! A strong, sweet, fresh odour seems to rise from it. . . ." The Emersonian note is sounded again and again by Isabel. She is truly the Young American so grandly pictured by the Concord idealist in his essay of that title, the Young American bred in a land "offering opportunity to the human mind not known in any other region" and hence possessed of an "organic simplicity and liberty, which, when it loses its balance, redresses itself presently. . . ." Witness the following passage of character-analysis, with its revelation of Isabel's shining beneficient Emersonianism:

Every now and then Isabel found out she was wrong, and then she treated herself to a week of passionate humility. After that she held her head higher than ever; for it was of no use, she had an unquenchable desire to think well of herself. She had a theory that it was only on this condition that life was worth living: that one should be of the best, should be conscious of a fine organization . . . *should move in a realm of light, of natural wisdom, of happy impulse, of inspiration fully chronic. It was almost as unnecessary to cultivate doubt of oneself as to cultivate doubt of one's best friend.* . . . The girl had a certain nobleness of imagination which rendered her a good many services and played her a good many tricks. She spent half her time in thinking of beauty, and bravery, and magnanimity; *she had a fixed determination to regard the world as a place of brightness, of free expansion, of irresistible action; she thought it would be detestable to be afraid or ashamed.* (Italics not in the original.)

Still more revealing is the exchange between Isabel and the thoroughly Europeanised Madame Merle on the subject of the individual's capacity for self-assertion in the face of outward circumstances:

Madame Merle: "When you have lived as long as I, you will see that every human being has his shell, that you must take the shell into account. By the shell I mean the whole envelope of circumstances. There is no such thing as an isolated man or woman; we're each of us made up of a cluster of circumstances. What do you call one's self? Where does it begin? Where does it end? It overflows into everything that belongs to me—and then it flows back again. I know that a large part of myself is in the dresses I choose to wear. I have a great respect for *things!*"

Isabel: "I don't agree with you. . . . I think just the other way. I don't know whether I succeed in expressing myself, but I know that nothing else expresses me. Nothing that belongs to me is a measure of me; on the contrary, it's a limit, a barrier, and a perfectly arbitrary one."*

In *The Portrait* James is still hesitating between the attitude of Madame Merle and that of Isabel, and his irony is provoked by the excessive claims advanced by both sides. But in years to come he is to be drawn more and more to the "European" idea of the human self, his finer discriminations being increasingly engaged by the "envelope of circumstances" in which it is contained.

Isabel is above all a young lady of principles, and her most intimate decisions are ruled by them. In refusing the proposal of the grandiose Lord Warburton, she wonders what ideal aspiration or design upon fate or conception of happiness prompts her

* Note the close parallel between Isabel's reply to Madame Merle and the Emersonian text. "You think me the child of my circumstances: I make my circumstances. Let any thought or motive of mine be different from what they are, the difference will transform my condition and economy. . . . You call it the power of circumstances, but it is the power of me." (*The Transcendentalist*)

to renounce such a chance for glamor and worldly satisfaction. Never had she seen a "personage" before, as there were none in her native land; of marriage she had been accustomed to think solely in terms of character—"of what one likes in a gentleman's mind and in his talk . . . hitherto her visions of a completed life had concerned themselves largely with moral images—things as to which the question would be whether they pleased her soul." But if an aristocratic marriage is not to Isabel's liking, neither is the strictly hometown alternative of marrying a business man. The exemplary Caspar Goodwood, who owns a cotton-mill and is the embodiment of patriotic virtue, likewise fails to win her consent.—"His jaw was too square and grim, and his figure too straight and stiff; these things suggested a want of easy adaptability to some of the occasions of life."

Isabel having so far lacked the requisite fortune to back up her assumption of the role of the heiress, her cousin Ralph provides what is wanting by persuading his dying father to leave her a large sum of money. "I should like to make her rich," Ralph declares. "What do you mean by rich?" "I call people rich when they are able to gratify their imagination." Thus Isabel enters the uppermost circle of her author's hierarchy, the circle of those favored few who, unhampered by any material coercion, are at once free to make what they can of themselves and to accept the fullest moral responsibility for what happens to them in consequence. Now the stage is set for the essential Jamesian drama of free choice. In this novel, however, the transcendent worth of such freedom is not yet taken for granted as it is in The Wings of the Dove and The Golden Bowl. There is the intervention, for instance, of the lady-correspondent Henrietta Stackpole, who is no passionate pilgrim but the mouthpiece, rather, of popular Americanism. It is she who questions Isabel's future on the ground that her money will work against her by bolstering her romantic inclinations. Henrietta is little more than a fictional convenience used to furnish the story with comic relief; but at this juncture of the plot she becomes the agent of a profound criticism aimed, in the last analysis, at James himself, at his own tendency to romanticise the values to which privilege lays claim. And what Henrietta has to say is scarcely in keeping with her habitual manner of the prancing

female journalist. Characteristically enough, she begins by remarking that she has no fear of Isabel turning into a sensual
woman; the peril she fears is of a different nature:

> "The peril for you is that you live too much in the world
> of your own dreams—you are not enough in contact with reality
> —with the toiling, striving, suffering, I may even say, sinning
> world that surrounds you. You are too fastidious, you have too
> many graceful illusions. Your newly-acquired thousands will
> shut you up more and more in the society of selfish and heart-
> less people, who will be interested in keeping up those illusions.
> . . . You think, furthermore, that you can lead a romantic life,
> that you can live by pleasing others and pleasing yourself. You
> will find you are mistaken. Whatever life you lead, you must
> put your soul into it—to make any sort of success of it; and
> from the moment you do that it ceases to be romance, I assure
> you; it becomes reality! . . . you think we can escape disagree-
> able duties by taking romantic views—that is your great illu-
> sion, my dear."

The case against the snobbish disposition of the Jamesian cul-
ture-seekers and their overestimation of the worldly motive has
seldom been so shrewdly and clearly stated. But Isabel is not
especially vulnerable to criticism of this sort. It is only in her
later incarnations that the heiress succumbs more and more to
precisely the illusions of which Henrietta gives warning—so
much so that in the end, when Maggie Verver appears on the
scene, the life she leads may be designated, from the standpoint
of the purely social analyst, as a romance of bourgeois material-
ism, the American romance of newly got wealth divesting itself
of its plebian origins in an ecstasy of refinement!

Henrietta's words, moreover, are meant to prefigure the
tragedy of Isabel's marriage to Gilbert Osmond, an Italianate
American, virtually a European, whom she takes to be what he
is not—a decent compromise between the moral notions of her
American background and the glamor of the European foreground. Osmond, whose special line is a dread of vulgarity, em-
ploys a kind of sincere cunning in presenting himself to Isabel
as the most fastidious gentleman living, concerned above all
with making his life a work of art and resolved, since he could
never hope to attain the status he actually deserved, "not to go
in for honors." The courtship takes place in Rome and in Flor-

ence, where Isabel is swayed by her impression of Osmond as a
"quiet, clever, distinguished man, strolling on a moss-grown
terrace above the sweet Val d'Arno . . . the picture was not brilliant, but she liked its lowness of tone, and the atmosphere of
summer twilight that pervaded it. . . . It seemed to speak of a
serious choice, a choice between things of a shallow and things
of a deep interest; of a lonely, studious life in a lovely land." But
the impression is false. Only when it is too late does she learn
that he had married her for her money with the connivance of
Madame Merle, his former mistress, who had undertaken to influence her in his behalf. This entrapment of Isabel illustrates
a recurrent formula of James's fiction. The person springing the
trap is almost invariably driven by mercenary motives, and, like
Osmond, is capable of accomplishing his aim by simulating a
sympathy and understanding that fascinate the victim and render her (or him) powerless.* Osmond still retains some features
of the old-fashioned villain, but his successors are gradually freed
from the encumbrances of melodrama. Merton Densher (*The
Wings of the Dove*) and Prince Amerigo (*The Golden Bowl*)
are men of grace and intelligence, whose wicked behavior is
primarily determined by the situation in which they find themselves.

Osmond reacts to the Emersonian strain in Isabel as to a
personal offence. He accuses her of wilfully rejecting traditional
values and of harboring sentiments "worthy of a radical newspaper or a Unitarian preacher." And she, on her part, discovers
that his fastidiousness reduced itself to a "sovereign contempt
for every one but some two or three or four exalted people whom
he envied, and for everything but half-a-dozen ideas of his own
. . . he pointed out to her so much of the baseness and shabbi-
ness of life . . . but this base, ignoble world, it appeared, was
after all what one was to live for; one was to keep it forever in
one's eye, in order, not to enlighten, or convert, or redeem, but

---

* It seems to me that this brand of evil has much in common with the
"unpardonable sin" by which Hawthorne was haunted—the sin of *using*
other people, of "violating the sanctity of a human heart." Chillingworth
in *The Scarlet Letter* is essentially this type of sinner, and so is Miriam's
model in *The Marble Faun*. In James, however, the evil characters have
none of the Gothic *mystique* which is to be found in Hawthorne. Their
motives are transparent.

to extract from it some recognition of one's superiority." Isabel's notion of the aristocratic life is "simply the union of great knowledge with great liberty," whereas for Osmond it is altogether a "thing of forms," an attitude of conscious calculation. His esteem for tradition is boundless; if one was so unfortunate as not to be born to an illustrious tradition, then "one must immediately proceed to make it."* A sense of darkness and suffocation takes hold of Isabel as her husband's rigid system closes in on her. She believes that there can be no release from the bondage into which she had fallen and that only through heroic suffering is its evil to be redeemed. On this tragic note the story ends.

Yet the heiress is not to be turned aside from her quest by such inevitable encounters with the old evils of history. On the lighted stage the bridegroom still awaits his new-world bride.

* The significance of Osmond's character has generally been underrated by the critics of James. For quite apart from his more personal traits (such as his depravity, which is a purely novelistic element), he is important as a cultural type in whom the logic of "traditionalism" is developed to its furthest limits. As a national group the American intellectuals suffer from a sense of inferiority toward the past, and this residue of "colonial" feeling is also to be detected in those among them who raise the banner of tradition. It is shown in their one-sided conformity to the idea of traditon, in their readiness to inflate the meanings that may be derived from it. Their tendency is to take literally what their European counterparts are likely to take metaphorically and imaginatively. My idea is that James tried to overcome this bias which he suspected in himself by objectifying it in the portrait of Osmond. To this day, however, the shadow of Gilbert Osmond falls on many a page of American writing whose author—whether critic, learned poet, or academic "humanist"—presents himself, with all the exaggerated zeal and solemnity of a belated convert, as a spokesman of tradition.

14 · The Lesson of the Master

HENRY JAMES's *Portrait of a Lady* (1880) was the first novel by an American that made, within the limits of its subject, full use of the novel form. By comparison, no previous American novel, even those of James, can claim to be fully "done." From James's point of view the older American romance-novelists had many faults. Some of these he singles out explicitly in his biography of Hawthorne, others, as was noted in Chapter I, he directly or indirectly deals with in his prefaces and critical writings. Cooper, Hawthorne, and Melville (actually James seems to know next to nothing of the last) relied too readily on extravagant events and startling characters. They failed to render experience fully. They failed to illustrate and dramatize connections and relations. They did not see (in the words of the Preface to *Roderick Hudson*) that for the true novelist "the continuity of things is the whole matter . . . of comedy and tragedy."

To read the first page of *The Portrait of a Lady* is to step into a world unfrequented by the earlier American novelists. A handsome pictorial representation, a fine old house, beautiful lawns and gardens, a group of people being set in motion—all these may be found in Cooper's *Satanstoe* or Hawthorne's *House of the Seven Gables*. But James's procedure is different from that of the earlier writers. The effect he seeks is more organic and

From *The American Novel and Its Tradition* (New York, 1957), pp. 117–37. Copyright © 1957 by Richard Chase. Reprinted by permission of Doubleday & Company, Inc., (New York) and of G. Bell & Sons, Ltd. (London).

self-contained. At the same time, there is more detail, more careful observation, for he has "researched" his subject—something which Hawthorne, as James said, tended to leave undone. We encounter at the very beginning the author's reference to his book as a "history" and we are perhaps reminded that in his essay "The Art of Fiction" (1884) he was to say that the novel should give the same impression of veracity as does history itself.

On the broad, sloping lawn of the mansion James calls Gardencourt we discover people taking tea, and they are finding it agreeable, not only because it tastes good but because drinking it is a mild ritual by which they show themselves to be a part of a way of life, a social order which we understand is to figure strongly in the book, as strongly as does the life of the Westchester aristocracy in *Satanstoe*. Yet the life of James's characters will be illustrated and dramatized with a far more exact and also a more poetic art than one can find in Cooper's novel.

To admit, as most readers would, that there is an element of poetry in *The Portrait of a Lady* is to admit that though it has all of the novelistic virtues, it has others too. There is a sense in which one might speak of the "poetry" of *Pride and Prejudice* or *Middlemarch*—a poetry of picture and scene, a poetry felt to belong to the organized effect of character, action, and setting. But this is, so to speak, novelistic poetry, of the kind every interesting novel has. *The Portrait* has it too, but it also has a further dimension of poetry, to understand which one must perceive that James's novel is akin to romance as the others are not.

It is an important fact about James's art that he gave up what he considered the claptrap of romance without giving up its mystery and beauty. Mr. Leavis in *The Great Tradition* is not interested in James as a romancer, but he nevertheless notes that James is a "poet-novelist" and says that he combines Jane Austen's skill of observing and dramatizing manners with Hawthorne's "profoundly moral and psychological . . . poetic art of fiction." This is very well put, and it supports the supposition of this chapter that a part of James's great program for improving the novel consisted of the reconstitution, on new grounds, of romance. Often one has difficulty in pinning down any one element of a James novel as belonging to romance because the

author has so completely subdued and transmuted it to suit his
exacting novelistic purposes. The element of romance becomes
generally subverted and assimilated; yet in turn it imparts the
glow of poetry to the realistic substance of the novel. Which is
to say in a different way what Mr. Leavis says in the following:

> James's own constant and profound concern with spiritual facts
> expresses itself not only in what obviously demands to be called
> symbolism, but in the handling of character, episode, and dia-
> logue, and in the totality of the plot, so that when he seems to
> offer a novel of manners, he gives us more than that and the
> "poetry" is major.

The conscious assimilation of romance into the novelistic
substance of The Portrait took place in two different ways. It
was assimilated into the language of the book and produced a
general enrichment of metaphor. It was also brought in in the
character of Isabel Archer, the heroine, who is to a considerable
extent our point of view as we read. Isabel tends to see things
as a romancer does, whereas the author sees things with the
firmer, more comprehensive, and more disillusioned vision of the
novelist. Thus James brings the element of romance into the
novel in such a way that he can both share in the romantic point
of view of his heroine and separate himself from it, by taking an
objective view of it.

The metaphors of The Portrait of a Lady do not often rival
the amazingly elaborate figures one encounters in James's later
works, but by contrast with the usual practice of the novel at
the time James wrote they are notably daring—so much so that
sometimes they seem to lead a life of their own within the spacious world of the book, although in each case we are led to see
the relevance of the metaphor to the course of events and to the
pattern of unfolding significance. There is a paradox, says James
in his Preface to The Portrait, in trying to write a fiction at once
so complex and so ambitious. The paradox is that a novel so
conceived must "positively . . . appear more true to its character
in proportion as it strains, or tends to burst, with a latent extravagance, its mould." Metaphor offered to James a kind of
repository or annex in which the latent extravagance of his imagination might take form. As has often been noticed the main
figures of speech in James's novel—although the variety is rich
—have to do with the house and the garden.

The metaphors are sometimes extravagant. For example we read of Isabel that "her imagination was by habit ridiculously active; when the door was not open it jumped out of the window." But that is a mere piece of fancy and reminds us less of the characteristic practice of James than of the quaint wit of Hawthorne. Ordinarily, James's metaphors, in *The Portrait* as elsewhere, are not quaint and concise. They are suggestively imaginative and they are likely to be given a tone of elevated levity which at once enjoys what is being said and takes note of its extravagance. As often as not the Jamesian metaphor shows that mixture of serious poetic imagination with humor which we find in other American writers, notably Melville, Mark Twain, and Faulkner. Although one would hardly mistake the style of any one of these writers for that of any other, all of them are fond of the serious, intricately sustained joke. Here is James speaking of Ralph Touchett's pose of facetious irony, which Isabel, in her earnest sincerity, finds baffling and also reprehensible. Sensing his inner despair and sorry that he is sickly, she wants to come directly to the "real" Ralph Touchett, but he himself explains the value of his pose:

"I keep a band of music in my ante-room. It has orders to play without stopping; it renders me two excellent services. It keeps the sounds of the world from reaching the private apartments, and it makes the world think that dancing's going on within." It was dance music indeed that you usually heard when you came within earshot of Ralph's band; the liveliest waltzes seemed to float upon the air. Isabel often found herself irritated by this perpetual fiddling; she would have liked to pass—

James finds the metaphor, once launched, too good to drop—

through the ante-room, as her cousin called it, and enter the private apartments. It mattered little that he had assured her they were a very dismal place; she would have been glad to undertake to sweep them and set them in order. It was but half-hospitality to let her remain outside.

The idea of leaving and entering a house, the contrast of different kinds of houses, the question of whether a house is a prison or the scene of liberation and fulfillment—these are the substance of the metaphors in *The Portrait of a Lady*. Figuratively speaking, the story told in the novel is of Isabel's leaving an American house—a way of life, that is—for a European house.

Ostensibly she conceives of this as an escape from frustrating and cramping confinement to a fuller, freer, more resonant and significant life. Actually, it is not hard to see that although James has much admiration and tenderness of feeling for his heroine, he gives her an element of perverse Yankee idealism of the sort that he was shortly to portray in the more exacerbated form of positively *perverted* idealism in Oliver Chancellor in *The Bostonians*. So that for all her dark-haired, gray-eyed beauty, her delightful young enthusiasm, and her zest for life, there is in Isabel a fatal susceptibility to a form of imprisonment worse than that she has escaped. Figuratively, the house in which she lives as the wife of Gilbert Osmond confines her in a hopeless imprisonment she could not consciously have imagined.

Our first sight of Isabel occurs when with her abrupt charm and her disarming candor she walks across the lawn at Gardencourt, the Touchetts' English estate, and presents herself to her cousin Ralph, his father, and Lord Warburton. But then in the form of a flash-back we are speedily acquainted with the general circumstances of Isabel's childhood and girlhood. We find her in the old family house at Albany talking with Mrs. Touchett and greeting with joy Mrs. Touchett's offer to take her to Europe. "To go to Florence," says Isabel, "I'd promise almost anything!" She sees in this offer an escape from the loneliness of the life she has known in the great, empty, dismal house. Yet now that escape is in view, Isabel admits that she does not hate the house or the circumstances of her early life, even though Mrs. Touchett dismisses the place as "very bourgeois." "I like places in which things have happened," says Isabel, "—even if they're sad things. A great many people have died here; the place has been full of life." And to Mrs. Touchett's query "Is that what you call being full of life?" she replies, "I mean full of experience—of people's feelings and sorrows. And not of their sorrows only, for I've been happy here as a child."

Still, the possibility of living a full life in Albany seems remote to Isabel. And the only considerable picture of her as a young girl that James gives us suggests that she had found the Albany house not so much the scene of human sufferings and joys as the somewhat bleak abode of a life of fantasy and reading, a life isolated from reality. Isabel had been accustomed to read and daydream in a room known as "the office" that lay beyond the library.

> The place owed much of its mysterious melancholy to the fact that it was properly entered from the second door of the house, the door that had been condemned, and that it was secured by bolts which a particularly slender little girl found it impossible to slide. She knew that this silent, motionless portal opened into the street; if the sidelights had not been filled with green paper she might have looked out upon the little brown stoop and the well-worn brick pavement. But she had no wish to look out, for this would have interfered with her theory that there was a strange, unseen place on the other side—a place which became to the child's imagination, according to its different moods, a region of delight or terror.

She is sitting in this room when Mrs. Touchett comes to see her, except that being now a young woman with undefined but strong purposes she is, on this fateful afternoon, not engaging in childish fantasy but, having given her mind "marching orders," she has sent it "trudging over the sandy plains of a history of German thought."

Despite her disorganized and tenuous education and the puritanism of her native Yankee temperament, Isabel is now ostensibly ready to pursue an enriched life of the emotions and of thought. A way of life characterized by its intricate amenity, its depth of emotion, and its richness of traditionally ordered experience cannot be symbolized by the house at Albany. But it can by the Tudor mansion of the Touchetts, to which Isabel is introduced when she arrives in England.

> Her uncle's house seemed a picture made real; no refinement of the agreeable was lost on Isabel: the rich perfection of Gardencourt at once revealed a world and gratified a need. The deep embrasures and curious casements, the quiet light on dark polished panels, the deep greenness outside, that seemed always peeping in, the sense of a well-ordered privacy in the centre of a "property"—a place where sounds were felicitously accidental, where the tread was muffled by the earth itself and in the thick mild air all friction dropped out of contact and all shrillness out of talk . . .

There is no paper in the windows of this house, no need to isolate oneself from the world outside. On the contrary the "greenness outside" seems "always peeping in" and the garden, where at important points in the novel Isabel will receive and reject proposals of marriage from Lord Warburton and Caspar Goodwood, seems as much a part of the house as does its own interior. Consequently, the garden makes an inevitable part of the general metaphor which represents the enriched sensibility of the heroine.

> She was always planning out her development, desiring her perfection, observing her progress. Her nature had, in her conceit, a certain garden-like quality, a suggestion of perfume and murmuring boughs. of shady bowers and lengthening vistas, which made her feel that introspection was, after all, an exercise in the open air, and that a visit to the recesses of one's spirit was harmless when one returned from it with a lapful of roses.

In a novel which describes a fall from innocence, it is suitable that the tragic action should be metaphorically mirrored in the heroine's mind by this imaginative conjunction of the garden and the ancient house, in which the garden stands for Isabel's Eve-like innocence and the house for a civilization that has lost its innocence but has acquired—along with its corruption—wisdom, maturity, and the whole involved and valuable accretion of culture. Thus Isabel is akin not only to the heroines of George Eliot, such as Hetty Sorrel, Maggie Tulliver, Rosamond Vincy, and Gwendolen Harleth, with whom James compares her in his Preface; nor is she akin only to Shakespeare's Portia, with whom James also compares Isabel, calling Portia "the very type and model of the young person intelligent and presumptuous." Isabel also resembles the strong-minded Rosalind in *As You Like It* and the innocent and expectant Miranda in *The Tempest*. And the particular charm of these girls is that they are "real," that they make positive demands on life, but that they are at the same time figures of romance. James is also thinking of the Miltonic archetype of all feminine innocence, as is suggested by his using, as Leon Edel points out, the language of *Paradise Lost* to describe Isabel as she sets out on her adventures: "The world lay before her—she could do whatever she chose."

Chapter 42 of *The Portrait* brings to its fullest realization, though not to its last refinement, the characteristic art of James, that art which I am attempting to define as an assimilation of romance into the substance of the novel. James describes this chapter by saying that, "It is obviously the best thing in the book, but it is only a supreme illustration of the general plan." In this chapter James was able to achieve supremely the "circuit" of the real and the ideal, of action and fantasy, and thus to capture along with the realistic substance of the story the wonder and beauty of romance while at the same time rejecting the conventional devices of romance.

Isabel, now the wife of Osmond, sits one evening by the fire in the drawing room of Osmond's house, and with a combination of disillusioned insight and darkly working imagination she recognizes for the first time the true character of her husband and the true nature of her predicament. The problem, as James sees it, is how to present an episode in which nothing happens except an "extraordinary meditative vigil" but which will have all the excitement of action and high adventure. The problem is how to make the "mystic conversion" of Isabel's adventures, which have actually been "mild," into "the stuff of drama," how, as he goes on to say, to produce "the maximum of intensity with the minimum of strain." The "circuit" of the real and the fantasied, the "mystic conversion" of which James speaks, is to be established not, certainly, through a mere retelling or summing-up of Isabel's "mild adventures," but by giving us her sense of them. "Without her sense of them, her sense *for* them, as one may say, they are next to nothing at all." Although there are no overt happenings in this chapter, it nevertheless, as James says,

> throws the action further forward than twenty "incidents" might have done. It was designed to have all the vivacity of incident and all the economy of picture. Isabel sits up, by her dying fire, far into the night, under the spell of recognitions on which she finds the last sharpness suddenly wait. It is a representation simply of her motionlessly *seeing,* and an attempt withal to make the mere still lucidity of her act as "interesting" as the surprise of a caravan or the identification of a pirate.

What occurs in Isabel's mind is the kind of disillusion and profoundly realistic perception of truth about oneself and one's situation that is called "tragic recognition." Yet it comes to her in images that belong as much to melodrama as to tragedy.

"Her soul was haunted by terrors," says James, "which crowded to the foreground of thought as quickly as a place was made for them." One of these terrors is the new image she has formed of her husband, an image which distinctly reminds us of one of the cold, selfish villains of Hawthorne, a Rappaccini or a Chillingworth. She thinks of Osmond's "faculty for making everything wither that he touched, spoiling everything for her that he looked at. . . . It was as if he had had the evil eye; as if his presence were a blight and his favor a misfortune."

She reflects that she had set out with her husband for "the high places of happiness." She had taken "all the first steps in the purest confidence," but now "she had suddenly found the infinite vista of a multiplied life to be a dark narrow alley with a dead wall at the end." The man who had so narrowed and enclosed her life, a creature of darkness, now steps forth into the light—"she had seen only half his nature then, as one saw the disk of the moon when it was partly masked by the shadow of the earth. She saw the full moon now—she saw the whole man."

But the full force of Isabel's recognition is appropriately conveyed by the metaphor of the house and the garden. She has escaped, to be sure, the isolation and girlish ignorance she had known at Albany, but she has lost the felicitous synthesis of innocence and experience symbolized as a possibility for her by Gardencourt. Her marriage, as she now sees, had made her the inhabitant of a different house.

> She could live it over again, the incredulous terror with which she had taken the measure of her dwelling. Between these four walls she had lived ever since; they were to surround her for the rest of her life. It was the house of darkness, the house of dumbness, the house of suffocation. Osmond's beautiful mind gave it neither light nor air; Osmond's beautiful mind indeed seemed to peep down from a small high window and mock at her.

And so Isabel comes to see that

> under all his culture, his cleverness, his amenity, under his good-nature, his facility, his knowledge of life, his egotism lay hidden like a serpent in a bank of flowers.

Her youthful innocence and good-will have been foully traduced, she has been the victim of an elegantly sordid conspiracy, the possibility of a full life she had envisioned has been spoiled. And we are left to recall, with a sense of its tragic irony, her early declaration to Lord Warburton that "I can't escape my fate"—that fate which Isabel had thought would consist of some rewarding involvement in life. For although she has rather grand aspirations, an essential stipulation of her fate, as she understands it, is that she shall never be exempt "from the usual chances and dangers, from what most people know and suffer." She has found knowledge and suffering no doubt, but of the grimmest sort. In her plight there can be no such clarion awakening and engagement of her human faculties as she had supposed might be the result of knowledge and suffering. Indeed there seems nothing left for her but a life of duty and abnegation. As we leave her at the end of the book she seems veritably to belong to the sisterhood of Hester Prynne.

But we know why Hester Prynne is made to suffer; conventional morality imposes on her its punishment for a sin of passion. For better or for worse, Isabel remains scrupulously virginal. She has been guilty of no misconduct in which we find any real justification for suffering. And we do, of course, want to find some measure of justification; otherwise we shall have to convict James of palming off on us under the guise of moral complexity what is morally speaking a mere melodrama of victimized innocence, a tale of merely senseless cruelty and pathos.

Is James himself subtly vindictive in his attitude toward Isabel? He clearly admires her for her almost redemptive American probity and moral spontaneity, and yet he just as clearly thinks her guilty of presumption, and of bad manners that are only just barely made tolerable by her ingenuous charm. Nor does James approve of her upbringing or of her father, one of those somewhat disorderly, nomadic Americans for whom he always shows a dislike. Isabel has been taught to "affront her destiny," as James says in his Preface; and this, one supposes, is less correct than *confronting* it. Even supposing, as there is some speculative ground for doing, that James has a neurotic involvement with his heroine which leads him to fear her female aggressiveness and thus to take satisfaction and to derive a feeling of security in showing her, though possessed of animal spirits, to be sexually cold, and in leading her, finally, to her cruel fate— even supposing on these or other grounds a genuine animosity on the part of James toward his heroine, the fact remains that this is surmounted by his admiration of her and his profound sympathy with her. And in any case Isabel is so completely created a character that she lives her life independently of the approval or disapproval the author may feel toward her, whether we deduce his feeling from the novel itself or from our knowledge of his life and temperament.

Sometimes moved, as one must be, by a desire for a more earthly and simple morality than James's usually is, one wishes that Isabel Archer were more like Kate Croy of *The Wings of the Dove* or even the unpleasantly named Fleda Vetch in *The Spoils of Poynton*, girls in whom the general quality of self-assertion has a sexual component. But despite her deeply repressed sexuality, Isabel remains among the most complex, the most fully realized, and the most humanly fascinating of James's characters. Consequently we cannot think her a mere case of victimized innocence. She has so many powers, imperfect though they are, of knowledge, of feeling, of imagination that her fate must surely issue in some crucial way from her being the sort of person she is. If she is disqualified for triumph, it is not in the obvious way of James's other victimized innocents, like Catherine Sloper in *Washington Square*, who is homely and timid, like Maisie in *What Maisie Knew* or little Miles and Flora in *The Turn of the Screw*, who are children, or like Milly Theale in *The Wings of the Dove*, who is dying of tuberculosis. Isabel's disqualification is that of heroines and heroes throughout tragic literature—a blindness to reality, a distortion of awareness, that puts her at the mercy of the perverse and self-destructive inner motives struggling in her for the upper hand.

Without attempting any sort of full discussion of Isabel and her troubles, one may note that she sees reality as the romancer sees it. This is obvious as a general proposition, since Isabel is patently romantic in the sense that she has highly imaginative dreams which prove to be beyond the possibility of fulfillment. A realistic young woman, or, for that matter, a conventionally romantic one, would have accepted Lord Warburton as a good catch, for he is, after all, an excellent man as well as a rich and noble lord. But Isabel has higher ideals than any she thinks can be realized by a life with Lord Warburton. Her personal ro-

mance includes strenuous abstractions that lead her to aspire
to far more than the conventional romance of marrying an English nobleman. She therefore perversely and no doubt quite
mistakenly decides that to marry Lord Warburton would be
to "escape" her "fate." "I can't escape unhappiness," she says.
"In marrying you I shall be trying to." And she continues by
saying that by marrying Lord Warburton she would be "turning away," "separating" herself from life, "from the usual
chances and dangers, from what most people know and suffer."
Lord Warburton's answer is one that would in the main turn
out to be true: "I don't offer you any exoneration from life or
from any chances or dangers whatever." He is brought by Isabel's
behavior to a true understanding of her, and he exclaims, "I never
saw a person judge things on such theoretic grounds." Her theory is that he is merely "a collection of attributes and powers,"
but this is clearly a false theory. Despite his being a hereditary
nobleman and so, bound to the formalities and duties of his
station in life, he presents himself to her with perfect candor
as a man, and not a lord, who needs and desires her. Thus Isabel's vague democratic objections to English aristocracy, which
in any case she seems generally to admire, are not the real reason why she rejects Lord Warburton. Nor when she does marry
does she choose a man notable for democracy. She rejects Lord
Warburton at the behest of her puritan spirituality, which leads
her to flee from the mere physical and social realities of life as
these would be should she marry him. Perversely and mistakenly,
her argument is that marriage to Lord Warburton would exempt
her from life. Better a collection of attributes and powers (which
in any case Lord Warburton is not) than a collection of sterile
tastes and appetites, which Gilbert Osmond certainly is. But
Isabel does not see Osmond for what he is until too late. (I am
assuming here as elsewhere that Isabel's choice is, for all practical purposes, between Warburton and Osmond. Ralph is in
love with her, but his illness disqualifies him. The persistent
Caspar Goodwood presents himself at intervals, but Isabel does
not see him as an actual possibility. She seems to conceive of
him as worthy but as rather stodgy in his conventional Massachusetts way. She scarcely thinks of him as being momentously
on the scene until at the very end of the novel when he pro-

poses to rescue her from Osmond and, in his vehemence, frightens her with his masculine aggressiveness by giving her, so far as the reader knows, her only kiss.)

How is it that the image Osmond presents to the world so easily commands Isabel's assent? This is a hard problem, but the answer may be suggested by observing that although Isabel's vision of things is neither that of self-interested common sense nor that of worldly romance in which poor girls marry great lords, it emphatically is that of the romance associated with the American tradition of puritanism and transcendentalism. Isabel subscribes to the American romance of the self. She believes that the self finds fulfillment either in its own isolated integrity or on a more or less transcendent ground where the contending forces of good and evil are symbolized abstractions. She sees her fate as a spiritual melodrama. Her grasp of reality, though manifold in its presumptions, is unstable, and her desire for experience is ambivalent. She rejects Lord Warburton ostensibly because she fears that marrying him will exempt her from life. But Ralph Touchett, who often speaks with the wisdom of the author, has no trouble in securing a contradictory admission from his amusing and perplexing cousin. At the end of a lengthy dialogue about her rejection of Lord Warburton, Ralph conjectures, "You want to drain the cup of experience," and gets out of Isabel this surprising answer, "No, I don't wish to touch the cup of experience. It's poisoned drink! I only want to see for myself." To which Ralph adds a comment in the partial truth of which we may see a link between Isabel and Osmond: "You want to see, but not to feel."

Ralph has hit upon a truth about his cousin. The kind of cold, amoral aloofness, the possibly morbid passion for observing life at a distance—these are real traits of Isabel's character. True, they are no more than strong strands in her fabric. But they are strong enough so that she responds to Osmond's talk about how "one ought to make one's life a work of art," without being aware of the inhumanity and the withering aestheticism such an idea may imply. Only when it is too late does she discover the cold malignancy of her husband. Only too late does she see that, apart from his need of the money she has inherited from her uncle, she is cherished by Osmond only to the extent that he

can consider her another art object in his collection. Only too
late does she understand the subtle corruption that leads Osmond to try to arrange his daughter's education so as to make
her life "a work of art." Listening to Osmond's plans for Pansy's
schooling, Isabel seems to see at last "how far her husband's
desire to be effective was capable of going—to the point of playing theoretic tricks on the delicate organism of his daughter."
In this way Isabel, who is herself every bit the theorist Lord
Warburton accused her of being, comes to understand the
perverse puritan impulse which Hawthorne called "the Unpardonable Sin." The sin is the same whether one's cold, theoretical manipulation of others has an aesthetic motive or as with
Hawthorne's Chillingworth or Ethan Brand a quasi-scientific
one.

Isabel's romance of the self, as was suggested above, requires that self-fulfillment shall take place only at a high level
of abstraction, where the disinterested pursuit of perfection may
be carried on. And although Ralph Touchett warns his cousin
that Osmond is a "sterile aesthete," she sees in him at once the
high priest, the devoted custodian, and martyr of the life of
perfection. She is very far from believing that the ordinary
vulgar circumstances of one's life have anything to do with
one's self. She finds it inconceivable and rather degrading that
anyone should suppose the self to be in any sort of dialectic
with the mere things one is surrounded by. In Chapter 19 there
occurs an important exchange between Madame Merle and
Isabel on this point. They have been talking about the inevitable
"young man with a mustache" who must figure in some way in
every young woman's life. Madame Merle speculatively inquires
whether Isabel's "young man with a mustache" has a "castle
in the Apennines" or "an ugly brick house in Fortieth Street."
And when Isabel says characteristically, "I don't care anything
about his house," Madame Merle replies, "That's very crude of
you." And she continues by saying,

> There's no such thing as an isolated man or woman; we're each
> of us made up of some cluster of appurtenances. What shall we
> call our "self"? Where does it begin? Where does it end? It
> overflows into everything that belongs to us—and then it flows
> back again. I know a large part of myself is in the clothes I

choose to wear. I've a great respect for *things!* One's self—for other people—is one's expression of one's self; and one's house, one's furniture, one's garments, the books one reads, the company one keeps—these things are all expressive.

This bit of worldly wisdom strikes Isabel as being worldly, all too worldly, but not as being wisdom. "I don't agree with you," she says. "I think just the other way. I don't know whether I succeed in expressing myself, but I know that nothing else expresses me. Nothing that belongs to me is any measure of me; everything's on the contrary a limit, a barrier, and a perfectly arbitrary one." To find the fulfillment of self through superiority to mere things and without attention to what others may think about what one does—this is the feat Isabel supposes Osmond to have accomplished. Actually as she comes tragically to see, Osmond is above all men enslaved by things and by what he supposes others to be thinking of him. "She had thought it a grand indifference, an exquisite independence. But indifference was really the last of his qualities; she had never seen anyone who thought so much of others."

The moral world shared by Isabel and Osmond—a world in which Lord Warburton has no place—is that of the high Emersonian self-culture. In the sordid elegance of Osmond's implacably willed hedonism we discover the final possibilities of corruption in this culture, which is of course no less subject to corruption than any other moral idealism. In Isabel's unhappy career we estimate the tragic implications of an idealism that in effect directs one to seek the rewards of the fully "lived life" without descending from one's high pedestal into its actual conditions. In Isabel's sincere presentation of her essentially spiritual quest as a quest for a real involvement in "the usual chances and dangers" of life lies the tragic irony of the story. And it has, furthermore, the advantage of verisimilitude since that is how an ambitious young woman in the latter part of the nineteenth century—spiritual puritan though she might be—would conceive of her quest, knowing it to be no longer inevitably the part of woman to isolate herself from the world either because of religious conviction or in the acquiescence to the conventions about woman's place.

Isabel Archer may be said to have the imagination of romance most notably in the sense that she responds to character intensely only when it conceives of itself at a high level of abstraction and when its acts are symbolic of ideal values. When this imagination is confronted by an appealingly complex human being, such as Lord Warburton, it sees only "a collection of attributes and powers." Like the romancer, Isabel refuses to impute significance to human actions unless they are conceived as being exempt from the ordinary circumstances of life, whereas the genuine novelist sees in ordinary circumstances the inescapable root condition of significant actions.

So, to carry the analogy only one step along, James in the end brings Isabel's point of view around from that of the romancer to that of the novelist. Like *The Blithedale Romance*, *The Portrait of a Lady* explores the limits of romance. But whereas Hawthorne seems to admit that he cannot be the true novelist and thus surrenders the imagination of the novelist to that of the romancer, James does the opposite, affirming the primacy of the novelist's imagination. But though he rejects romance as a moral view of the world, he assimilates into the very substance of the novel, by means of metaphor and the charm of the heroine herself, the appeal of romance. Thus he is able to meet superabundantly the requirement for the novel which he calls in the Preface to *The American* satisfying "our general sense of the ways things happen" and at the same time he is able to provide the novel with the poetry of romance.

So much, and as it would seem, no more is to be done with *The Portrait of a Lady* as a romance. In James's books one catches hold of the romance only just as it is disappearing into the thicket of the novel. Thus it is a thankless task to pursue too long and arduously something that is always being assimilated into something else. James is not a romancer like Hawthorne or Melville; he is a novelist to the finger tips.

It is true that, compared with any English novelist one might mention, James shows a strikingly varied interest in the literary forms associated with romance. He is not interested in pastoral idyls, to be sure. But many of his novels, as Jacques Barzun has pointed out, have a strong element of melodrama, from the early *Washington Square* to the late *Wings of the Dove*. Yet none of his fictions end in the sheer horror produced by the unresolved tensions of melodrama. This is true, for example, of the late short novel *The Other House*. In the first two thirds of the book we have the conflict of a "good" woman and a "bad" woman, a tale of frustrated love and revenge, and the drowning by the bad woman of a little girl. But even this thriller runs afoul of Jamesian complications before we are through with it. It turns out that the villainous woman is not, after all, guilty of unalloyed villainy. It is shown that she has attractive qualities, and it is shown that although she committed a particularly repulsive murder, the moral question finally involves the conscious or unconscious complicity in the crime by several of the people around her. The conclusion of the book is rather feeble and unsatisfactory, but the crime is made to seem that of a social class and a particular way of life, a crime that is compounded by everyone's agreeing to hush it up. By this time the tale has become quasi-tragic and our minds are directed as in the plays of Ibsen, which influence *The Other House*, to a social problem, the corruption of the bourgeoisie. The abstract actions, the stirring contradictions, the relative freedom from social and moral perplexities that we look for in melodrama—all these are excitingly present in *The Other House*, but they do not see James through to the end. Instead he characteristically makes the attempt to assimilate the purely melodramatic elements of the story into a novelistic conception. *The Other House* is an instructive investigation, from the Jamesian point of view, of the limits of melodrama.

A more striking departure from the practice of the English novelists (for, after all, Dickens and Conrad, among others, make use of melodrama) is James's use of a symbolistic or allegorical poetry in the late novels—notably *The Wings of the Dove* and *The Golden Bowl*. That these novels are akin to poetry has long been recognized. For example, Stephen Spender once compared *The Golden Bowl* illuminatingly with Eliot's poems. And many people have noted a certain ritualistic poetry of sacrifice and elegy in *The Wings of the Dove* and have seen in this story of the betrayal and death of a blameless young woman a resemblance to Racine's *Iphigenia* and Shakespeare's *Othello*. And Quentin Anderson's argument that *The Ambassadors*, *The Wings of the Dove*, and *The Golden Bowl* constitute in

their cumulative significance a "divine novel" allegorically presenting James's version of his father's Swedenborgian theology
is an important discovery.

Nevertheless, it seems to me that the foregoing discussion
of *The Portrait of a Lady* marks out in a general way the borders
beyond which an examination of James's more poetic dimension
cannot go without becoming irrelevant to the question of James
as a master of the craft of the novel. Even in reading a book
which has so beautiful a central conception as *The Wings of
the Dove* one is not recompensed by the allegory for the
vexation of finding a novel which is so attenuated and prolix.
One reads it, that is, stubbornly *as a novel*. One sets out with
high hopes and is immediately gratified by the unsurpassable
rendering, at the beginning, of Kate Croy and her incomparable
father; one is impressed and interested by Mrs. Lowder and her
household; one gives a slightly baffled assent to Merton Densher;
one finds the diaphanous Milly Theale beautiful and touching.
But then the *longueurs* set in, along with the infinitely syn-
tactical language which seems to engross no recognizable experience, and we are forced to settle for two fine scenes: Milly
confronting the Bronzino portrait at Lord Mark's country house
and Densher standing in the rain outside the Venetian café
recognizing through the window Lord Mark. In short the meta-
phorical effects of *The Wings of the Dove*, which contain a sort
of half-rendered allegory, do not strike one, like those in *The
Portrait of a Lady*, as forming a positively valuable component
of the whole. They strike one, rather, as negative facts—attenu-
ations of the naturalistic substance of the novel. It is not possible
for James, given his characteristic genius, to render an allegory
in the form of a novel. But it is possible for him to weaken a
novel by giving it an elusive aura of allegory. This at least is
what one feels in actually reading the book. The allegory assumes substance and significance when it is considered as a
part of the history of ideas, but that is another matter.

William Bysshe Stein

15 · The Portrait of a Lady: Vis Inertiae

> James knows almost nothing of women but the
> mere outside; he never was married. This new
> writer not only knows women, but also ladies;
> the rarest of literary gifts.
>
> HENRY ADAMS to JOHN HAY (1881)

THIS DISMISSIVELY curt judgment, as right and wrong as it is,
opens up a new approach to an understanding of the characterization of Isabel Archer in *The Portrait of a Lady*. There
seems little doubt that Adams had this novel in mind; for in a
letter to Charles Milnes Gaskell a few months earlier, not long
after the publication of the work in 1881, he confesses: "I
frankly broke down on *The Portrait of a Lady*." James's upstart
young "lady" has, of course, affected many modern critics in the
same way and probably for the same reason. As the subversive
italics of *"ladies"* suggest, Adams looks upon the title with
humorous suspicion as if it were treason against the nature of
woman, a betrayal of the lineage of Eve. And so, too, he views
Isabel, or so one might guess. He assumes that James wants the
reader to take her suffering seriously and to steep himself in her
moral predicament. Logically, Adams resents this defamation
of woman. Isabel, in his eyes, is a fleshless robot, a contemptu-
ous prig who flaunts her impotent femininity in the guise of
innocence. Thus he feels that James knows nothing about
woman's instinctual life. And he has a right to think this, I
would say, if he really believes that *The Portrait* offers a characterization of woman consistent with universal female psychology. But here he is wrong. Failing to credit his lifelong
friend with a wit as sardonic as his own, he overlooks the tone

From *Western Humanities Review*, XIII (Spring 1959), 177–90. Reprinted by permission of the *Western Humanities Review* and of the author.
Copyright © 1959 by the University of Utah.

of deprecation in the title of the novel. He allows his cosmopolitan sophistication to blind him to the mock sympathy of James's narrator; for at times the latter sheds this mask to tip off the reader to his purpose. In effect, he burlesques the Victorian authorial intrusions, say, of someone like Trollope. And one can, I think, interpret the following passage in this light. It is deliberately couched in a series of descriptive contradictions in order to convey the utter absurdity of the terminal caveat:

> Sometimes she went so far as to wish that she might find herself some day in a difficult position, so that she should have *the pleasure of being as heroic as the occasion demanded.* Altogether, with her meagre knowledge, her inflated ideals, her confidence at one innocent and dogmatic, her temper at once exciting and indulgent, her mixture of curiosity and fastidiousness, of vivacity and indifference, *her desire to look very well and to be if possible even better,* her determination to see, to try, to know, her combination of the delicate, desultory, flame-like spirit and the eager and personal creature of conditions: she would be an easy victim for scientific criticism if she were not intended to awaken on the reader's part an impulse more tender and more purely expectant.[1]

With this inadequate intellectual, emotional, and moral equipment it is no wonder that James, in the preface to the New York Edition of the novel, punningly envisions her as "affronting her destiny." For in her conduct she never seems to forget her belief that sacrifice is a pleasure. She smirkingly applies this principle in her rejection of the marriage proposals of Warburton and Goodwood; then, after her estrangement from Osmond, she invariably self-dramatizes her unhappiness before her friends, in her studied reticence perversely enjoying her role of a Victorian Griselda.

In the revisions of *The Portrait* James betrays the awareness that his original characterization of Isabel has failed to communicate her simpering inanity. As a consequence, forgetting his deprecation of scientific scrupulosity, he deliberately proceeds to undermine the "purely expectant" view of her fate. Long before Adams had outlined the problem of sexual inertia in *The Education,* James realized, perhaps unconsciously, that he had given it dramatic embodiment in Isabel. Whether he wanted to or not, it seems highly probable that in his acquaint-

ance with Adams over the years he had been influenced by the
former's cynical estimation of American women, especially their
renunciation of a dynamic role in history. There is even the
chance that he may have seen and read the manuscript of *The
Education* before its private publication in 1907. At any rate,
his retouched portrait of Isabel is, I think, clearly influenced by
Adams' caricature of the American woman. This does not mean,
however, that this involved any radical alteration of her character. She already had many of the traits which Adams associated with the evolution of the sexless woman. She was oblivious
to her role in nature, the *vis inertiae* with which the female had
long controlled the world. Instead, like the male, she was
obsessed with the abstraction of independence and freedom.
Indeed, she wanted to compete with the male on his terms
and with his kind of power. She, as in the case of Henrietta
Stackpole, resented any surrender to the primal instincts of her
sex. Her friend's renunciation of intellectual equality with the
male for mere marriage was more than she could understand:

> Henrietta, after all, *had confessed herself human and feminine,*
> Henrietta whom she had hitherto regarded as a light keen
> flame, a disembodied voice. It was a disappointment to find
> that she *had personal susceptibilities,* that she *was subject to
> common* passions, and that her intimacy with Mr. Bantling
> had not been completely original. (II, 400, italics mine.)

This passage, occurring as it does just before Ralph's death,
anticipates Isabel's flight from the passionate embrace of Goodwood; for, quite obviously, she has ceased to believe in the drive
of female sexuality. Or perhaps, as in her early exhibitions of
Victorian priggishness, she had unconsciously willed herself into
sexlessness to achieve the relationship between the sexes which
Adams so aptly describes: "Already the American man sometimes felt surprised at finding himself regarded as sexless; the
American woman was oftener surprised at finding herself regarded as sexual." [2] These striking parallels in thought, as I see
it, ultimately motivated James to introduce into his revisions
the metaphor or trope of energy and force which pervades *The
Education.*

The heroine's attitude toward normal emotions figures a

betrayal of her womanhood, for she relinquishes nature's definition of her authority. Victim and victimizer of herself, she
becomes vulnerable to outward energies and forces. She molds
her fate in the pattern of flight until she willingly returns to her
cage of respectability and propriety in which Osmond has im-
prisoned her sterile femininity. Consistent with this view of the
heroine, James's first application of Adams' trope of force is
pitched on a piercing note of irony. Appropriately, it is associated with Ralph Touchett who provides her with the freedom
to realize herself. In the original version of the novel James
generalizes Ralph's impression of Isabel's redoubtable charm:
" 'A character like that,' he said to himself, 'is the finest thing
in nature.' " [3] His revision takes cognizance of her benefactor's
delusion that she is the incarnation of an American Venus, a
woman who, mentally, had never donned Eve's fig-leaves: " 'A
character like that,' he said to himself—'a real little passionate
force to see at play is the finest thing in nature.' " (1, 86.) This
misconception of her personality controls the next development
of action. To illustrate the absurdity of Ralph's valuation James
immediately introduces a new and old suitor. Intimating a proposal by Warburton, she responds to it with "an appreciable
shock." And as James carefully points out for the reader, "her
coldness was not the calculation of effect—a game she played
in a much smaller degree than would have seemed probable to
many critics. It came from a certain fear." (1, 113.) What does
this passage argue? Is it Isabel's virginal purity? Is it her emotional immaturity? Is it her innocence? Or is it, as I believe, her
refusal to acknowledge her own sexuality? That latter inference
seems valid; for, before Warburton presses his suit, James deliberately and insidiously reveals Isabel in another situation
which involves a furtive reference to sexuality. Henrietta's jest
that her friend is in her relationship with Goodwood concealing
"a grand passion" is greeted with "rather a cold smile." (1, 137).
Further evidence of Isabel's efforts to desexualize her relations
with men is present in her rationalization of Warburton's declaration of love: "[He] repeated in the kindest, tenderest, pleas-
antest voice Isabel had ever heard, and looking at her with eyes
charged with the light of passion that had sifted itself clear of

the baser parts of emotion—the heat, the violence, the unrea-
son." (I, 148.)

It would appear, I suppose, from the citations that this
essay is developing into a case history of sexual frigidity. This is
not, however, a Freudian trespass. If anyone is to be forgiven,
it is James and Adams. I merely follow them in an attempt to
understand the phenomenon of the nineteenth-century American woman as history shaped her. I mean by this that manners
and customs in this period, according to *The Education* and
The Portrait, were tending to redefine the role of woman in
determining the life-goals of civilization. Artificial values, like
money and social station, usurped her biological autonomy,
falsifying her responsibilities to herself and to mankind. She was
persuaded that the material progress of the times was in the
process of giving her a freedom and independence equal to the
male's. But this emancipation was an illusion. It cut her off from
her instinctual self-reliance; it rendered her dependent upon the
productive energy of the male. James, for instance, treats this
topic in a comic manner in his delineation of Mrs. Touchett.
Her husband's wealth and social prestige, but particularly the
first, alienate her from the primal sources of her emotional
identity. As a consequence, she devotes herself to the pursuit of
freedom outside the pale of womanhood, a selfish monetary and
social security which induces a spurious sense of superiority and
self-satisfaction. Mr. Touchett, it seems to me, is aware of this
dislocation when he protests Ralph's cultivated indifference to
Isabel:

> "You look at things in a way that would make everything
> wrong. What sort of a cousin is a cousin that you had never
> seen for more than twenty years of her life? We're all each
> other's cousins, and *if we stopped at that the human race would
> die out*. It's just the same with your bad lung. You're a great
> deal better than you used to be. All you want is to lead a natu-
> ral life. It is a great deal more natural to marry a pretty young
> lady that you're in love with than it is to remain single on false
> principles." (I, 259, italics mine.)

This statement is virtually a matriarchal pronouncement. It renounces the efficacy of abstract values. It is a plea straight from
the heart of eternal nature. It likewise explains why he is morally

shocked when Ralph indicates his desire to be amused with the manner in which Isabel works out her plan of freedom. This situation parallels Adams' observation on the changes or perversions wrought in woman by human control over nature:

> He had seen artificial energy to the amount of twenty or five-and-twenty million steam horse-power created in America since 1840, *and as much more economized,* which had been socially turned over to the American woman, she being the chief object of social extravagance, and the household the only considerable object of American extravagance.[4]

In both quotations we witness the neutralizing of the sexual *vis inertiae* of woman, its conversion into empty social energy. Money with the idleness and boredom it provides defrauds her of the primordial power with which she once ruled the world. She thus becomes a mere possession of the male, an expensive and expendable luxury.

In the novels prior to *The Portrait* James also centers on the insidious influences of social and economic independence upon the normal emotional existence. In *Roderick Hudson,* for example, Rowland Mallet is the prototype of Ralph Touchett. Though for a different reason, the disease of puritanical inhibition, he seeks to experience love and life vicariously through his patronage of the sculptor Roderick Hudson. His wealth, whetting the appetites of Roderick, delivers him to his doom. In *The American* Christopher Newman, who stupidly exalts the power of money over the power of instinct, tries to buy a wife who will correspond to the indiscriminate standards of his fortune. Ultimately his vulgarity—and innocence cannot explain it away—victimizes Claire de Cintré and himself. While the effects of wealth on Catherine Sloper in *Washington Square* close her off from emotional fulfillment, in *Daisy Miller* the freedom provided by riches destroys her. In drawing these parallels it is not my purpose to wage ideological warfare with capitalism. Rather I merely wish to indicate that in these and James's later writings, as for example *The Bostonians* and *The Golden Bowl,* money always tends to depose love from its natural, democratic authority. Less and less, the magnetism of primitive woman is permitted to express itself in a prosperous and artificial society; more and more, it compromises itself and

172 AMERICAN AFFINITIES

is compromised. And as Adams would have it, the emancipation from responsibility which it seems to promise is a threat to the continuation of the human race:

> The woman had been set free—volatilized like Clark Maxwell's perfect gas; almost brought to the point of explosion, like steam. One had but to pass a week in Florida, or on any of a hundred huge steamers, or walk through the Place Vendome, or join a party of Cook's tourists to Jerusalem, to see that woman had been set free; but these swarms were ephemeral, like clouds of butterflies in season, blown away and lost, while the reproductive sources lay hidden.[5]

Adams here states explicitly what James suggestively implies in *The Portrait*. In a world created by male ingenuity there is no place for woman. Where before she shaped her life in accordance with the demands of nature and her own human nature, she now seeks to understand her destiny in the abstractions of art and religion. Her ancient primordial energy, over the centuries gradually enervated by participation in the affairs of the masculine world, has at last reduced her to the innocuousness of static electricity. Her ardors are inflamed by the affectations of thought, not by the fever of blood. No longer is she the aggressive proponent of instinctual values; she has been forced into retreat by disloyalty to her invulnerable sexuality.

This fact is brought into focus in another of James's revisions in which the imagery of energy generates association with Adams' perspective on historical reality. In this case he examines the impact of Goodwood's physical presence upon Isabel. The incident, of course, also functions to explain her reaction to Warburton's earlier proposal. But of particular interest is Goodwood's transformation into an overpowering projection of the dynamics of the masculine world. His identity is inextricably linked with the male's dominance of the processes of civilization. He is a disciple of the machine. He commands power by his ability to organize, to administer, and guide. He epitomizes the superiority of intellectual will over the groping, undirected impulses of instinct. What this power brings into being is an empty leisure which deprives woman of her self-reliance. Like Isabel, she is granted a pseudo-freedom which installs self-distrust and fear. And it is before this impersonal authority that the heroine compromises herself; this is seen even in James's first recreation of Isabel's dilemma of independence:

> [F]or it was part of the influence he had upon her that he seemed to take from her the sense of freedom. There was something too forcible, something oppressive and restrictive, in the manner in which he presented himself. She had been haunted at moments by the image of his disapproval. . . . The difficulty was that more than any man she had ever known . . . , Caspar Goodwood gave her an impression of energy. She might like it or not, but at any rate there was something strong about him. . . . The idea of a diminished liberty was particularly disagreeable to Isabel at the present.[6]

This description is generalized in character; it *suggests* an awareness of the external pressures in the cultural environment which operate to frustrate Isabel. However, James's creative imagination has not been able to crystalize this impression clearly. It is still amorphous, a feeling rather than an absorbed intuition. The revision clearly shows what I mean; for Isabel's recollection of Goodwood is translated directly into the imagery of physics, the idiom as it were of this machine culture. His vitality is a thing of mass, weight, and power, something like the impersonal potential of a fire-and-steam driven mechanism:

> [F]or it was part of the influence he had upon her that he seemed to deprive her of the sense of freedom. There was a *disagreeably strong push*, a kind of *hardness* of presence, in his way of rising before her. She had been haunted at moments by the image, *by the danger*, of his disapproval. . . . The difficulty was that more than any man . . . , Caspar Goodwood expressed for her *an energy*—and she had felt it as *a power*—that was of his very nature. . . . it was a matter of the spirit that sat in his *clear-burning eyes* like some tireless watcher at a window. She might like it or not, but he insisted, ever, with the *whole weight* and *force*: even in one's usual contact with him one had to reckon with that. The idea of a diminished liberty. . . . (1, 162, italics mine.)

What Isabel envisions here is less a man than the type of individual which her civilization developed as its paragon. It is against this imposture of humanity that her instincts rebel.

In another perspective, of course, James wants his reader to interpret this description in the sexual sense, for it betrays the American woman's abandonment of her own feminine integrity and self-containment. Isabel, ironically, is repelled by the energy of aggressive emotions which the machine-man has usurped and warped. This is illustrated in still another revision in which James's original statement of her rejection of Goodwood is couched in conventional sympathy, "Caspar Goodwood, of all men, ought to enjoy the whole devotion of some tender woman," [7] but then is rewritten to communicate her fear of ravishment by a ruthless animal force: "He oughtn't to stride about lean and hungry, however—she certainly felt *that* for him." (I, 224.) The first version of the novel transcribes Isabel's sense of release from Goodwood's intimidating strength as an exercise of her power to resist him:

> She was not praying; she was trembling—trembling all over. She was an excitable creature, and now she was much excited; but she wished to resist her excitement, and the attitude of prayer, which she kept for some time, seemed to help her to be still. She was extremely glad Caspar Goodwood was gone; there was something exhilarating in having gotten rid of him. As Isabel became conscious of her feeling . . . ; it was part of her emotion; but it was a thing to be ashamed of—it was profane and out of place.[8]

In the New York Edition her instinctive sexual response to his fierce attraction is transformed into a tableau of her conquest of passion, not—and of this one must take special note—by virtue of her purity but by a denial of the emotional authority of the response insofar as it had any meaning for her as woman:

> She was not praying; she was trembling—trembling all over. Vibration was easy to her, was in fact too constant with her, and she found herself now humming like a smitten harp. She only asked, however, to put on the cover, to case herself again in brown holland, but she wished to resist her excitement, and the attitude of devotion, which she kept for some time, seemed to help her to be still. She intensely rejoiced that Caspar Goodwood was gone; there was something in having thus got rid of him that was like the payment, for a stamped receipt, of some debt too long on her mind. As she felt the glad relief . . .
> (I, 232.)

Her posture in this passage is peculiarly arresting, like a nun at her devotions. And when this connotation is connected with the metaphor of commerce, the combination seems to imply that

she has now *bought* her freedom from all violent emotional attachments. She has defied her own nature and her own womanhood. She has purchased an intellectual virginity. An American
Lysistrata, she discounts her inherited, prepotent sexuality to
claim the peace and the emancipation that her culture has substituted in the ancient rule of women.

How effective this contraception of passion is may be seen
in James's next report of Isabel's reaction to a confrontation of
the same two suitors. Significantly enough, at this point she is
independent of man in every sense; she is now in the possession
of the fortune which Ralph has had willed to her. In James's
initial delineation of this state there is no suggestion of her
double triumph over natural energy, her own and her suitors':

> [B]ut at times, as she listened to the murmur of the Mediterra-
> nean waves, her glance took a backward flight. It rested upon
> two figures which, in spite of increasing distance, were still suf-
> ficiently salient; they were recognizable without difficulty as
> those of Caspar Goodwood and Lord Warburton. It was strange
> how quickly these gentlemen had fallen into the background of
> our young lady's life.[9]

James revises only the last sentence in this passage, but it, I
think, quite plausibly may be connected with his previous inter-
calations of the trope of force: "It was strange how quickly
these images of energy had fallen into the background of our
young lady's life." (I, 322.) This complacency, particularly
James's phrasing of it, is a crucial anticipatory detail. It foreshadows Isabel's capitulation to the passive wooing of Osmond;
for, in his attitudes and manner, he is the negation not only of
the force of sexual passion but also of the coercive dynamics of
the competitive fields of politics and economics which, both as
a reflection of her previous wooers and of the world of male
domination, had threatened her cultivation of the illusion of
female freedom. To establish the validity of this interpretation,
I would like, for a moment, to allude to James's description of
Osmond's mountain home. Originally he, in one phase of her
reaction to the place, merely comments on its rather grim
austerity: "There was something rather severe about the place;
it looked somehow as if, once you were in it, it would not be
easy to get out. For Isabel, however, there was of course yet no

thought of getting out, but only of advancing." [10] In the revision
James appears to affiliate it with its owner, at least in terms of
the way the action develops. Its aloofness from the activity of
the city below and from the values cherished by this world
projects the passive and quiescent egotism of Osmond. It becomes the symbol of the phenomenon of male *vis inertiae*, as
the alteration of the first sentence shows: "There was something
grave and strong in the place; it looked somehow as if, once you
were in it, it would need *an act of energy to get out.*" (I, 364,
italics mine.) Here the physical surrogate of Osmond's self-exile
from society, as opposed to the rather offensive quality of the
first description, is rendered inviting to Isabel. This is to say
that Isabel's attraction for the house in James's restatement
foreshadows her attempt to find in it a refuge for her uncertain
womanhood.

Thus when its owner finally proposes to her, she emotionally meets the announcement with a kind of puerile elation,
consistent, or so it seems to me, with Adams' derisive remark
that the American woman could appreciate "sex for sentiment,
never for force." [11] This applies particularly to James's first version which contrasts with the aggressive rejections previously of
Goodwood and Warburton:

> The tears came into Isabel's eyes—they were caused by an
> intenser throb of that pleasant pain I spoke of a moment ago.
> There was an immense sweetness in the words he had uttered;
> but, morally speaking, she retreated before them—facing him
> still—as she had retreated in two or three cases we know in
> which the same words had been spoken.[12]

James's renovations of this text are curious. Force and sentiment
collide, generating a far more valid moral rationalization than
the original statement:

> The tears came into her eyes: this time they obeyed the sharp-
> ness of the pang that suggested to her somehow *the slipping of
> a fine bolt—backward, forward,* she could n't have said which.
> The words he had uttered . . . invested him as with the golden
> air of early autumn; but, morally speaking, she retreated before
> them. . . . (II, 18, italics mine.)

Without insisting upon a Freudian interpretation of this response, I think that the reader must associate it with the

fantasies induced by her refusal to acknowledge the physical basis of love. This hallucinatory experience cannot be ignored. It reveals a compulsive fear of sexuality in which puritanical inhibition attires itself in the modest robes of morality. James's additional elucidation of her confused feelings on this occasion is, in the first version of the novel, traced to a credible inertia of innocent virginity:

> "O, don't say that, please," she answered at last, in a tone of entreaty which had nothing of conventional modesty, but which expressed the dread of having . . . to choose and decide. What made her dread great was precisely the force which, as it would seem, ought to have banished all dread—the consciousness of what was in her own heart. It was terrible to have to surrender to that.[13]

But in the revision the analysis of this state is astonishingly reorientated. The love in her heart is viewed equivocally. Indeed James virtually asserts that it is self-deception. And when he resorts to the imagery of the counting-house in order to convey this nuance of her feelings, he degrades it into a fatal narcissism:

> What made her dread great was precisely the force which, as it would seem, ought to have banished all dread—the sense of something within herself, deep down, *that she supposed to be inspired and trustful passion*. It was there like a large sum stored in a bank—which there was terror in having to begin to spend. If she touched it, it would all come out. (ɪɪ, 18, italics mine.)

Perhaps I may be judged too harsh in my indictment, but one cannot, I think, overlook James's reiteration of her delusion that she has a stupendous wealth of personality to offer to the world. Her daydreams, from our moment of first acquaintance with her in the seclusion of a room in her Albany home, are compounded of fatuous illusions. Indication of this is found in her reaction to Ralph's acid ridicule of her lover: "a mingled sentiment, to which the angry pain excited by his words and *the wounded pride* of having needed to justify a choice of which she felt only *the nobleness and purity*, equally contributed." (ɪɪ, 74, italics mine.) Even granting the logic of her angered vanity, I cannot find any reason for not attaching more importance to James's rubric on self-adulation. It is a rationalization that one might forgive in the heroine of a sentimental novel. But in a work which purports to be a psychological study of human behavior —and the preface for the novel is clear enough on this point— it must be viewed as an abnormal quirk of character.

In a recent article which attempts to cope with the ambiguities of Isabel's conduct, James is said to be working "in the tradition of the limited heroine" [14] in which his purpose is to define her traits in "a developing portrait." [15] The use of this technique is assumed to explain the abortive speculations of all other critics. While I accept the validity of this statement of narrative method, I must confess that I can make little out of it in regard to what James is trying to communicate to his reader in terms of theme. It is here, I think, that Adams provides the frame of reference in which we must interpret what is being said. For one of the paradoxes of James's characterization, even accepting the idea of the developing portrait, is that it circles back upon itself. From the beginning to the end of the story Isabel does not change. Only her situations change. In this process we are confronted with James's treatment of the stagnant emotions of the Victorian female. This articulation of artistic intention is also supported by the mode of characterization, especially in the exploitation of *ficelles*. This latter term, applying as it does to characters which mediate the direct knowledge which James gives us of Isabel, helps to illuminate my perspective on the action and to identify it as a comedy of self-deception.

The heroine's career is fatefully launched by Ralph's misconception of her conviction of individual freedom. Her closest friend Henrietta, much like Ralph, looks upon her as a reflection of her own emancipation. Serena Merle, on the other hand, totally misconstrues Isabel's acquisition of her fortune, in terms of her own ruthless ambitions picturing it as a product of design, not of Ralph's delusions. Warburton, in the final analysis, is charmed by his illusion of her mechanical spontaneity. Her American suitor Goodwood, bent upon obsessive possession of her, almost like Newman's desire for Claire de Cintré, is the victim of his own forceful courting, for he undermines completely Isabel's faith in her own femininity. It is only the Countess Gemini who instinctively perceives what is wrong with

her brother's wife. A woman who has never discovered any reason why she should betray the spirit of her mythic ancestress
Eve, she immediately centers upon Isabel's perfidity to her own
sex: " 'You've such a beastly pure mind. I never saw a woman
with such a pure mind!' cried the Countess." (II, 362.) It is
interesting to note that James revised the first part of this dialogue simply by adding one word, the qualifying "beastly" that
discloses Isabel's "quaint" sterility. This aspect of the heroine's
abeyant passion is also adumbrated in her marital relations with
Osmond who, in his own self-love, tolerantly and happily accepts her timid role of wifehood. Though on one occasion she
appears to protest this status vehemently, " 'We don't live decently together!' " (II, 357) there is ample reason in context to
question the sexual implications of the outburst at any rate if
we are to go along with any view at all of her innate virginal
reticence.

But having briefly outlined this state of collective misunderstanding of the heroine, it is to the earlier of James's fore-
shadowings of her destiny that we must turn for corroboration
of my position. In one of Mr. Touchett's meditations upon her
character we encounter incontrovertible evidence, I think, of the
artist's disposition to delineate her as another victim of the
social and financial freedom that transformed Mrs. Touchett
into a masculine simulacrum of woman:

> Like the mass of American girls Isabel had been encouraged to
> express herself; her remarks had been attended to; she had been
> expected to have emotions and opinions. Many of her opinions
> had doubtless but a slender value, *many of her emotions passed
> away in the utterance*; but they had left a trace in giving her *the
> habit of seeming at least to feel and think*, and in imparting
> moreover to her words when she was really moved that prompt
> vividness which so many people had regarded as a sign of su-
> periority. Mr. Touchett used to think that she reminded him
> of his wife when his wife was in her teens. It was because she
> was fresh and natural and quick to understand, to speak . . .
> that he had fallen in love with Mrs. Touchett. (I, 74.)

Isabel, in other words, is a product of a later generation's indiscriminate meddling with the natural impulses of the female
nature; for, in tolerating a sense of intellectual license even more
extreme than in Mrs. Touchett's early womanhood, it has given

the young girl, a type that the American culture was developing, a distorted notion of what demands life made upon her sex. As Adams would have it, the male's infatuation with the historical forms of human existence had seduced woman into treason against herself: "He could not run his machine and a woman too; he must leave her, even though his wife, to find her own way, and all the world saw her trying to find her way by imitating him." [16] This description corresponds with Mrs. Touchett's public and private engagement to her role of wife, and it also comprehends the kind of freedom which Isabel's inheritance provided, the time and the leisure to brood on the abstract ambitions of the emancipated woman. Indeed her marriage to Osmond is the inevitable consequence of this defection from the biological function of woman in nature, the fulfillment of herself as a wife and a mother. It seems to me that James's silence throughout the book on the death of her child clearly indicates her preoccupation with the social aspect of marriage. She had not wed a man but rather a paragon of taste and decorum, seeking security in an artificial order of existence in which all values were arbitrarily defined. In the process she had renounced the fate that was ordained for her when Eve, bored with the static innocence of the Garden of Eden, flirted with the urbane serpent.

This last analogy is not used facetiously. It leads me to a necessary consideration of the garden symbolism in the story, an artifice of setting in so many of James's novels in which he is concerned with emotional perversion. As William Troy has so aptly declared, the garden in The Portrait "is the dwelling place of the unknown terror that is actually in herself [Isabel]—the terror of experience which at the end she rationalizes in terms of moral obligation." [17] It is not, however, the counterpart of the Garden of Eden; for Gardencourt is a product of civilization, the vibrant energy of nature brought under discipline and domestication. But lurking behind this façade of culture is the wild, rebellious primitive, the force within herself and without herself in the shape of her lovers from which she flees. Ashamed of the Eve in her genetic constitution, she affects a self-blinded innocence; she assumes the role of woman which has been assigned to her by, to use Adams' pertinent phrase, "the monthly-

magazine-made American female" (Is he punning on one
word?).[18] She declines to acknowledge the biological *vis inertiae*
of her sex, a force far stronger than any with which the male
can affront nature in her eternal garden.

And it is on this note of awareness that James terminates
the novel, adducing the trope of energy which has distinguished
this one pattern of his revisionary practices. The incident in
question, of course, is her final meeting with Goodwood, and it
recapitulates in meaning her initial meeting with him in Gardencourt. It likewise affirms, I submit, my conviction that the
movement of action is circular, an inevitability in the light of
Isabel's failure to develop emotionally. Her recoil from his passionate embrace marks the pathetic triumph of conventional
moralism over instinctive integrity. It, at the same time, com-
memorates the period in history when the American woman
surrendered the innate prerogatives of her destiny to the mechanical aggressiveness of the American male. The episode in
the garden, at least in terms of James's revisions, is framed in
two major movements. The first embraces her psychologically
hysterical fear of Goodwood, the threat to her enshrined terror
of experience, but in the edition of 1881 it is empty of dramatic
impact. His question as to why she should return to the "ghastly
form" of her marriage is met with " 'To get away from *you!* ' "
But this response, as James points out, is a fatuous rationalization, for it "expressed only a little of what she felt. The rest was
that she had never been loved before. It wrapped her about; it
lifted her off her feet." [19] The New York Edition retains
the order of the first two parts of the comment; but the last
sentence is altered in order to ascertain the communication of
James's feeling in regard to Isabel's desperate need to cling to
her narcissistic innocence:

> She had believed it, but this was different; this was the hot
> wind of the desert, at the approach of which the others dropped
> dead, like mere sweet airs of the garden. It wrapped her about;
> it lifted her off her feet, while the very taste of it, as of some-
> thing potent, acrid and strange, forced open her set teeth. (II,
> 433-34.)

The imagery of this revision suggests that physical love for Isabel
would be a fatal experience. Her fantasy inverts the fruitful

symbol of the garden into a blighting wind from the desert, and
thus James reveals to the reader the waste land of emotions
which has dried up her erotic spontaneity.

The main turn of events in this encounter centers upon her
reaction to her lover's compulsory kiss. Originally the description
was restricted to the heroine's personal feeling: "He glared at
her a moment through the dusk, and the next instant she felt
his arms about her, and his lips on her lips. His kiss was like a
flash of lightning; when it was dark again, she was free." [20] The
revision likewise stresses her individual response, but this time
it is related directly to the overwhelming energy of Goodwood.
And, in line with my previous observation on Isabel's patho-
logical narcissism, the intercalary imagery implies, almost like a
similar scene in T. S. Eliot's "Prufrock," that the very thought of
mutual love is akin to emotional suicide:

> His kiss was like white lightning, a flash that spread, and spread
> again, and stayed; and it was extraordinarily as if, while she took
> it, she felt each thing in his hard manhood that had least
> pleased her, each aggressive fact of his face, his figure, his pres-
> ence, justified of its intense identity and made one with this
> act of possession. So had she heard of those wrecked and under
> water following a train of images before they sink. But when
> darkness returned *she was free*. (II, 436, italics mine.)

More than anything else, in the manner of James's usual handling of coarse innuendoes, this passage emphasizes the ani-
malistic sexual virility of Goodwood. It, in Isabel's mind, is
associated with brutal rape; and, as the analogy of drowning so
eloquently argues, it is a foreshadowing of death. This means
that for Isabel to give herself voluntarily in an act of love would
be to lose the sense of deluded innocence by which she identifies
herself. In the freedom which she attains for herself she succeeds
in her rebellion against maternity, the problem of American
women which so absorbed Adams. And in Isabel, even as the
former was afraid, the *vis inertiae* of female sexuality succumbs
to the irresponsible force of a male who has also lost his sense
of function in a culture which has destroyed the natural basis of
relationship between the opposite sexes. And the enveloping
action in this novel, the deaths of the male Touchetts who make
Isabel's freedom possible, anticipates this climax. The promis-

cuous charity of a rootless and sterile commercialism passes a sentence of doom upon the redemptive feminine in twentieth-century culture. James's portrait of Isabel, like Adams' *Education,* is certainly a prophecy that has come true in our own times.

Notes

1. Parenthetical page references hereafter are to the Modern Library edition (New York, 1951), I, 69, italics mine.
2. *The Education of Henry Adams* (New York, 1946), p. 447.
3. (New York, 1881), p. 52. Hereafter I will refer to this edition as *1881.*
4. *The Education,* p. 444, italics mine.
5. *The Education,* p. 444.
6. *1881,* pp. 98–99.
7. *1881,* p. 137.
8. *1881,* p. 142.
9. *1881,* p. 196.
10. *1881,* p. 221.
11. *The Education,* p. 385.
12. *1881,* p. 271.
13. *1881,* pp. 271–72.
14. Oscar Cargill, "*The Portrait of a Lady:* A Critical Reappraisal," *Modern Fiction Studies,* III (Spring, 1957), 30. (See Chapter 20 in this book for an expanded version of the same essay.)
15. *Ibid.,* p. 32.
16. *The Education,* p. 445.
17. "The Altar of Henry James," included in *The Question of Henry James,* ed. F. W. Dupee (New York, 1945), p. 269.
18. *The Education,* p. 384.
19. *1881,* p. 517.
20. *1881,* p. 519.

VI. Methods Revealed

Ernest Sandeen

16 · The *Wings of the Dove* and The *Portrait of a Lady:* A Study of Henry James's Later Phase

I

Whatever Henry James's feelings may have been toward his favorite "Albany cousin," Mary ("Minny") Temple, while she lived, it is clear that at her death in 1870, she left with him an indelible image that made available to him as a writer large areas of human experience. This image figured more or less obscurely in several of his stories and minor female characters but according to his own testimony was most fully and consciously operative in his creation of Isabel Archer in *The Portrait of a Lady* and of Milly Theale in *The Wings of the Dove.*[1]

Certainly there was the danger in either of these novels that James's view of the human situation which the symbol of Minny Temple revealed might be distorted by his strong personal feelings for Minny herself. He confessed to his "tenderness of imagination" about Milly Theale in the "Preface" to *Wings* which he wrote for the New York Edition of his works. Yet when he came to create this later heroine, James was able to assimilate his private sentiments more completely into his art than he had been when he had created Isabel Archer.

In both *Portrait* and *Wings* the Minny Temple image points toward the same effect, and the sequence of events by which the two protagonists are led to their destiny is basically the same. Isabel and Milly are American girls, they are intelligent and sensitive, and they are equipped with wealth and

From *PMLA*, LXIX (December, 1954), pp. 1060–75. Reprinted by permission of the Modern Language Association of America and of the author.

personal charm. They are introduced into the great world of European society and there they enjoy a brilliant hour of triumph which includes the luxury of declining the "ordinary" form of success, marriage to a member of the English nobility. However, after they form what they believe are attachments of their own free choice, they discover that they have been betrayed by persons interested chiefly in their wealth.

The essential element in this common pattern is the ironic disparity between the great endowments of the heroine and the defeat she suffers, between the high hopes entertained for her and the dismal reality that overtakes her. From the first, James's picture of his cousin Minny had been refracted through his sense of her incongruous relation to the world. At the time when he was trying to adjust himself to the new fact of her death what impressed him most about the living Mary Temple as he remembered her was "that life—poor narrow life—contained no place for her." [2] "Her character may be almost literally said to have been without practical application to life." [3]

In view of the correspondences between the stories of Isabel Archer and Milly Theale it is not surprising that the two casts of characters surrounding the principals should be roughly equivalent to each other. The resemblances are not in their personal qualities, however, but only in the literary functions they serve. For example, Henrietta Stackpole when placed beside her fellow-journalist, Susan Shepherd Stringham of *Wings*, appears more distinctly than ever as a caricature. Yet the two women stand in much the same relation to the heroine. Both betray an admiration for her which rises to a kind of anxious idolatry, and both assume the role of confidante, though Susan is more securely placed in that position than Henrietta.

Again, Mrs. Touchett of *Portrait* could never be confused, as a person, with Maud Manningham Lowder of *Wings*, but James uses both of them for the same purpose. As matrons of European society, they furnish a social entree for the heroine and thus make possible her initial success and her eventual failure. Although Lord Mark is a more cynical portrait of the English aristocracy than Lord Warburton, each is used to develop the irony attaching to the heroine's refusal of his offer of marriage in favor of a more humble and what she believes, mistakenly, is a more genuine petition. Most obviously parallel are the two pairs of "villains," Madame Serena Merle and Gilbert Osmond in *Portrait*, Kate Croy and Merton Densher in *Wings*. Yet the sinister quality in Merle and Osmond, restrained as it is, is converted to a more sympathetic form of frailty in Croy and Densher.

The crucial difference between the two novels, the one which registers most of the other differences, is that in *Wings* there is no character to correspond to Ralph Touchett in *Portrait*. This omission in *Wings* dramatizes James's development of the story which Minny Temple had given him.

Ralph Touchett is not literally an autobiographical character but he is closely related to his author. In respect to Isabel Archer, Ralph himself plays the part of an author contriving her destiny from within the story as James contrives it from without. Like a genuine artist Ralph presumes to arrange Isabel's future from no ulterior motive, but simply as a greatly interested and sympathetic spectator. He wants merely "to put a little wind in her sails," "to see her going before the breeze."[4] Specifically what he wants to do is what James does for so many of his characters and for the same reason, i.e., Ralph wants to furnish Isabel with money so that she may be free to use her inner resources to the full, unhampered by external needs, as she goes forward to confront her destiny. The only good Ralph expects for himself, he says, is "that of having met the requirements of my imagination" (III, 265).

James has allowed Ralph the means of meeting these requirements. Shortly before his father's death, Ralph persuades the senior Touchett to alter his will in such a way that a fortune of some £70,000, to be diverted from Ralph's own inheritance, will be left to Isabel. The episode suggests that in the new vicarious life he was giving his cousin, James wished to grant her the advantages she had yearned for but had lacked in real life. "You remember," he wrote of her to his brother, "how largely she dealt in the future—how she considered and planned and arranged." One of Minny Temple's ardent ambitions, never fulfilled, was to travel in Europe. Perhaps bad conscience in part intensified James's wish to give Minny, in her literary dimension, what she had always desired, and on an economic scale that would empower her to experience the best. "But here I am," he exclaimed when he had first heard of her death, "plucking all the sweetest fruits of this Europe which was a dream among her many dreams—while she had 'gone abroad' in another sense!" Still, he could not help thinking that her longing for Europe, particularly England, was mistaken. "Every time that I have been out during the last three days," he told William, "the aspect of things has perpetually seemed to enforce her image by simple contrast and difference. . . . She was a breathing protest against English grossness, English compromises and conventions—a plant of pure American growth."[5] These words could be read, in retrospect, as a prediction that Isabel Archer's European experience would have an unfortunate conclusion. And the fact is that in the novel the fortune which Ralph has secretly arranged for Isabel is a curse. Far from liberating her as Ralph intended, it delivers her into the hands of fortune-hunters, and she falls a victim to them, it must be admitted, with astonishing ease.

Ralph Touchett is related to James's memory of Mary Temple in another, more oblique way. Because the image from which Isabel Archer emerged was marked by disease and early death, it is an interesting circumstance that not Isabel but Ralph Touchett is afflicted with this disease of consumption and dies of it near the end of the story. The substitution suggests that Ralph plays the role of scapegoat, of atoning redeemer, as it were. But his close relation to his author indicates that he plays this role by proxy, as if James in the person of Ralph Touchett had entered his own story to take upon himself the disease which cut short his cousin's earthly career and so had made possible for her a new life in Isabel Archer.

To be sure, a practical purpose is served by Ralph's affliction. It eliminates him as a suitor of Isabel and therefore, whatever his feelings for her may be, it is certain that what he does for her springs from disinterested motives. Yet here again an autobiographical parallel obtrudes. At the time when James might have regarded Mary Temple with the eyes of a lover, he was himself an invalid and therefore, he believed, not qualified as a suitor. He complained to William after Minny's death: "She never knew how sick and disordered a creature I was and

I always felt that she knew me at my worst. I always looked forward with a certain eagerness to the day when I should have regained my natural lead, and friendship on my part, at least, might become more active and masculine." However, as time went on, he slowly crawled "from weakness and inaction and suffering into strength and health and hope" while she sank "out of brightness and youth into decline and death." Of all his sad reflections upon Minny's death, he told his brother, the saddest was "this view of the gradual change and reversal of our relations . . ."[6] It would seem that James symbolically nullified this reversal in *Portrait* by means of the character Ralph Touchett.

Again, in Ralph's contradictory statements concerning his attitude toward Isabel, James might be taken to represent his own strong but obscure feelings about Mary Temple. "Every one was supposed, I believe, to be more or less in love with her," James explained to his brother; ". . . I never was, and yet I had the great satisfaction that I enjoyed *pleasing* her almost as much as if I had been." Three days before, however, James had written to his mother: "It is no surprise to me to find that I felt for her an affection as deep as the foundations of my being."[7] Ralph Touchett shows much the same apparent inconsistency when he expresses his sentiments about Isabel Archer. To his father he flatly asserts, "No, I'm not in love with her," although he confesses that he would be "if certain things were different" (III, 258), a reference to his uncertain health. Yet in his final meeting with Isabel when he is dying, Ralph whispers to her, ". . . if you've been hated you've also been loved. Ah but, Isabel— *adored!*" (IV, 417).

A comparison of *The Portrait of a Lady* with *The Wings of the Dove* brings out the literary weaknesses which the character Ralph Touchett represents in the former novel. He is seen, in this perspective, as an expression of James's great personal tenderness for the woman who lived in his memory and was the archetype for his heroine. It may have been that James's private emotions were as strong when he wrote *Wings*, but here they were not condensed and personified as they had been in *Portrait;* they were, instead, absorbed into the main channels of his protagonist's story. The absence in *Wings* of any character like Ralph Touchett means that James, in effect, has absented himself. A connection is at once suggested between this absence and the greater artistic "toughness" with which James projects the Minny Temple myth in the later novel. The result is the greater depth and the wider range of Milly Theale's tragedy as compared with Isabel Archer's. In brief, the character Ralph Touchett testifies negatively to the truth of the dictum that "the more perfect the artist, the more completely separate in him will be the man who suffers and the mind which creates; the more perfectly will the mind digest and transmute the passions which are its material."[8]

A simple economy of means in *Wings* makes a counterpart to Ralph Touchett superfluous: the functions he might perform do not exist. In the first place, no one is needed to arrange a large inheritance for Milly Theale at an appropriate moment in the story, because Milly is introduced at the outset as a great heiress. There is nothing of the "from-rags-to-riches" theme in *Wings* which, in a greatly refined form, dominates Isabel's early career. In *Portrait* James betrays an idealist's anxiety to justify his heroine's wealth. Isabel must first prove her great qualities and when she has passed the test to the satisfaction of all who observe her, including the reader, she is rewarded as people like her undoubtedly deserve to be but seldom are. James has been careful to motivate the process but an air of contrivance hovers over it, at best. Isabel's inheritance figures, in the last analysis, as the author's management of plot; it never becomes a part of her character.

No apology is offered for Milly Theale's great fortune. She is not required to "earn" it, and yet it is treated frankly as an important source of the power which everyone feels in her presence. Milly manages her wealth with an ease which is at once grand and unself-conscious. She is not at all made uncomfortable by her money; she is not, like Isabel, looking for someone to share the moral responsibility of her good luck. Of course, Milly's greatness is ultimately a matter of character, but no one can think of her personal qualities as altogether detached from her riches. The impression which people have of Milly is that if her fortune is immense, she appears to be equal to it. Even Susan Stringham, Milly's companion, who adores and almost worships Milly, perceives that money is an intrinsic element in her picture of this American "princess." Susan recognizes it as "the truth of truths that the girl couldn't get away from her wealth. . . . it was in the fine folds of [her] helplessly expensive little black frock . . . it was in the curious and splendid coils of [her] hair, 'done' with no eye whatever to the *mode du jour* . . . it lurked between the leaves of [her] uncut but antiquated Tauchnitz volume. . . . She couldn't dress it away, nor walk it away, nor read it away, nor think it away; she could neither smile it away in any dreamy absence nor blow it away in any softened sigh. She couldn't have lost it if she had tried—that was what it was to be really rich. It had to be *the* thing you were" (XIX, 121).

Another instance of James's greater artistic hardness in *Wings* is his willingness to subject his heroine to the same early death which belonged to his memory of Minny Temple. Once again, he has no need for a Ralph Touchett. Milly is not provided with a patron-guardian who is also a sacrificial victim, and this explains in part why she is a more profoundly tragic figure than Isabel Archer. James's hardheaded acceptance of Milly's fortune as great human power complements his refusal to rescue her from the doom to which Minny Temple had condemned her. It is the combination of her wealth and his disease, of the promise of an illimitable future and the threat of an impending death, that makes Milly peculiarly vulnerable, within and without, to the deception she encounters. The menace of death sharpens her natural desire for a love which she does not want to buy with her money. Yet "wouldn't her value," it dawns upon her, "for the man who should marry her, be precisely in the ravage of her disease? *She* mightn't last, but her money would" (XX, 149). If she were an heiress in perfect health, or if she were mortally ill without a fortune, she would not provoke the fate which she eventually suffers.

The harsh realities surrounding Milly Theale are not blurred and softened. Her predicament is more terrible and more pitiable than Isabel Archer's, and it is also more convincing. In order to throw herself into the trap set by Madame Merle and Gilbert Osmond, Isabel has to defy the suspicion and disapproval of all her friends. When she becomes engaged to Osmond,

she is warned of her danger by Mrs. Touchett and by Ralph
Touchett in very plain language, to say nothing of the less dis-
interested opposition of Caspar Goodwood, Lord Warburton
and Henrietta Stackpole. The forces of deception ranged against
Milly Theale are much more formidable. The conspiracy to
delude Milly may be engineered by Kate Croy and Merton
Densher, but it is one in which everyone in the story, except Lord
Mark, eventually takes a part.

Everyone sees in Milly's developing relations with Densher
an opportunity either for himself or for someone else. Maud
Lowder, who according to her lights has her niece's best interest
at heart, finds in the "affair" a chance to end Kate's infatuation
with Densher and to promote a better match between Kate and
Lord Mark. But Sir Luke Strett, Milly's physician, who takes
both a personal and a professional interest in Milly's own wel-
fare, also favors the attachment. Paradoxically, Milly's most loyal
friend, Susan Stringham, is willing to carry the deception as far
as anyone else, farther in fact that Merton Densher is willing
to carry it. Of course, her motives are of the best. She believes
that love—even if only a delusion—may help Milly to live or,
at the very least, give her the sense of having lived if it cannot
repair her health. For these good reasons, then, Susan urges Merton Densher to deny to Milly's face Lord Mark's charge that
Densher and Kate are engaged—a charge which Susan plainly
believes to be true. But Densher refuses to countenance this
depth of deceit.

It cannot be denied that the responsibility for the plot to
beguile Milly Theale comes back to Kate Croy and Merton
Densher. In their purely functional roles in the action these
two greatly resemble Madame Merle and Gilbert Osmond of
Portrait. In a pattern of precedence in guilt which recalls Genesis
the woman in each novel conceives the plan to delude the heroine, and the man at the woman's urging tries to carry it out. But
in character the two couples have little in common. The Gothic
tinges which distinguish Merle and Osmond from the other
characters in *Portrait* have been elaborately subdued in the portraits of Kate and Merton. Much art and space are given over
in *Wings* to blending the darker guilt of Kate Croy and her

lover into the general gray of human frailty which surrounds the
heroine and which here and there dulls even her luminosity.
Merle and Osmond look upon each other with the mild contempt of those who share the memory of a "romantic" experience long ago gone stale. Their common interest is their illegitimate daughter and each parent looks upon her in a way
which reveals only a self-centered concern. Kate and Merton,
though terribly knowing and sophisticated, still represent "young
love"; they see each other in respect to the future, not the past,
and much is forgiven them because even their least worthy actions spring from their genuine loyalty to each other.

It is true that Kate perceives in Milly's situation a chance
to have her cake and eat it too, to marry the man she loves and
at the same time enjoy the fortune she covets. Then she will be
free of her Aunt Maud who promises her the wealth she desires
but only on condition that she reject Densher and marry Lord
Mark. Ideally, of course, Kate should sacrifice to her love all
prospects of material well-being. But it is characteristic of James's
maturity in *Wings* to emphasize the complexity and the limitations of human behavior. James takes pains, for example, to
dramatize Kate's economic responsibilities to others. If she married Densher in opposition to her aunt's will, Kate would, in
effect, abandon to final poverty her widowed sister, Mrs. Condrip, with her brood of children, to say nothing of abandoning
her father to the disreputable stratagems by which he manages
to live on nothing a year. There are further considerations which
weaken the case against Kate Croy. There is, first, the indis-
putable fact of her nature that she finds her proper self only in
a setting of opulence. When Densher meets her in the limited
context of her sister's house, he recognizes the glaring incongruity which she poses against such a backdrop. Further, her love
for Densher being sincere and deep, Kate's willingness to share
him with another woman even temporarily exacts from her a
genuine sacrifice. Finally, Kate believes as Susan Stringham does,
that Densher's paying court to Milly will be of benefit to the
dying girl. She is convinced that she can serve Milly's interests
at the same time as she serves her own.

James has placed Maud Lowder's large figure in such a position as to shade Kate Croy from the glare of unambiguous, solitary guilt. The real contest, in fact, is between these two evenly matched adversaries, not one between the worldly-wise English girl and the guileless American girl. Actually it is Mrs. Lowder who first sets in motion the scheme to mislead Milly Theale. Kate perceives at once how her aunt intends to make use of Milly in order to promote her own plans, i.e., to fob off on Milly the penniless, unpedigreed Densher so that the way will be clear for Kate to marry Lord Mark. Kate decides not to expose the scheme—though she is tempted to do so—but instead, with Densher's help, to encourage it and so finally beat Mrs. Lowder at her own game. In brief, Kate's primary objective is not to deceive her friend Milly but to outwit her Aunt Maud.

Merton Densher carries out the design upon Milly's innocence, yet he is even less culpable than Kate Croy, his instigator. At first he stumbles unwittingly into her intrigue, believing that she wants him merely to make sure of a convenient meeting place for the two of them in Milly's rooms. At a later stage Kate argues that he should take the trouble to solace Milly because it is the least he can do for a girl who is probably very ill. Whatever Kate's scheme is, he feels that he must back her up in it, though he is puzzled to find that Mrs. Lowder and Mrs. Stringham encourage him in his attentions to Milly quite as much as Kate does. When he begins to understand the part he is expected to play, he discovers that without being exactly false he has nevertheless gone too far.[9] Before he fully realizes it, he has "turned his corner" and retreat seems impossible. Kate gives him a chance to escape but he swears blind obedience to her wishes. He will see the deception to the end: when Mrs. Lowder and Kate return to London, he will remain in Venice and will visit Milly every day. He will even marry her if she will have it so, but only if she takes the initiative.

However, if he is to endure this ordeal alone, Densher feels justified in demanding some proof of equality with Kate in love and responsibility. He asks her to spend a night with him in his rooms and she complies. In essence what Merton is asking of Kate is whether she wants merely the money which she believes he can get out of Milly or whether she wants him *and* the money. In their final meeting, bringing the novel to a close, the alternatives which he offers are more grimly distinct. Merton will give Kate the fortune that Milly has left to him or he will marry her. He will not do both.

The real guilt of Densher and Kate Croy is not excused, condoned, or diminished, but their motives are made understandable and are shown to be not altogether evil. What is more, all of the other people, even the least selfish, are implicated in the attempt to delude the heroine. Milly herself is implicated in her delusion: she has the innocence of the dove but fails in the wisdom of the serpent. If the plan had succeeded, it seems probable, as all her deceivers hoped, that it would have worked for Milly's benefit. Even as it turned out, it may be true—though Kate who suggests the possibility is trying to rationalize her own position—that despite her cruel disillusionment Milly actually got from her relation with Densher what she so desperately wanted from life—"The peace of having loved. . . . Of having *been* loved. . . . Of having . . . realized her passion" (xx, 332).

Lord Mark who exposes the plot and tells Milly the truth about Kate and Merton is far from being an idealist who cannot endure the thought of duplicity. In fact, of all the persons in the story he shows the least moral discrimination and principle. Indifferent to the effect of his revelation upon Milly, he speaks merely in order to be avenged on Densher who is the cause, he suspects, for his proposals to Kate and Milly being refused. It should be added that both of his proposals are dishonest and cynically materialistic in intention.

Such moral ambiguities and complexities reveal James's growing appreciation of the fine shadings in human motives and of the paradoxes and anomalies in human behavior. They do not mean, as has been asserted, that James was inclined in his later years to dissolve ethical values in purely aesthetic enthusiasms. At the same time, however, his greater sensitivity to moral distinctions is indicated by a refinement of his art. *Wings* is a more profound criticism of life than *Portrait* because in the later novel James shows greater artistry and detachment in developing the Minny Temple image. As has been shown, the presence of the character Ralph Touchett in *Portrait* suggests that in this story James was disposed to a romantic softness that blunted his tragic effects and came close to sentimentalizing the moral realities of Isabel Archer's world.

In *Wings* James's perception of the human scene is at once wider in scope and more accurate in detail. Without losing any of Isabel Archer's concreteness, Milly Theale loses much of Isabel's limited particularity. Even as a representative American figure, Milly rises to a higher level of significance than Isabel. Though she remains fragile and flower-like, Milly is consistently displayed as "the heiress of all the ages."

But the "international light" does not shine with great intensity in *Wings*. Milly Theale is much more important as a figure that dramatizes the whole human condition, the story of man's great powers for adventure and achievement enacted under the shadow of mortality. The broadly human implications of Milly's doom are poetically elaborated. When Milly went to the great physician, Sir Luke Strett, for a physical examination, she received what must surely be one of the most subtly expressed diagnoses on record. It was not, however, too subtle for Milly; she realized at once the great danger hovering over her. Emerging from the Doctor's office, she went for a long walk through the poorer sections of London. For this jaunt she wanted no close companion. "She literally felt, in this first flush, that her only company must be the human race at large, present all round her, but inspiringly impersonal, and that her only field must be, then and there, the grey immensity of London" (xix, 247). She ended up in the Regent's Park,

> round which on two or three occasions with Kate Croy her public chariot had solemnly rolled. But she went into it further now; this was the real thing; the real thing was to be quite away from the pompous roads, well within the centre and on the stretches of shabby grass. Here were benches and smutty sheep; here were idle lads at games of ball . . . here were wanderers anxious and tired like herself; here doubtless were hundreds of others just in the same box. . . . All she thus shared with them made her wish to sit in their company; which she so far did that she looked for a bench that was empty, eschewing a still emptier chair that she saw hard by and for which she would have paid, with superiority, a fee. (xix, 250)

Both *Portrait* and *Wings* exemplify that "idea of treachery, the 'Judas complex'," which Graham Greene points to as James's "ruling passion"[10] and which was imbedded perhaps in his memory of Minny Temple. But in *Wings* the treason is more firmly rooted in the general fallibilities of human nature. As was noted before, Susan Stringham, the very picture of the faithful friend whose loyalty is fortified with all the rigor of the New England conscience, is at last as entangled in Milly's deception as Kate Croy, the type of the faithless friend. Merton Densher and Lord Mark are also brought together in the same community of human weakness, though the moral distance between them is scrupulously kept. When he learns that Lord Mark has callously disabused Milly of her illusion for the sake of personal revenge, Merton is outraged. He is filled with the indignation of a superior virtue and moral delicacy, yet in view of the part he has been playing, who is he to throw the first stone? Lord Mark has wished to marry Milly simply in order to inherit her money after her death, an event he believes is very near. Merton in deluding Milly has at least been acting out of a sincere love for Kate Croy, a woman he would marry in a minute whether she had money or not. Yet it is Merton Densher, after all, who deceives Milly and it is Lord Mark who tells her the truth.

The final effect of these ironies is to suggest a total human complicity in error and guilt. Both Isabel Archer and Milly Theale are cruelly deceived, but in Isabel's story there are clearly marked deceivers; in Milly's there is only deception. Isabel is betrayed by two morally specified human beings; Milly is betrayed by human nature.

II

Just as notable as the absence in *Wings* of a counterpart to Ralph Touchett is the absence in *Portrait* of any sustained metaphors of the kind that run through the later novel. Again, the difference is crucial, one that marks the greater depth and reach of Milly Theale's story. The two figures, "princess" and "dove," which are used to reveal the heroine and to emphasize the incongruity which is the essence of her tragedy, give to *Wings* a symbolic range which *Portrait* does not have. These pervasive images do not have the effect of reducing the story to abstract allegory but they do add to it certain common associations of thought and feeling which tend to universalize it. It is immediately apparent that the two figures are ordinary to the point of cliché. All who remember their childhood reading feel at once familiar with a heroine who is also a princess, and the dove is a commonly accepted symbol of innocence. James takes advantage of the wide currency which these simple figures have to ring his own changes upon them and to enrich them with his own ironic effects.

It is Susan Stringham who gives Milly the title of "Princess"; it names what Milly stands for in Susan's view—a gracious, charming embodiment of power. With her beauty, intelligence, youth and immense fortune Milly is about to realize her inheritance, which is nothing less than all the best of all the ages. But it turns out that Milly is a princess who loses everything—love, even at last the illusion of love, even life itself. Susan's title for Milly underscores the irony of Milly's tragedy. But the princess image has another, less austere association. Milly wields her sceptre with an unconscious ease that suggests a wand and relates her to the heroines of fairy tales. In fact, Milly *is* a royal figure of fairyland who for a time is overwhelmed by those sinister principalities and powers which also exist in fairyland, as every child knows. At last, however, her influence can be felt in beautiful triumph over the forces that deceive and kill.[11]

The other image under which Milly Theale appears, that of a dove, refers to the opposite pole of the axis around which her tragedy revolves. The figure suggests her innocence, her weakness, her capacity to be beguiled. It is therefore appropriate that this analogy should come from the realistic imagination of Kate Croy. Susan may see Milly in the light of gentle, triumphant power; Kate sees her as a potential victim.

The first time Kate calls Milly a dove, she does so with dramatic suddenness, and yet the metaphor bursts out of the context of their conversation logically enough. After suggesting that her Aunt Maud has plans in mind for Milly as well as for herself, Kate issues an exasperated warning: "We're of no use to you—it's decent to tell you. You'd be of use to us, but that's a different matter. My honest advice to you would be . . . to drop us while you can." Milly does not gather the full import of what Kate has said but she is nevertheless frightened. The

next morning it occurs to her "that she had felt herself alone
with a creature who paced like a panther." When Kate observes,
a moment later, "Oh you may very well loathe me yet!" Milly
breaks down. "Why do you say such things to me?" she asks.
The abrupt question has an immediate softening effect upon
Kate and she replies, "Because you're a dove." And she kisses
Milly, "not with familiarity or as a liberty taken, but almost
ceremonially and in the manner of an *accolade*; partly as if,
though a dove who could perch on a finger, one were also a
princess with whom forms were to be observed." To a certain degree Milly was aware that the image was appropriate. It seemed
to her "an inspiration. . . . revealed truth; it lighted up the
strange dusk in which she lately had walked. *That* was what
was the matter with her. She was a dove. Oh, *wasn't* she?" (XIX,
281–283). But Milly here is thinking only of Maud's attempt
to use her to pry information out of Kate about Densher's where-
abouts. She has not yet begun to penetrate the shadows of duplicity that surround her.

The next time Kate has occasion to return to the dove image
she is with Densher and the two of them are watching Milly
as she entertains her guests in her hired Venetian palace. Here
Kate blends the figure of Milly's innocence with an emblem of
Milly's power which is more substantial than Susan's transcendent one—a "long, priceless chain" of pearls which Milly is wearing, "wound twice around the neck." "She's a dove," Kate observes, "and one somehow doesn't think of doves as bejewelled.
Yet they suit her down to the ground." "Yes—down to the
ground is the word," Merton replies and he begins to reflect
upon Kate's metaphor.

Milly was indeed a dove; this was the figure, though it most
applied to her spirit. Yet he knew in a moment that Kate was
just now . . . exceptionally under the impression of that element
of wealth in her which was a power, which was a great power,
and which was dove-like only so far as one remembered that
doves have wings and wondrous flights, have them as well as
tender tints and soft sounds. It even came to him dimly that
such wings could in a given case—*had*, truly, in the case with
which he was concerned—spread themselves for protection.
Hadn't they, for that matter, lately taken an inordinate reach,

and weren't Kate and Mrs. Lowder, weren't Susan Shepherd and he, wasn't *he* in particular, nestling under them to a great increase of immediate ease? (xx, 217–218)

The title of the novel indicates that this shift in focus from the dove to the wings of the dove is an important one. The wings image, insofar as it implies "wondrous flights," signifies effortless superiority to earthly forces, and can readily be associated with the picture of a fairy princess. But another meaning is brought out when the dove is seen to spread her wings, not for flight, but for the protection of others. Of course, this new value also merges easily into the image of the storybook heroine.

All these possibilities of the figure are played upon and further extended near the end of the story when Mrs. Lowder refers to Milly's "wings" in a conversation with Densher. She is discussing the news of Milly's death, actually the first report of it he has had, although Mrs. Lowder believes that he has already been informed. It is therefore a solemn moment for Merton Densher.

> "Our dear dove then, as Kate calls her, has folded her wonderful wings."
> "Yes—folded them."
>
> . . . .
>   "Unless it's more true," she . . . added, "that she has spread them the wider."
> He again but formally assented, though, strangely enough, the words fitted a figure deep in his own imagination. "Rather, yes—spread them the wider."
> "For a flight, I trust, to some happiness greater—!"
> "Exactly. Greater," Densher broke in. (xx, 356)

Here the dominant idea, that of flight, is one which Densher previously introduced when musing upon Kate's use of the dove image. In Mrs. Lowder's picture of her folding her wonderful wings, Milly is seen coming to rest after her "wondrous flight," and the quickly reversed image which follows suggests a flight still more wondrous, one which blends into the conventional figure of the redeemed soul ascending to heaven or being borne to heaven on the wings of angels.

Mrs. Lowder's reference to Milly's flight contains an allu-

sion which James probably intended her to be ignorant of, for
if she knew of the allusion, she would not be likely to use the
image at all. It cannot be assumed, however, that James was
likewise unaware of it. He must have hoped that the reader
would recognize the phrase which he made the title of his story
and would be able to restore it to its context. Psalm 55 is typical
in that the psalmist asks God to destroy the enemies that surround him. But the enemy in this Psalm is of a peculiarly
treacherous kind.

> And I said, Oh that I had wings like a dove! for then
> would I fly away, and be at rest.
> Lo, then would I wander far off, and remain in the wil-
> derness. . . . for I have seen violence and strife in the city. . . .
> Wickedness is in the midst thereof: deceit and guile de-
> part not from her streets.
> For it was not an enemy that reproached me; then I could
> have borne it: neither was it he that hated me that did magnify
> himself against me; then I would have hid myself from him:
> But it was thou, a man mine equal, my guide, and mine
> acquaintance.
> We took sweet counsel together. . . .
> He hath put forth his hands against such as be at peace
> with him: he hath broken his convenant.
> The words of his mouth were smoother than butter, but
> war was in his heart: his words were softer than oil, yet were
> they drawn swords.

James has led Mrs. Lowder to utter what she does not
know, and her portrayal of Milly's death as the flight of a dove
to a place of greater happiness is therefore steeped in irony.
Through the long latter part of the novel when she is suffering
most, Milly Theale is never brought before the reader in person
—an achievement in literary tact which James points to with
some pride in his "Preface." But the Biblical allusion which
Mrs. Lowder unknowingly introduces suggests how Milly during
her last days might have seen herself in the figure of the soaring
dove. After learning how she had been betrayed, after she had,
in Susan's phrase, also Biblical, "turned her face to the wall,"
it is easy to imagine that she might have yearned for "wings like
a dove" in order to escape from the city of deceit and guile and
to fly from those who pretended to be her friends—Mrs. Lowder

herself, Merton Densher and Kate Croy. She had taken "sweet counsel" with those who broke their covenant; their "words were softer than oil, yet were . . . drawn swords."

It is appropriate that Kate Croy who invented it should be the last to recall Milly Theale under the image of the dove. In the final "scene" in the novel as Kate and Merton assess the effect which Milly has had upon their relations to each other, Kate declares that Milly died for them so that they might understand her.

> "I used to call her, in my stupidity—for want of anything better—a dove. Well she stretched out her wings, and it was to *that* they reached. They cover us."
> "They cover us," Densher said.
> "That's what I give you," Kate gravely wound up. "That's what I've done for you." (xx, 404)

Here Kate is revising her original concept of Milly as an innocent victim in favor of an image less condescending. In fact she has adopted the symbol of Milly's royal protective power which occurred to Densher when he first heard Kate describe Milly as a dove. What impresses Kate now is that although Milly discovered the deception practised upon her, she nevertheless willed most of her fortune to the man she knew would marry Kate Croy. This is what Kate means by saying that Milly's wings cover her and Densher. As far as results are concerned, the plot that failed has succeeded and Kate promptly takes credit for her management of the affair: "That's what I give you. . . . That's what I've done for you."

But Kate discovers a moment later that the happy consummation is not to be. Densher will not allow her to have both him and Milly's money. That is to say, in their relation to each other, Kate and Merton are as they were before Milly appeared, except that these two, as Kate lucidly observes, will never again be as they were. It is Milly who has made the profound difference. Returning good for evil she has proved her superiority but she has also had her revenge: without intending it she has heaped coals of fire upon the heads of those who tried to wrong her. It has turned out that Susan Stringham was right and Kate Croy was mistaken; Milly Theale was not a helpless dove but a princess magnificent in power.

Notes

1. For the story of the relationship between Henry James and Mary Temple and an account of its effect upon James's fiction, see Leon Edel, *Henry James: The Untried Years, 1843–1870* (Philadelphia and New York, 1953), pp. 226–238, 323–333.

2. R. C. LeClair, "Henry James and Minny Temple," *AL*, xxi (1949), 40.

3. F. O. Matthiessen, *The James Family, Including Selections from the Writings of Henry James Senior, William, Henry and Alice James* (New York, 1947), p. 260. Hereafter referred to as *James Family*.

4. *The Novels and Tales of Henry James*, New York ed. (New York, 1907–17), iii, 260, 262. Parenthetical documentation in my text is from this edition.

5. *James Family*, pp. 263, 261, 263.

6. *James Family*, pp. 261, 260. Leon Edel, *Henry James: The Untried Years*, pp. 235–238, 326–330, suggests that this consciousness of a reversal of Henry's and Minny's roles is related to the "vampire theme" which James developed in certain of his stories.

7. *James Family*, p. 260; LeClair, p. 40. Leon Edel, *Henry James: The Untried Years*, p. 344, dates the letter from James to his mother, 26 March 1870, which LeClair dates 29 March 1870. Edel, p. 331, contends that James both loved and feared Minny Temple: "Minny alive had been a constant reminder to Henry of his inarticulateness and his fear to assert himself. Minny gradually sinking into decline could renew his strength. Dead, Minny was Henry's, within the crystal walls of his mind. . . . He did not have to marry Minny and risk the awful consequences—and no one else could . . . Minny was now permanently his, the creature of his dreams."

8. T. S. Eliot, "Tradition and the Individual Talent," in *Selected Essays*, new ed. (New York, 1950), pp. 7–8.

9. Densher never tells Milly a downright lie about his relationship with Kate. Kate herself may be less scrupulous; at least, Milly tells Lord Mark that Kate has sworn she is not engaged. Yet the reader is never allowed to catch Kate telling Milly an unambiguous falsehood. For the most part, Kate and Merton in misleading Milly depend upon the power of suggestion and the untruth provided by others, e.g., by Mrs. Lowder and Mrs. Condrip.

10. *The Lost Childhood and Other Essays* (London, 1951), p. 44

11. F. O. Matthiessen, *Henry James: The Major Phase* (New York, 1944), p. 59, says that in *Wings* James "is evoking essentially the mood of a fairy tale."

William H. Gass

17· The High Brutality of
Good Intentions

> *"The great question as to a poet or a novelist
> is, How does he feel about life? what, in the
> last analysis, is his philosophy?"*
>
> HENRY JAMES

"ART," Yeats wrote in his essay on "The Thinking of the Body,"
"bids us touch and taste and hear and see the world, and shrinks
from what Blake calls mathematic form, from every abstract
thing, from all that is of the brain only, from all that is not a
fountain jetting from the entire hopes, memories, and sensa-
tions of the body." Yet the world that we are permitted to touch
and taste and hear and see in art, in Yeats's art as much as in
any other, is not a world of pure Becoming, with the abstractions removed to a place safe only for philosophers; it is a world
invested out of the ordinary with formal natures, with types and
typicals, by abstractions and purest principles; invested to a
degree which, in comparison with the real, renders it at times
grotesque and always abnormal. It is charged with Being. Touching it provides a shock.

The advantage the creator of fiction has over the moral
philosopher is that the writer is concerned with the exhibition
of objects, thoughts, feelings and actions where they are free
from the puzzling disorders of the real and the need to come
to conclusions about them. He is subject only to those calculated disorders which are the result of his refusal, in the fact of
the actual complexities of any well-chosen "case," to take a stand.
The moral philosopher is expected to take a stand. He is expected to pronounce upon the principles of value. The writer of
fiction, in so far as he is interested in morals, rather than, for

From *Accent*, XVIII (Winter, 1958), 62–71. Reprinted by permission of
Kerker Quinn for *Accent* and of the author. © 1958 by *Accent*.

instance, metaphysics, can satisfy himself and the requirements of his art by the exposure of moral principle in the act, an exposure more telling than life because it is, although concrete, concrete in no real way—stripped of the irrelevant, the accidental, the incomplete—every bit of paste and hair and string part of the intrinsic nature of the article. However the moral philosopher comes by his conclusions, he does not generally suppose (unless he is also a theologian) that the world is ordered by them or that the coming together of feelings and intents or the issuance of acts or the flow of consequences, which constitute the moral facts, was designed simply in order to display them.

It is the particular achievement of Henry James that he was able to transform the moral color of his personal vision into the hues of his famous figure in the carpet; that he found a form for his awareness of moral issues, an awareness that was so pervasive it invaded furniture and walls and ornamental gardens and perched upon the shoulders of his people a dove for spirit, beating its wings with the violence of all Protestant history; so that of this feeling, of the moving wing itself, he could make a *style*. This endeavor was both aided and hindered by the fact that, for James, art and morality were so closely twined, and by the fact that no theory of either art or morality had footing unless, previous to it, the terrible difficulties of vision and knowledge, of personal construction and actual fact, of, in short, the relation of reality to appearance had been thoroughly overcome. James's style is a result of his effort to master, at the level of his craft, these difficulties, and his effort, quite apart from any measure of its actual success with these things, brought to the form of the novel in English an order of art never even, before him, envisioned by it.

Both Henry James and his brother were consumed by a form of The Moral Passion. Both struggled to find in the plural world of practice a vantage for spirit. But William was fatally enmeshed in the commercial. How well he speaks for the best in his age. He pursues the saint; he probes the spiritual disorders of the soul; he commiserates with the world-weary and encourages the strong; he investigates the nature of God, His relation to the world, His code; he defends the possible immortality of

the soul and the right to believe: and does all so skillfully, with
a nature so sensitive, temperate and generous, that it is deeply
disappointing to discover, as one soon must, that the lenses of
his mind are monetary, his open hand is open for the coin, and
that the more he struggles to understand, appreciate, and rise,
the more instead he misses, debases, and destroys.

> In the religion of the once-born the world is a sort of rectilinear
> or one-storied affair, whose accounts are kept in one denomina-
> tion, whose parts have just the values which naturally they ap-
> pear to have, and of which a simple algebraic sum of pluses and
> minuses will give the total worth. Happiness and religious
> peace consist in living on the plus side of the account. In the
> religion of the twice-born, on the other hand, the world is a
> double-storied mystery. Peace cannot be reached by the simple
> addition of pluses and elimination of minuses from life. Natu-
> ral good is not simply insufficient in amount and transient,
> there lurks a falsity in its very being. Cancelled as it all is by
> death if not by earlier enemies, it gives no final balance, and
> can never be the thing intended for our lasting worship.[1]

Even when William, in a passage not obviously composed with
the bookkeeper's pen, makes a literary allusion, as here:

> Like the single drops which sparkle in the sun as they are flung
> far ahead of the advancing edge of a wave-crest or of a flood,
> they show the way and are forerunners. The world is not yet
> with them, so they often seem in the midst of the world's affairs
> to be preposterous . . .[2]

it turns out to be a covert reference to "getting and spending."

Henry James was certainly aware that one is always on the
market, but as he grew as an artist he grew as a moralist and his
use of the commercial matrix of analogy[3] became markedly
satirical or ironic and his investigation of the human trade more
self-conscious and profound until in nearly all the works of his
maturity his theme is the evil of human manipulation, a theme
best summarized by the second formulation of Kant's categorical imperative:

> So act as to treat humanity, whether in thine own person or in
> that of any other, in every case as an end withal, never as a
> means only.

Nothing further from pragmatism can be imagined, and if we
first entertain the aphorism that though William was the su-

perior thinker, Henry had the superior thought, we may be led
to consider the final effect of their rivalry,[4] for the novels and
stories of Henry James constitute the most searching criticism
available of the pragmatic ideal of the proper treatment and
ultimate worth of man. That this criticism was embodied in
Henry James's style, William James was one of the first to recognize. "Your methods and my ideals seem the reverse, the one
of the other," he wrote to Henry in a letter complaining about
the "interminable elaboration" of *The Golden Bowl*. Couldn't
we have, he asks, a "book with no twilight or mustiness in the
plot, with great vigour and decisiveness in the action, no fencing
in the dialogue, no psychological commentaries, and absolute
straightness in the style?"[5] Henry would rather have gone, he
replies, to a dishonored grave.

The Portrait of a Lady is James's first fully exposed case of
human manipulation; his first full-dress investigation, at the level
of what Plato called "right opinion," of what it means to be a
consumer of persons, and of what it means to be a person consumed. The population of James's fictional society is composed,
as populations commonly are, of purchasers and their purchases,
of the handlers and the handled, of the users and the used.
Sometimes actual objects, like Mrs. Gereth's spoils, are involved
in the transaction, but their involvement is symbolic of a buying
and a being sold which is on the level of human worth (where
the quality of the product is measured in terms of its respon-
siveness to the purchaser's "finest feelings," and its ability to
sound the buyer's taste discreetly aloud), and it is for this reason
that James never chooses to center his interest upon objects
which can, by use, be visibly consumed. In nearly all of the later
novels and stories, it is a human being, not an object, it is first
Isabel Archer, then Pansy, who is the spoil, and it is by no means
true that only the "villains" fall upon her and try to carry her
off; nor is it easy to discover just who the villains really are.

Kant's imperative governs by its absence—as the hollow
center. It is not that some characters, the "good" people, are
busy being the moral legislators of mankind and that the others,
the "bad" people, are committed to a crass and shallow pragmatism or a trifling estheticism; for were that the case *The Portrait* would be just another skillful novel of manners and James

would be distinctly visible, outside the work, nodding or shaking his head at the behavior of the animals in his moral fable. He would have managed no advance in the art of English fiction. James's examination of the methods of human consumption goes too deep. He is concerned with all of the ways in which men may be reduced to the status of objects and because James pursues his subject so diligently, satisfying himself only when he has unravelled every thread, and because he is so intent on avoiding in himself what he has revealed as evil in his characters and exemplifying rather what he praises in Hawthorne who, he says, "never intermeddled,"[6] the moral problem of *The Portrait* becomes an esthetic problem, a problem of form, the scope and course of the action, the nature of the characters, the content of dialogue, the shape and dress of setting, the points-of-view, the figures of speech, the very turn and tumble of the sentences themselves directed by the problem's looked-for solution, and there is consequently no suggestion that one should choose up sides or take to heart his criticism of a certain society nor any invitation to discuss the moral motivations of his characters *as if* they were surrogates for the real.

The moral problem, moreover, merges with the esthetic. It is possible to be an artist, James sees, in more than paint and language, and in *The Portrait*, as it is so often in his other work, Isabel Archer becomes the unworked medium through which, like benevolent Svengali, the shapers and admirers of beautifully brought out persons express their artistry and themselves. The result is very often lovely, but it is invariably sad. James has the feeling, furthermore, and it is a distinctly magical feeling, that the novelist takes possession of his subject through his words; that the artist is a puppeteer; his works are the works of a god. He constantly endeavors to shift the obligation and the blame, if there be any, to another: his reflector, his reverberator, his sensitive gong. In *The Portrait* James begins his movement toward the theory of the point-of-view. The phrase itself occurs incessantly. Its acceptance as a canon of method means the loss of a single, universally objective reality. He is committed, henceforth, to a standpoint philosophy, and it would seem, then, that the best world would be that observed from the most sensitive, catholic, yet discriminating standpoint. In this way, the esthetic problem reaches out to the metaphysical. This marvelous observer: what is it he observes? Does he see the world as it really is, palpitating with delicious signs of the internal, or does he merely fling out the self-capturing net? James struggles with this question most obviously in *The Sacred Fount* but it is always before him. So many of his characters are "perceptive." They understand the value of the unmolded clay. They feel they know, as artists, what will be best for their human medium. They will *take up* the young lady (for so it usually is). They will *bring* her *out*. They will *do for* her; *make something of* her. She will be *beautiful* and *fine*, in short, she will inspire *interest, amusement,* and *wonder*. And their pursuit of the ideally refractive medium parallels perfectly Henry James's own, except he is aware that his selected lens dare not be perfect else he will have embodied a god again, and far more obnoxious must this god seem in the body of a character than he did in the nib of the author's pen; but more than this, James knows, as his creations so often do not, that this manipulation is the essence, the ultimate germ, of the evil the whole of his work condemns, and it is nowhere more brutal than when fronted by the kindest regard and backed by a benevolent will.

The Portrait of a Lady, for one who is familiar with James, opens on rich sounds. None of his major motifs is missing. The talk at tea provides us with five, the composition of the company constitutes a sixth, and his treatment of the setting satisfies the full and holy seven. The talk moves in a desultory fashion ("desultory" is the repetitive word) and in joking tones ("That's a sort of joke" is the repetitive phrase) from health and illness, and the ambiguity of its value, to boredom, considered as a kind of sickness, and the ambiguity of its production.[7] Wealth is suggested as a cause of boredom, then marriage is proposed as a cure. The elder Touchett warns Lord Warburton not to fall in love with his niece, a young lady recently captured by his wife to be exhibited abroad. The questions about her are: has she money? is she interesting? The jokes are: is she marriageable? is she engaged? Isabel is the fifth thing, then—the young, spirited material. Lord Warburton is English, of course, while the Touchetts are Americans. Isabel's coming will sharpen the contrast, dramatize the confrontation. Lastly, James dwells lovingly on the ancient red brick house, emphasizing its esthetic appeal, its traditions, its status as a work of art. In describing the grounds he indicates, too, what an American man of money may do: fall in love with a history not his own and allow it, slowly, to civilize him, draw him into Europe. Lord Warburton is said to be bored. It is suggested that he is trying to fall in love. Ralph is described as cynical, without belief, a condition ascribed to his illness by his father. "He seems to feel as if he had never had a chance." But the best of the ladies will save us, the elder Touchett says, a remark made improbable by his own lack of success.

The structure of the talk of this astonishing first chapter foreshadows everything. All jests turn earnest, and in them, as in the aimless pattern of the jesters' leisure, lies plain the essential evil, for the evil cannot be blinked even though it may not be so immediately irritating to the eye as the evil of Madame Merle or Gilbert Osmond. There is in Isabel herself a certain willing-ness to be employed, a desire to be taken up and fancied, if only because that very enslavement, on other terms, makes her more free. She refuses Warburton, not because he seeks his own sal-vation in her, his cure by "interest," but rather because marriage to him would not satisfy her greed for experience, her freedom to see and feel and do. Neither Warburton nor Goodwood ap-peals as a person to Isabel's vanity. She is a great subject. She will make a great portrait. She knows it. Nevertheless Isabel's ambi-tions are at first naive and inarticulate. It is Ralph who sees the chance, in her, for the really fine thing; who sees in her his own chance, too, the chance at life denied him. It is Ralph, finally, who empowers her flight and in doing so draws the attention of the hunters.

Ralph and Osmond represent two types of the artist. Os-mond regards Isabel as an opportunity to create a work which will flatter himself and be the best testimony to his taste. Her intelligence is a silver plate he will heap with fruits to decorate his table. Her talk will be for him "a sort of served dessert." He will rap her with his knuckle. She will ring. As Osmond's wife, Isabel recognizes that she is a piece of property; her mind is attached to his like a small garden-plot to a deer park. But Ralph obeys the strictures *The Art of Fiction* was later to lay down. He works rather with the medium itself and respects the given.

His desire is to exhibit it, make it whole, refulgent, round. He
wants, in short, to make an image or to see one made—a portrait. He demands of the work only that it be "interesting." He
effaces himself. The "case" is his concern. *The Portrait's* crucial
scene, in this regard, is that between Ralph and his dying father.
Ralph cannot love Isabel. His illness prevents him. He feels it
would be wrong. Nevertheless, he takes, he says, "a great interest" in his cousin although he has no real influence over her.

> "But I should like to do something for her . . . I should like to
> put a little wind in her sails . . . I should like to put it into her
> power to do some of the things she wants. She wants to see the
> world for instance. I should like to put money in her purse."

The language is unmistakable. It is the language of Iago. Ralph
wants her rich.

> "I call people rich when they're able to meet the requirements
> of their imagination. Isabel has a great deal of imagination."

With money she will not have to marry for it. Money will make
her free. It is a curious faith. Mr. Touchett says, "You speak as
if it were for your mere amusement," and Ralph replies, "So it
is, a good deal." Mr. Touchett's objections are serenely met.
Isabel will be extravagant but she will come to her senses in
time. And, Ralph says,

> ". . . it would be very painful to me to think of her coming to
> the consciousness of a lot of wants she should be unable to
> satisfy. . . ."
> "Well, I don't know . . . I don't think I enter into your
> spirit. It seems to me immoral."
> "Immoral, dear daddy?"
> "Well, I don't know that it's right to make everything so
> easy for a person."[8]
> "It surely depends upon the person. When the person's
> good, your making things easy is all to the credit of virtue. To
> facilitate the execution of good impulses, what can be a nobler
> act? . . ."
> "Isabel's a sweet young thing; but do you think she's so
> good as that?"
> "She's as good as her best opportunities . . ."
> "Doesn't it occur to you that a young lady with sixty
> thousand pounds may fall a victim to the fortune-hunters?"
> "She'll hardly fall a victim to more than one."

"Well, one's too many."

"Decidedly. That's a risk, and it has entered into my calculation. I think it's appreciable, but I think it's small, and I'm
prepared to take it . . ."

"But I don't see what good you're to get of it. . . ."

"I shall get just the good I said a few moments ago I
wished to put into Isabel's reach—that of having met the requirements of my imagination. . . ."

The differences between Gilbert Osmond and Ralph Touchett
are vast, but they are also thin.

Isabel Archer is thus free to try her wings. She is thrown
upon the world. She becomes the friend of Madame Merle, "the
great round world herself": polished, perfect, beautiful without
a fault, mysterious, exciting, treacherous, repellent, and at bottom, like Isabel, identically betrayed; like Isabel again, seeking
out of her own ruin to protect Pansy, the new subject, "the
blank page," from that same round world that is herself. It is
irony of the profoundest sort that "good" and "evil" in their
paths should pass so closely. The dark ambitions of Serena
Merle are lightened by a pathetic bulb, and it is only those whose
eyes are fascinated and convinced by surface who can put their
confident finger on the "really good." Ralph Touchett, and we
are not meant to miss the appropriateness of his name, has not
only failed to respect Isabel Archer as an end, he has failed to
calculate correctly the qualities of his object. Isabel is a sweet,
young thing. She is not yet, at any rate, as good as her best
opportunities. The sensitive eye was at the acute point blind.
Ralph has unwittingly put his bird in a cage. In a later interview, Isabel tells him she has given up all desire for a general
view of life. Now she prefers corners. It is a corner she's been
driven to. Time after time the "better" people curse the future
they wish to save with their bequests. Longdon of *The Awkward
Age* and Milly Theale of *The Wings of the Dove* come immediately to mind. Time after time the better artists fail because
their point-of-view is ultimately only *theirs,* and because they
have brought the esthetic relation too grandly, too completely
into life.

In the portrait of Fleda Vetch of *The Spoils of Poynton*
James has rendered an ideally considerate soul. Fleda, a person
of modest means and background, possesses nevertheless the

true sense of beauty. She is drawn by her friend Mrs. Gereth into the full exercise of that sense and to an appreciation of the ripe contemplative life which otherwise might have been denied her. Yet Fleda so little awards the palm to mere cleverness or sensibility that she falls in love with the slow, confused, and indecisive Owen Gereth. Fleda furthermore separates her moral and her esthetic ideals. Not only does she refuse to manipulate others, she refuses, herself, to be manipulated. The moral lines she feels are delicate. She takes all into her hands. Everyone has absolute worth. Scruples beset and surround her and not even Mrs. Gereth's righteousness, the warmth of her remembered wrongs, can melt them through. The impatience which James generates in the reader and expresses through Mrs. Gereth is the impatience, precisely, of his brother: for Fleda to act, to break from the net of scruple and seize the chance. It would be for the good of the good. It would save the spoils, save Owen, save Mrs. Gereth, save love for herself; but Fleda Vetch understands, as few people in Henry James ever do, the high brutality of such good intentions. She cannot accept happiness on the condition of moral compromise, for that would be to betray the ground on which, ideally, happiness ought to rest. Indeed it would betray happiness itself, and love, and the people and their possessions that have precipitated the problem and suggested the attractive and fatal price.

It is not simply in the organization of character, dialogue, and action that Henry James reveals The Moral Passion, nor is it reflected further only in his treatment of surroundings[9] but it represents itself and its ideal in the increasing scrupulosity of the style: precision of definition, respect for nuance, tone, the multiplying presence of enveloping metaphors, the winding around the tender center of ritual lines, like the approach of the devout and worshipful to the altar, these circumlocutions at once protecting the subject and slowing the advance so that the mere utility of the core is despaired of and it is valued solely in the contemplative sight. The value of life lies ultimately in the experienced quality of it, in the integrity of the given not in the usefulness of the taken. Henry James does not peer through experience to the future, through this future to the future futures, endlessly down the infinite tube. He does not

find in today only what is needful for tomorrow. His aim is
rather to appreciate and to respect the things of his experience
and to set them, finally, free.

Notes

1. William James, *The Varieties of Religious Experience*, Modern
Library, New York, p. 163. God does a wholesale not a retail business, p.
484. The world is a banking house, p. 120. Catholic confession is a method
of periodically auditing and squaring accounts, p. 126. Examples could be
multiplied endlessly, not only in *The Varieties* but in all his work. In *The
Varieties* alone consult pages: 28, 38, 39, 133, 134, 135, 138, 330, 331,
333, 340, 347, 429fn, 481, 482.
2. *Ibid.*, p. 450.
3. Mark Schorer's expression, "Fiction and the Matrix of Analogy,"
The Kenyon Review, xi, No. 4 (1949). The commercial metaphor pervades James's work and has been remarked so frequently that it scarcely
requires documentation.
4. Leon Edel develops this theme in the first volume of his biography,
Henry James: The Untried Years, 1834–1870.
5. Quoted by R. B. Perry, *The Thought and Character of William
James*, 2 vols., Boston (1935), Vol. I, p. 424.
6. *The American Essays of Henry James*, ed. by Leon Edel, Vintage,
New York (1956), "Nathaniel Hawthorne," p. 23.
7. Illness, in James's novels, either signifies the beautiful thing (the
Minny Temple theme) or it provides the excuse for spectatorship and
withdrawal, the opportunity to develop the esthetic sense (the Henry James
theme).
8. A remark characteristic of the self-made man. In the first chapter,
Mr. Touchett attributes Warburton's "boredom" to idleness. "You
wouldn't be bored if you had something to do; but all you young men are
too idle. You think too much of your pleasure. You're too fastidious, and
too indolent, and too rich." Caspar Goodwood is the industrious suitor.
9. When, for instance, in *The Portrait* Gilbert Osmond proposed to
Isabel, the furnishings of the room in which their talk takes place seem to
Osmond himself "ugly to distress" and "the false colours, the sham splendour . . . like vulgar, bragging, lying talk"—an obvious commentary by the
setting on the action.

Sister M. Corona Sharp, O.S.U.

18·From *The Confidante in Henry James*

THE PORTRAIT OF A LADY (1881) is remarkable for many merits, including the indirect juxtaposition of two confidantes. The contrast between Henrietta Stackpole and Madame Merle, alluded to in the author's Preface, is more dramatic than the distinctions made between Mrs. Prest and Miss Tina Bordereau in "The Aspern Papers." In receiving fuller treatment, the confidantes in *The Portrait* are differentiated not only in their technical use, but also in their moral and cultural backgrounds.

In the Preface James gives more attention to Henrietta than to any other character, except of course the heroine herself. In discussing the function of Henrietta, he compares her with Maria Gostrey, "then in the bosom of time," and a better example of what Miss Stackpole sets out to be.[1]

> Each of these persons is but wheels to the coach; neither belongs to the body of the vehicle, or is for a moment accommodated with a seat inside. There the subject alone is ensconced, in the form of its "hero and heroine," and of the privileged high officials, say, who ride with the king and queen. . . . Maria Gostrey and Miss Stackpole then are cases, each, of the light *ficelle*, not of the true agent; they may run beside the coach "for all they are worth," they may cling to it till they are out of breath (as poor Miss Stackpole all so vividly does), but neither, all the while, so much as gets her foot on the step, neither ceases for a moment to tread the dusty road (p. 55).

From *The Confidante in Henry James: Evolution and Moral Value of a Fictive Character* (South Bend, 1963), pp. 67–96. Reprinted by permission of the University of Notre Dame Press and of the author. © 1963 by the University of Notre Dame Press.

Although Miss Stackpole came to the author's mind along with the other characters, as "the definite array of contributions to Isabel Archer's history," yet her position remains inferior from the start: she is never a true agent in the drama of the novel (p. 53). James admits the incongruity between her ancillary function and her ample treatment, offering as an excuse "an excess of [his] zeal," an example of his weakness to "*overtreat*, rather than *undertreat*" his subject (p. 57), and an effort to embellish the novel by "cultivation of the lively. . . . Henrietta must have been at that time a part of my wonderful notion of the lively" (p. 57). It is true that this *ficelle* provides most of the humor in *The Portrait*, the rest of it being contributed by her friend, Mr. Bantling, by Mrs. Touchett, and by the Countess Gemini. But Henrietta's other function of confidante and admonisher of the protagonist is ignored by James in the Preface; it is simply left for the reader to discover for himself.

The basic difference between Henrietta and Madame Merle is indicated in the same part of the Preface: Henrietta is running beside the coach, while the latter lady, "seated, all absorbed but all serene, at the piano" at Gardencourt, presents to the heroine the sudden recognition of "a turning point in her life" (p. 56). To what extent Madame Merle becomes "the agent" in Isabel Archer's life will presently be taken up. Just now a remark on the contrasted mode of influence may be linked with James's own image of the coach. As Henrietta is running along on the outside, her influence can only be seen as external upon Isabel, whereas Madame Merle, seated within the coach—if one may extend James's metaphor—exercises a deep and thorough influence both exterior and interior, the full extent of which the heroine does not fathom until the end of the novel.

The great difference between the two confidantes originates in their diverse purposes in the author's plan. Henrietta, who figures largely in the first part of the novel, which takes place in England and Paris, is used by James to analyze Isabel verbally and to be the first of her friends to predict her disaster. Equipped with utter frankness and fearlessness, Henrietta sees Isabel both from the outside and the inside. In spite of her warnings, however, she does not succeed in altering Isabel's life.[2] On the other hand, James's purpose for Madame Merle is to implement his heroine's downfall through the subtlety of her betrayal. Madame Merle dominates the later sections of the novel, before and after Isabel's marriage, which occur in Italy. The novel is a study of knowledge: knowledge gained through experience; knowledge hidden by deceit; knowledge distorted by prejudice. Isabel's tragic irony is the loss of happiness through knowledge. While Henrietta relentlessly uncovers ugly facts, it is in Madame Merle's interests to conceal them. Instead of criticizing Isabel, she builds up her already sublime ego. It is characteristic, and fateful, that the heroine should ignore the first and listen to the second confidante.

Seen with the critical eyes of Ralph Touchett, Henrietta's first appearance has the comic touches of the light *ficelle* the author meant her to be:

> She was a neat plump person, of medium stature, with a round face, a small mouth, a delicate complexion, a bunch of light brown ringlets at the back of her head and a peculiarly open, surprised-looking eye. The most striking point in her appearance was the remarkable fixedness of this organ, which rested without impudence or defiance, but as if in conscientious exercise of a natural right, upon every object it happened to encounter. . . . She rustled, she shimmered, in fresh, dove-coloured draperies . . . she was as crisp and new and comprehensive as a first issue before the folding. From top to toe she had probably no misprint.[3]

The remarkable fixedness of her eyes is doubtless intended to symbolize the bumptiousness with which she makes her way across England and the Continent, and the general simplistic American view of life, which James frequently satirized. Not only is Ralph critical of Miss Stackpole, but Mrs. Touchett objects strongly to the loudness of this enterprising woman:

> "I don't like Miss Stackpole—everything about her displeases me; she talks so much too loud and looks at one as if one wanted to look at *her*—which one doesn't. I'm sure she has lived all her life in a boarding-house, and I detest the manners and the liberties of such places" (p. 88).

This blunt and tactless friend of Isabel does not succeed at first in obtaining any great confidences from the girl. Miss Archer is questing for a more profound experience of life—and

Henrietta certainly is very easily understood. Still, she has been for "Isabel . . . a proof that a woman might suffice to herself and be happy" (p. 55). Her convictions about conscience and duty appeal to the heroine. In defending her to Ralph Isabel states:

> "I'm afraid it's because she's rather vulgar that I like her. . . . it's because there's something of the 'people' in her. . . . she's a kind of emanation of the great democracy—the continent, the country, the nation. I don't say that she sums it all up, that would be too much to ask of her. But she suggests it; she vividly figures it" (pp. 86–87).

But Isabel finds that in an English setting, Henrietta can be very annoying. Her behavior at Gardencourt is often embarrassing; and her espousal of Caspar Goodwood's cause Isabel finds to be lacking in delicacy. Also, her criticism of Isabel's newly acquired ideas proves to be irritating to the independent girl. New ideas, Henrietta declares in a pontifical tone, " 'shouldn't interfere with the old ones when the old ones have been the right ones' " (p. 97). In her estimation, poor Ralph is suspect for his expatriate urbanity; and she holds forth to him on the American virtue of simplicity. " 'We take everything more naturally over there, and, after all, we're a great deal more simple. I admit that; I'm very simple myself. . . . I'm quite content to be myself; I don't want to change' " (p. 107).

That Isabel's new ideas are removing her from the state of simplicity causes alarm for her staunch American friend. To remedy this evil she applies to Ralph for help:

> "You had bitter stir yourself and be careful. Isabel's changing every day; she's drifting away—right out to sea. I've watched her and I can see it. She's not the bright American girl she was. She's taking different views, a different colour, and turning away from her old ideals. I want to save those ideals. . . . I've got a fear in my heart that she's going to marry one of these fell Europeans, and I want to prevent it" (p. 108).

It will be prevented by getting Isabel to marry her old suitor from Massachusetts, who, with undashed hopes, has pursued her to Europe. " 'He's the only man I have ever seen whom I think worthy of Isabel' " (p. 109). " 'I know her well enough to know that she would never be truly happy over here, and I wish her

to form some strong American tie that will act as a preserva-
tive' " (p. 110).

The sincerity of Henrietta's desire to save her friend " 'from
drowning' " is very creditable. It springs from her innate simplicity, which dreads any change whatever. Also, her interest in
Caspar's suit is prompted by a sincere sympathy for the young
man, similar to the interest of Mrs. Tristram in her candidate. In
her meddlesome way Henrietta even forces Ralph to invite Caspar Goodwood to Gardencourt. But despite her forwardness,
Henrietta is not too obtuse to discover Ralph's love for Isabel.
In pointing it out she serves the technical purpose of exposition,
since Ralph would certainly never confess his feelings to anyone
before doing so to Isabel herself on his deathbed.

One of Henrietta's big comic scenes is enacted with Lord
Warburton before her departure from Gardencourt. Although
it is one of James's digressions in favor of "the lively," and hence
has nothing to do with Henrietta's role of confidante, a claim
to its usefulness as an interlude can still be made, for it precedes
a tense scene between Isabel and the Lord (Chapter XIV).

Miss Stackpole's subsequent and swift friendship with Mr.
Bantling in London adds more details to her comic role. In his
appreciative company she simply effervesces. The men in whom
Henrietta is interested, Goodwood and Bantling, are a commentary on her own character. As indicated in their revealing
names, both men are paragons of Henrietta's cardinal virtue—
simplicity. Isabel has called Caspar " 'very simple-minded' "
(p. 90), and together Ralph and Isabel estimate Bantling as
" 'a very simple organism' " and Henrietta as " 'a simpler one
still' " (p. 128). These judgments made by Isabel on her first
confidante and the latter's friends form the basis of contrast with
her second confidante and her friend. To the reader this basis
is quite clear; but to Isabel, ironically, the values of the second
group are not so accurately defined.

Henrietta's simplicity is even more evident in the little ruse
which she plays on Isabel to obtain a private hearing for Caspar. It is the entire extent of her plot to marry Isabel to the
rugged young businessman, and in its naïveté scarcely compares
with Madame Merle's machination. But it is true to her character, to which any deception is quite foreign. Her greeting to

Isabel after the surprise interview with Caspar is: " 'Has he
been here, dear?' the latter yearningly asked" (p. 143). The
note of vicarious pleasure is unmistakable, which Isabel's an-
noyance does not in the least disturb. It is her mistake, however,
to try to force confidences from Isabel:

> "I hope you don't mean to tell me that you didn't give
> Mr. Goodwood some hope."
> "I don't see why I should tell you anything; as I said to
> you just now, I can't trust you. . . ."
> "You don't mean to say you've sent him off?" Henrietta
> almost shrieked.
> "I asked him to leave me alone; and I ask you the same,
> Henrietta" (p. 144).

Isabel obviously is in no mood for recriminations, but Henrietta rides roughly over any precautionary considerations: " 'Do
you know where you're drifting? . . . You're drifting to some
great mistake' " (p. 144). The seriousness of this warning is
prompted by utter devotion of friendship, and the lively journalist, instead of indulging righteous anger at its rejection, hu-
morously responds to Isabel's witty retort about Mr. Bantling's
arrangements:

> "Do you know where you're drifting, Henrietta Stack-
> pole?" . . . .
> "I'm drifting to a big position—that of the Queen of
> American Journalism. If my next letter isn't copied all over the
> West I'll swallow my pen-wiper!" (p. 145).

But the confidante—still without obtaining confidences—is
more than ever determined to pursue Mr. Goodwood's cause.
In a short subsequent scene with Ralph she discloses her intention to " 'tell him not to give up. If I didn't believe Isabel would
come round,' Miss Stackpole added—'Well, I'd give up myself.
I mean I'd give her up!' " (p. 148). It is important for Henrietta's role that she should not give Isabel up. For near the
end of the novel the author will use her sympathetic ministra-
tions to his heroine when her need for a confidante is greatest.
The present scene (Chapter 17) is the last to be dominated by
Miss Stackpole for a long time. The following nine chapters are
devoted, with only two exceptions, to the second confidante,
Madame Merle.

Isabel had told Ralph that she liked " 'people to be totally
different from Henrietta' " (p. 87), and in Madame Merle she
undoubtedly finds such a person. The ideal represented by this
woman instantly captivates her imagination:

> Our heroine had always passed for a person of resources and
> had taken a certain pride in being one; but she wandered, as
> by the wrong side of the wall of a private garden, round the
> enclosed talents, accomplishments, aptitudes of Madame Merle.
> She found herself desiring to emulate them, and in twenty such
> ways this lady presented herself as a model. . . . It took no great
> time indeed for her to feel herself, as the phrase is, under an
> influence. "What's the harm," she wondered, "so long as it's a
> good one? The more one's under a good influence the better.
> The only thing is to see our steps as we take them—to under-
> stand them as we go. That, no doubt, I shall always do" (p.
> 163).

This aura of mystery surrounding Madame Merle, which Mrs.
Touchett calls " 'her great fault,' " is enhanced by her classic
appearance and aristocratic bearing:

> It was a face that told of an amplitude of nature and of quick
> and free motions and, though it had no regular beauty, was in
> the highest degree engaging and attaching. Madame Merle was
> a tall, fair, smooth woman; everything in her person was round
> and replete. . . . Her grey eyes were small but full of light and
> incapable of stupidity—incapable, according to some people,
> even of tears; she had a liberal, full-rimmed mouth which when
> she smiled drew itself upward to the left side in a manner that
> most people thought very odd, some very affected and a few
> very graceful. . . . Madame Merle had thick, fair hair, arranged
> somehow "classically" and as if she were a Bust, Isabel judged
> —a Juno or a Niobe; and large white hands, of a perfect shape.
> . . . [She might have ranked] as . . . a baroness, a countess, a
> princess (pp. 151–152).

Just as Henrietta is decked out for high comedy, so her rival is
endowed with the features and elegance of classical tragedy.
Here is a woman capable of ruling kingdoms and destined to
witness their collapse. So completely has she assimilated the
traditions of the "old, old world," that no marked American
trait remains visible. Her bid for Isabel's friendship on grounds
of American origin falls flat. Isabel can only wonder "what
Henrietta Stackpole would say to her thinking so much of this

perverted product of their common soil, and had a conviction
that it would be severely judged. Henrietta would not at all sub-
scribe to Madame Merle; for reasons she could not have defined
this truth came home to the girl" (p. 163).

Yet Madame Merle, she feels certain, would instantly "strike
off some happy view" of Miss Stackpole; she "was too humorous, too observant, not to do justice to Henrietta, and on becoming acquainted with her would probably give the measure
of a tact which Miss Stackpole couldn't hope to emulate" (pp.
163–164). Isabel's estimate of their mutual impressions is later
borne out during their actual meeting in Florence.

The extent to which Madame Merle captivates Isabel's confidence is determined by her striking singularity. The girl's romantic sense thrills because she

> had never encountered a more agreeable and interesting figure
> than Madame Merle; she had never met a person having less of
> that fault which is the principal obstacle to friendship—the air
> of reproducing the more tiresome, the stale, the too-familiar
> parts of one's own character (p. 161).

There is an unconscious reference here to Henrietta, whose
sense of duty and staunch American independence are indeed
familiar parts of Isabel's own character. And the implicit comparison continues when Isabel notices that Madame Merle "was
not natural . . . her nature had been too much overlaid by cus-
tom and her angle too much rubbed away. She had become too
flexible, too useful, was too ripe and too final. . . . She was
deep . . ." (p. 165). In Madame Merle there is a totally new
creature to meet, and she becomes Isabel's only confidante until
the time of the latter's marriage. In spite of her silence over Lord
Warburton and Caspar Goodwood,

> the gates of the girl's confidence were opened wider than they
> had ever been; she said things to this amiable auditress that she
> had not yet said to anyone. Sometimes she took alarm at her
> candour; it was as if she had given to a comparative stranger
> the key to her cabinet of jewels. These spiritual gems were the
> only ones of any magnitude that Isabel possessed, but there was
> all the greater reason for their being carefully guarded. After-
> wards, however, she always remembered that one should never
> regret a generous error and that if Madame Merle had not the
> merit she attributed to her, so much the worse for Madame
> Merle (p. 161).

Undoubtedly, the measure of confidence bestowed by Isabel commits her in like measure to the power of the confidante. Madame Merle extracts more from Isabel in a few weeks than Henrietta does in years. This she does by showing keen interest in all that concerns Isabel, without however pumping her in the officious manner of Miss Stackpole.

> She preferred for the present to talk to Isabel of Isabel, and exhibited the greatest interest in our heroine's history, sentiments, opinions, prospects. She made her chatter and listened to her chatter with infinite good nature. This flattered and quickened the girl, who was struck with all the distinguished people her friend had known . . . (p. 166).

The important thing in these confidences is not the factual details, but the laying bare of the girl's soul, which enables the older woman to read it most clearly. She gains knowledge of Isabel's idealism and generosity—both her strength and her weakness—and this knowledge gives her immediate power over the girl. Casually she leads into the topic of her American friend living in Italy, who is outstanding for nothing except his daughter: " 'But he has a little girl—a dear little girl; he does speak of *her*. He's devoted to her, and if it were a career to be an excellent father he'd be very distinguished' " (p. 169). These details she knows will influence Isabel's deeply sensitive heart: and the effect of the girl's first visit to his home later verifies her confidante's foreknowledge.

In presenting the picture of Madame Merle James does two things—he shows her impression made on Isabel, and he shows the reader the masks with which she makes that impression. Her most important masks are those of the trustworthy confidante, in whose heart secrets lie forever buried, and the sympathetic, just listener, who can find good in everyone, even the impossible Countess. Her dabbling in art and art-collecting is another mask. But the mask that underlies all the others is her small position among the great people of the world:

> She had known great things and great people, but she had never played a great part. She was one of the small ones of the earth; she had not been born to honours; she knew the world too well to nourish fatuous illusions on the article of her own place in it. She had encountered many of the fortunate few and was perfectly aware of those points at which their fortune differed from

hers. But if by her informed measure she was no figure for a
high scene, she had yet to Isabel's imagination a sort of greatness. To be so cultivated and civilised, so wise and so easy, and
still make so light of it—that was really to be a great lady, especially when one so carried and presented one's self (p. 164).

In the role of highly-trained lady-in-waiting upon the great,
Madame Merle merits the applause of her youthful spectator,
who notes in her life the functions pertaining to her role. When
not engaged in her voluminous correspondence, nor in painting water-colors which she freely gives away, nor in playing
the piano with perfect consideration for her listeners, she busies
herself with rich embroidery, with playing cards, or in conversation. "She laid down her pastimes as easily as she took them
up. . . . She was in short the most comfortable, profitable, amen-
able person to live with" (p. 165).

Another feature of Madame Merle's exterior masks is her
philosophy of clothes:

> "I know a large part of myself is in the clothes I wear. I've a
> great respect for *things!* One's self—for other people—is one's
> expression of one's self; and one's house, one's furniture, one's
> garments, the books one reads, the company one keeps—these
> are all expressive" (pp. 172–173).

It is the born actress discussing the histrionic value of her cos-
tumes and disguises; and it illuminates her use of masks throughout the novel.

In contrast with this lady and her masks, undisguised Henrietta, whose creed of honesty might be published in any head-
line, reappears briefly on the scene in Paris. Madame Merle has
just shown the reader her controlled pleasure over Isabel's inheritance; Miss Stackpole's opinion on the contrary is that

> "it will certainly confirm your dangerous tendencies . . . The
> peril for you is that you live too much in the world of your own
> dreams. . . . You're too fastidious; you've too many graceful
> illusions. Your newly-acquired thousands will shut you up more
> and more to the society of a few selfish and heartless people
> who will be interested in keeping them up. . . . you think you
> can lead a romantic life . . ." (pp. 184–185).

In renewing her warnings, Henrietta functions as the *ficelle*
designed to prognosticate for the "center." Her arguments
against the romantic life trouble and frighten Isabel, although

they do not materially alter her course. Her reaction has none-theless deepened since the scene in Pratt's Hotel when she listened to similar remarks. This change in Isabel's attitude marks a development in both her character and in her relation to her confidante. Her being frightened now foreshadows her confession of bitter sorrow later.

With the removal of the principals to Italy the activities of the two confidantes is considerably altered. Allowed only three brief appearances, simple Henrietta is relegated to her journal-istic pursuits in other quarters; while Madame Merle closes in on Isabel in the realization of her plot. The reader feels that Isabel has moved out of Henrietta's sphere into the domain of the subtle expatriates. Mrs. Touchett and Ralph, having lived longer in Europe than Henrietta, are now used by the author as the more capable voices of warning to Isabel.

Madame Merle is given such free scope that she becomes the center of consciousness in the scene with Osmond (Chapter XXII).[4] The exposition given in this scene sets the stage for the unfolding of the plot to marry Isabel to Osmond. An air of intimacy is discernible in this private interview, yet the woman's motives lie so deeply concealed that her secret is safeguarded until the author is ready to reveal it to his heroine near the end of the novel. But cues are given to the reader here, which later fall in place. One of these is Madame Merle's pain over Pansy's not liking her. The depth of her deception in getting the girl to marry the father of her own child is equalled only by the suavity of her power of suggestion. In recommending him to Isabel's attention, she does not omit touching lightly on the girl's most vulnerable spot, her vanity:

> He had his perversities—which indeed Isabel would find to be the case with all men really worth knowing—and didn't cause his light to shine equally for all persons—Madame Merle, how-ever, thought she could undertake that for Isabel he would be brilliant. He was easily bored, too easily, and dull people always put him out; but a quick and cultivated girl like Isabel would give him a stimulus which was too absent from his life (p. 207).

When Osmond presents himself in the prearranged call on his ally in order to meet Miss Archer, James again resorts to the imagery of the theater to enhance the duplicity of the confidante:

> Isabel took on this occasion little part in the talk; she scarcely
> even smiled when the others turned to her invitingly; she sat
> there as if she had been at the play and had paid even a large
> sum for her place. . . . They talked of the Florentine, the
> Roman, the cosmopolite world, and might have been distin-
> guished performers figuring for a charity. It had all the rich
> readiness that would have come from rehearsal. Madame Merle
> appealed to her as if she had been on the stage, but she could
> ignore any learnt cue without spoiling the scene . . . (p. 209).

But Isabel is unaware of watching a rehearsed performance. She
lacks the insight of Ralph who "had learned more or less in-
scrutably to attend, and there could have been nothing so 'sustained' to attend to as the general performance of Madame
Merle" (p. 212). Through Ralph's consciousness, rather than Isabel's, the reader gains insight into Madame Merle's frustration.
The beautiful classical type now appears merely as a small businessman's widow, who is accepted by people like the latest
best-seller. James deliberately undercuts the earlier impression
to prepare for the final revelation of her melodramatic involvement with Osmond. Her life is, after all, only bourgeois tragedy.

Madame Merle's ambitions, thwarted until now, converge
with a quiet but fierce determination to see her plot through to
consummation. In the third scene written from her point of
view (Chapter 25) she engages the Countess Gemini in conversation, and coolly blackmails her into silence in respect to
warning Isabel. Everywhere she is the self-possessed, suave con-
triver, who needs only to prevent obstacles from arising. Left to
herself, Isabel will most probably enter into the marriage, and
Madame Merle does leave her considerably to herself and to
Osmond. She does, however, convey to Isabel in sympathetic
terms the exposition of Osmond's and the Countess's background. In doing this she subtly injects the warning that one
could not believe a word the Countess says. This is to safeguard
the plot in case the Countess should try to betray it after all.

During this time Henrietta makes one of her brief appearances in Florence, and her meeting with Madame Merle gives
only a sketchy and unilateral view of their differences:

> Madame Merle surveyed [Henrietta] with a single glance, took
> her in from head to foot, and after a pang of despair deter-
> mined to endure her. She determined indeed to delight in her.

She mightn't be inhaled as a rose, but she might be grasped as
a nettle. Madame Merle genially squeezed her into insignifi-
cance, and Isabel felt that in foreseeing this liberality she had
done justice to her friend's intelligence (p. 236).

In may be inferred that Henrietta, having been squeezed into
oblivion, fails to express her views of Madame Merle. The simplicity of the journalist is no doubt baffled by the consummate
aplomb of the woman of the world. The contrast between the
two confidantes, begun in their very names, and continued
through the descriptions of their appearance, their manner and
speech, culminates in the nature of their ambitions and the
essential features of their characters. All these differences point
up the distinction between their technical roles. Madame Merle
with all her skill sits at ease inside the coach, while Henrietta
pants along on the outside. The deeply concealed alliance between Madame Merle and Gilbert Osmond complements the
simple plan of Henrietta in favor of Caspar Goodwood. Isabel
sees through the simple plan; but she never suspects duplicity
in Madame Merle until it is too late.

Madame Merle however begins to doubt the beneficence of
her plot before Isabel does. In the brief scene between herself
and Osmond (Chapter 26), she reveals her terror at the abyss
yawning at Isabel's feet—the abyss of Osmond's selfishness
and cruelty: " 'I'm frightened at the abyss into which I shall
have cast her' " (p. 239). It is the redeeming feature of Madame
Merle's character that in spite of her readiness to exploit Isabel,
she can still sympathize with her as a fellow victim. " 'That fine
creature,' " the term she applied to her, indicates her admiration
for the girl.

The two scenes between Madame Merle and Osmond reveal the character of the confidante more plainly than her scenes
with Isabel. With her former lover, her masks are down, and
the suppressed pathos wells up. Her role as betrayer requires
these brief dialogues "behind the scenes," in order to keep the
reader *au courant*, for revelation of the plot can scarcely be
made through Isabel, the victim, who is the "center" throughout the greater part of the novel. These scenes also mark a progression in Madame Merle's own downfall. By this time the
woman of many accomplishments and much social success has

begun to doubt her greatest achievement. Osmond taunts her: " 'You can't draw back—you've gone too far.' 'Very good [she replies]; but you must do the rest yourself' " (p. 239).

James's study of the confidante-"center" relation in *The Portrait* revolves around his favorite theme of the American innocent acquiring experience. Isabel, the innocent heroine, stands midway between Henrietta, the isolationist armed with high-sounding prejudices, and Madame Merle, the expatriate who has surrendered to cosmopolitan cynicism. Through the confidential relation James facilitates the progress of his heroine from ignorance to disillusionment. As she moves out of Henrietta's orbit into Madame Merle's, the girl meets life and experiences the death of her idealistic ambitions.

Meanwhile the confidantes develop as well. Henrietta, the friend of Isabel's American years, outstrips her in coming to terms with Europe. They are her terms, certainly; but she finds on foreign soil the happiness and fulfillment which Isabel misses. In a reverse manner, Madame Merle, although versed in evil, discerns new depths in the sinister soul of Osmond. At the sight even she recoils. In this threefold way the author delineates the passage of the woman's heart from one stage to another. The progress of the confidantes is like an obbligato to the melody of the heroine's growth in awareness.

Because of the isolation created by Isabel's egotism, there is little collaboration between herself and her confidantes in their separate expansion of consciousness. Each one makes her way independently of the other. Still, Madame Merle, in using Isabel as her tool, does achieve her later understanding through the misery of the young woman. It is not, of course, a result of friendship. Once exploitation appears friendship dies. In most cases the Jamesian confidante is exploited. Here it is the confider. But the result is the same.

On the Eastern tour Isabel begins to discover the divergence in morality between Madame Merle and herself: ". . . our young woman had a sense in her of values gone wrong or, as they said at the shops, marked down" (p. 269). The consummate performance is slackening. Here and there the young woman notices that a corner of the curtain is never lifted on Madame Merle's past. In pondering this woman's depth she is now shocked, now dismayed, and increasingly filled with foreboding. Isabel's confidante—as none other—is an index of life. Minor satellites to Madame Merle are Mrs. Tristram, Mrs. Costello, and Lady Davenant. By studying these women their confiders could learn all they need to know about life; it is part of their tragedy that they lack a quick perception for clues of worldliness. James knew the smooth, hardened society woman very well. Many times he portrays the type in his international fiction. She is seldom a person to inspire confidence. As soon as Isabel awakens to this hardness in her friend her confidence begins to wane.

On her part, Madame Merle has shown herself an expert psychologist in estimating Isabel's need to confide. The confidences she elicits from the first days at Gardencourt until the end of the Eastern tour meet a psychological need on Isabel's part, and a strategic one on her own. In spite of her many friends, Isabel is always lonely. Isolated in part by her romantic ideals, in part by her egotism, she naturally allows admittance to her heart only to those who appeal to the ideals or flatter the egotism. Not until the end, when she has been purified by suffering, does she admit Henrietta and Ralph to her secrets; for up to this point she has resisted their advice and warnings.

After their return from the East the engagement takes place; and from then on Madame Merle's role in Isabel's life is wholly changed. An estrangement sets in between the two women; but Madame Merle interests herself more noticeably in Pansy. The first scene in this latter part of the novel showing Madame Merle transpires with Mr. Rosier, who begs her assistance in furthering his suit for Pansy. Madame Merle functions as Rosier's confidante, but offers him no sympathy and only scant advice. James also uses her to provide the reader with some information about the past three years which the narrative has skipped.

Madame Merle is next seen sailing through Isabel's drawing rooms as though claiming proprietorship:

> The other rooms meanwhile had become conscious of the arrival of Madame Merle, who, wherever she went, produced an impression when she entered. How she did it the most attentive spectator could not have told you, for she neither spoke

loud, nor laughed profusely, nor moved rapidly, nor dressed
with splendour, nor appealed in any appreciable manner to the
audience. Large, fair, smiling, serene, there was something in
her very tranquillity that diffused itself, and when people
looked round it was because of a sudden quiet (p. 307).

She continues to create her atmosphere, especially in conversation with Isabel's husband, the subject being, upon different
occasions, a suitable husband for Pansy. Her assumption of
authority in the matter is made obvious first to Rosier, then
gradually to Isabel herself. The contrast now is not between
confidantes, but between confidante and confider. As the former continues to shine upon others in the radiance of her
cautious success, the lackluster of the latter deepens. Ralph
perceives that "if [Isabel] wore a mask it completely covered her
face. There was something fixed and mechanical in the serenity
painted on it; this was not an expression, Ralph said—it was
a representation, it was an advertisement" (p. 323).

Isabel notes the rift widening between herself and her old
confidante. At first, the young woman had kept her admiration
for the "rich sensibility" contained under the fine self-possession
of her "highly cultivated friend," and more especially for her
art of living "entirely by reason and by wisdom" (p. 331). But
by the time Madame Merle has returned to Rome from her
various travels, the third year of wedded life has elapsed for
Isabel, and she has outgrown her admiration for Madame
Merle's perfect demeanor.

She also perceives a difference, a detachment in her old
friend. With her aunt's accusation that Madame Merle made
her marriage still in mind, Isabel begins to wonder about her
scrupulosity in keeping away. In any case, in her generosity
Isabel is as yet unwilling to blame Madame Merle for her own
unhappiness.

The serenity of Madame Merle's scenes comes, however,
closer to being shattered the nearer she approaches the subject
of Pansy's marriage to Lord Warburton. In Chapters 40 and
49 she engages her erstwhile confider in a verbal fencing match
over this issue. The first of these scenes follows directly upon
Isabel's surprising Madame Merle with Osmond in her own
drawing room, and receiving a new impression of their relation.

But before she has time to reflect on this new impression, Osmond has hastily withdrawn and Madame Merle has launched into her exploratory discussion. Her aim is to discover the extent of Warburton's attachment to Pansy. To Isabel she says: "'. . . you've infinitely more observation of Lord Warburton's behaviour than I.'" Isabel responds: "'. . . Lord Warburton has let me know that he's charmed with Pansy.'" After stifling her "treacherous impulse" to betray her mother's joy at this, Madame Merle quietly resumes: "It would be very delightful; it would be a great marriage. It's really very kind of him'" (p. 339).

Having declared she will no longer encourage Mr. Rosier, for whose suit we know she had entertained some hope, Madame Merle winds up:

"I want to see her married to Lord Warburton."
"You had better wait till he asks her."
"If what you say is true, he'll ask her. Especially," said Madame Merle in a moment, "if you make him."
"If I make him?"
"It's quite in your power. You've great influence with him."
Isabel frowned a little. "Where did you learn that?"
"Mrs. Touchett told me. Not you—never!" said Madame Merle, smiling.
"I certainly never told you anything of the sort."
"You *might* have done so—so far as opportunity went—when we were by way of being confidential with each other. But you really told me very little; I've often thought so since."
Isabel had thought so too, and sometimes with a certain satisfaction. But she didn't admit it now—perhaps because she wished not to appear to exult in it. "You seem to have an excellent informant in my aunt," she simply returned (pp. 339–340).

Madame Merle then tells her how she learned from Mrs. Touchett of Isabel's declining the Lord's offer, and concludes with a glib suggestion: "'But if you wouldn't marry Lord Warburton yourself, make him the reparation of helping him to marry some one else'" (p. 340). The grotesqueness of this suggestion is entirely a breach in Madame Merle's etiquette and a deep flaw in her polish. It indicates the violent urge of the mother's interest, which stops at nothing. Isabel has already perceived that she is "too much interested" in Pansy's love-affairs, and she resists the pressure exerted by both Madame Merle and Osmond.

Once more James clears the stage, and shifts the confidantes around. It is now Henrietta's turn to enter. She arrives, determined, "perfectly unchanged," "brisk and business-like," and calls on the Countess in Florence. James brings Henrietta to the Countess for expository purposes. She seeks preliminary information about Isabel's present predicament, but she does not gain much light from Amy's morally garbled views. Having herself felt Osmond's dislike, Henrietta is going to urge Isabel " 'to make a stand' " with her husband; and she will try to see for herself whether Isabel is unhappy. Another reason for this scene is to create colorful contrast between these two minor characters, thereby brightening the last part of the novel, which at this point is growing very dark and ominous. The frivolity and spitefulness of the Countess bring out in Henrietta Stackpole only more dignity, gravity, and determination to be of assistance. Even this woman's misery touches Henrietta's good heart: ". . . there was nature in this bitter effusion [of the Countess]" (p. 374).

The first, but lesser confidante then journeys to Rome to have her big scene with the protagonist. It is Isabel's confession of unhappiness, and marks the zenith of Henrietta's role as confidante.

> She was a woman, she was a sister; she was not Ralph, nor Lord Warburton, nor Caspar Goodwood, and Isabel could speak.
> "Yes, I'm wretched," she said very mildly. She hated to hear herself say it; she tried to say it as judicially as possible.
> "What does he do to you?" Henrietta asked, frowning as if she were enquiring into the operations of a quack doctor.
> "He does nothing. He doesn't like me."
> "He's very hard to please!" cried Miss Stackpole. "Why don't you leave him?"
> "I can't change that way," Isabel said.
> "Why not, I should like to know? You won't confess that you've made a mistake. You're too proud" (pp. 399–400).

Isabel denies this and repeats that " 'One can't change that way.' " Henrietta counters: " 'You *have* changed, in spite of the impossibility' " (p. 400). It is her old theme—disaster is met in

change, while safety lies in not changing. The only remedy for
an unwise change is to change back again. By leaving Osmond
Isabel would be able to return to America and freedom once
more. Henrietta's own unchanged condition counterpoints with
the imperturbability of Madame Merle on the one side, and the
complete change in Isabel on the other. The utter honesty of
her advice to her friend acts as a foil to the counsel offered by
the Countess: "Don't try to be too good. Be a little easy and
natural and nasty; feel a little wicked, for the comfort of it, once
in your life!' " (p. 447). But Isabel rejects both the clean break
advocated by the wholesome American newspaperwoman and
the spiteful revenge suggested by the tainted expatriate. Besides
illuminating further both women's characters, the function of
this scene is to prepare for Isabel's final confession to Ralph.

The second visit of Miss Stackpole to Isabel proves unsatisfactory to herself. Not only does she fail to rescue Isabel, but
distinctly she realizes the latter's desire to be rid of her. " 'Oh,
you do give me such a sense of helplessness!' " (p. 410). That
disappointment is very bitter for a woman of Henrietta's generous and efficient nature. She has listened to Isabel's confidences, but to no practical purpose. And the correspondent who
put Europe in her pocket is nothing if not practical. The admirable woman who captivated Mr. Bantling and put him to work
in the interests of the reading public, meets with complete failure in accomplishing anything for her friend. Technically, her
role as *ficelle* is now finished.

But perhaps the saddest aspect of this scene is the moral rift
widening between them. After recognizing that Madame Merle
had a moral code differing from her own, Isabel could find some
comfort in a superior feeling. But now, the other confidante is
found to support an alien code as well: and Isabel is struck
" 'with the offhand way in which [Henrietta] speak[s] of a
woman's leaving her husband' " (p. 410). But Henrietta appeals
for her justification to the practice common in " 'our Western
cities, and it's to them, after all, that we must look in the
future' " (p. 410). The freedom of the wife to abandon her husband rests on Henrietta's modern views of emancipation.[5]
From the presentation of her arguments one feels that James
inclines toward Isabel's choice of supporting the older code.

Once she realizes her failure to convince Isabel, Henrietta wastes no time in packing up to leave; whereupon Madame Merle re-enters to have her last big scenes with her erstwhile confidante.

Returning from a visit to Naples she finds Lord Warburton departed and her dreams of a great marriage for Pansy wrecked. In Chapter 49 she accosts Isabel in their most critical scene. Madame Merle's smile "at the left corner of her mouth," that sign used several times by James to objectify the sinister element in her character, is noticeable as the scene opens. Isabel sees at once

> that her visitor's attitude was a critical one. Madame Merle, as we know, had been very discreet hitherto; she had never criticised; she had been markedly afraid of intermeddling. But apparently she had only reserved herself for this occasion, since she now had a dangerous quickness in her eye and an air of irritation which even admirable ease was not able to transmute. She had suffered a disappointment which excited Isabel's surprise—our heroine having no knowledge of her zealous interest in Pansy's marriage; and she betrayed it in a manner which quickened Mrs. Osmond's alarm. More clearly than ever before Isabel heard a cold, mocking voice proceed from she knew not where, in the dim void that surrounded her, and declare that this bright, strong, definite, worldly woman, this incarnation of the practical, the personal, the immediate, was a powerful agent in her destiny. She was nearer to her than Isabel had yet discovered, and her nearness was not the charming accident she had so long supposed (p. 420).

This intuitional perception made by Isabel marks the approaching climax of her full insight into the character of her former friend. Although Isabel had really told her very little, still her confidences had sufficed to bind her to the woman who has been "a powerful agent in her destiny." The polished surface of this woman is cracking further than in the previous scene, forced open by "a nameless vitality" surging up within her being. It is perhaps the best dramatization of Madame Merle's character, and a scene that definitely gives her the advantage over her antagonist. Borne up by her vitality and spurred on by her acute disappointment, elated also by the strength of her position, she confronts Isabel in a new role—that of the truly superior being, superior not only in manner and bearing, but infinitely superior in the thing that next to money most ensures power: knowledge. This woman *knows* more than Isabel, whose fumbling for the clue she can easily afford to smile down upon. What Madame Merle knows is of course her own connection with Osmond and his child, and the exploitation she has made of Isabel. But one thing is lacking in her fund of information, something the knowledge of which will give her even more power over her tool. Unscrupulously she inquires:

> "Just this: whether Lord Warburton changed his mind quite of his own movement or because you recommended it. To please himself I mean, or to please you. Think of the confidence I must still have in you, in spite of having lost a little of it," Madame Merle continued with a smile, "to ask such a question as that!" (p. 422).

Isabel will tell the truth if she says anything: never for a moment does Madame Merle doubt that, and by means of this honesty her enemy hopes to convict her out of her own mouth:

> "And don't you see how well it is that your husband should know it? . . . it would make a difference in his view of his daughter's prospects to know distinctly what really occurred. If Lord Warburton simply got tired of the poor child, that's one thing, and it's a pity. If he gave her up to please you it's another. That's a pity too, but in a different way. Then, in the latter case, you'd perhaps resign yourself to not being pleased— to simply seeing your stepdaughter married. Let him off—let us have him!" (p. 422).

At the height of her power, seated grandly with her mantle gathered about her and "a faint, agreeable fragrance" around her person, Madame Merle delivers this, her finest speech, with theatrical effect. The weight of the accumulated impression is too much for Isabel. A horror has seized her:

> "Who are you—what are you? . . . What have you to do with my husband? . . . What have you to do with me?" . . .
> Madame Merle slowly got up, stroking her muff, but not removing her eyes from Isabel's face. "Everything!" she answered.
> Isabel sat there looking up at her, without rising; her face was almost a prayer to be enlightened. But the light of this woman's eyes seemed only a darkness. "Oh misery!" she murmured at last; and she fell back covering her face with her

hands. It had come over her like a high-surging wave that Mrs.
Touchett was right—Madame Merle had married her (p. 423).

The relation between the confidante and her confider has
reached its utmost stage. Madame Merle, who supplanted Mrs.
Touchett in guiding Isabel into the ways of the great world, has
finally brought her to the end of that "wonderful" road—to the
brink of knowledge of good and evil—to the uttermost cleavage
between loyalty and betrayal, between friendship and exploitation. The woman whose role began in the simple guise of confidante and guide, stands now fully revealed as the principal agent
in the protagonist's life. Mrs. Tristram tries to function in this
capacity, but fails. Mrs. Assingham tries, and for a time succeeds, but finally is relegated to the background. Madame Merle
alone among James's confidantes remains supreme mistress of
the protagonist's fate. Her shapely hand is discernible even in
Isabel's final decision to return to Rome; for it was she who
primed the latter to her selfless devotion to the child. Even
though she fails in her last attempt to secure Lord Warburton,
or to extract the answer from Isabel to her last question, she still
triumphs over the latter's fate, and to the end she is almost completely mistress of herself.

The only time we see her falter much is in her third and last
scene with Osmond (Chapter 49.). Broaching the subject of
Isabel's state of shock as she has just observed it, Madame Merle
suddenly bursts into passionate remorse:

> "It was precisely my deviltry that stupefied her. I couldn't help
> it; I was full of something bad. Perhaps it was something good;
> I don't know. You've not only dried up my tears; you've dried
> up my soul.
> You made me as bad as yourself.
> Your wife was afraid of me this morning, but in me it was really
> you she feared" (pp. 427–428).

For Madame Merle herself this utterance represents a revelation
of Osmond's character: " '. . . it's only since your marriage that
I've understood you' " (p. 428). And with this understanding
has come the most bitter recognition of the falseness and futility
of her position. She has clung to Osmond for the good she could
do him and the child. " 'It's that . . . that made me so jealous of
Isabel. I want it to be *my* work,' she added, with her face, which

had grown hard and bitter, relaxing to its habit of smoothness"
(p. 429). But Osmond coldly counsels her to leave that to him,
and departs. Madame Merle is left to face her frustration alone:
" 'Have I been so vile all for nothing?' " (p. 429).

This last scene with Osmond shows a different Madame
Merle from the self-assured lady who has glided through the
novel. The author's sympathy with even this most unscrupulously designing woman is evident in these quiet touches to her
character. Readjusting her masks, however, she appears in the
parlor of Pansy's convent where she shares two final scenes with
Isabel. Both women have come to visit Pansy, who has been sent
back by her father to reflect more keenly on her duty of submis-
sion to himself. As Madame Merle enters, "Isabel saw that she
was more than ever playing a part [yet] it seemed to her that
on the whole the wonderful woman had never been so natural"
(p. 449).

Isabel, knowing now her secret from the Countess, has no
desire to speak to her; and so Madame Merle's first speech
flows on

> with much of the brilliancy of a woman who had long been a
> mistress of the art of conversation. But there were phases and
> gradations in her speech, not one of which was lost upon Isa-
> bel's ear. . . . She had not proceeded far before Isabel noted a
> sudden break in her voice, a lapse in her continuity, which was
> in itself a complete drama. This subtle modulation marked a
> momentous discovery—the perception of an entirely new atti-
> tude on the part of her listener. Madame Merle had guessed in
> the space of an instant that everything was at an end between
> them, and in the space of another instant she had guessed the
> reason why. The person who stood there was not the same one
> she had seen hitherto, but was a very different person—a person
> who knew her secret. This discovery was tremendous, and from
> the moment she made it the most accomplished of women fal-
> tered and lost her courage. But only for a moment. Then the
> conscious stream of her perfect manner gathered itself again
> and flowed on as smoothly as might be to the end (p. 450).

These lines begin the "picture" conveying the present relation between the unmasked confidante-traitor and her victim.
It is one of the finest passages in the novel. It surveys a whole
little drama of expectancy, loss of confidence, fear of exposure,

on the part of Madame Merle; and the recognition, brief triumph, and passing revenge, on the part of Isabel. For the latter, however, the feeling of revulsion overflows all else as she sees how she was used as a common tool. Her only revenge is to remain silent, so that "the cleverest woman in the world [was left] standing there within a few feet of her knowing as little what to think as the meanest" (p. 451).

So, in the life-and-death game which has engaged these two women—the struggle for superior knowledge—Isabel seems to be the final victor. She "would never accuse her, never reproach her; perhaps because she never would give her the opportunity to defend herself" (p. 451). The "cleverest woman in the world" has indeed been baffled, and she seats "herself with a movement which was in itself a confession of helplessness" (p. 451).

But during the interval between the two scenes, while Isabel is visiting Pansy, Madame Merle remains alone in the parlor. When Isabel returns, the older woman has regained her poise and has her last trump card ready. It is her last chance to reassert her waning superiority, because it is one bit of information still lacking to Isabel. Imparting it will set her at a definite and final disadvantage, for it is calculated to infuse bitterness into the last human relation offering Isabel comfort: the devotion of her dying cousin.[6]

"Your cousin did you once a great service. . . . He made you a rich woman."

"*He* made me—?"

Madame Merle appearing to see herself successful, she went on more triumphantly: "He imparted to you that extra lustre which was required to make you a brilliant match. At bottom it's him you've to thank. . . . Yes, it was your uncle's money, but it was your cousin's idea."

Isabel stood staring; she seemed to-day to live in a world illumined by lurid flashes. "I don't know why you say such things. I don't know what you know."

"I know nothing but what I've guessed. But I've guessed that" (p. 456).

Isabel never learns that Madame Merle's guess was based on information supplied again by Mrs. Touchett. The two weapons wielded so effectively by her enemies, the knowledge of her rejection of Lord Warburton and now this guess of Madame

Merle's, constitute the irony of her suffering coming to her partially through the communicativeness of her taciturn aunt. With supreme self-control she turns to her foe and speaks her only words of revenge:

> "I believed it was you I had to thank!"
>   Madame Merle dropped her eyes; she stood there in a kind of proud penance. "You're very unhappy, I know. But I'm more so."
>   "Yes, I can believe that. I think I should like never to see you again" (p. 456).

For Madame Merle to admit herself unhappy is to admit defeat. The announcement of her departure for America sounds like a new adventure, quite stripped of its glamor. In this way a dazzling role terminates. The "true agent" has accomplished her work, but not in the way she had hoped. Her frustration contrasts with the new life of promise beckoning to Henrietta.

Isabel meets this lady upon her arrival in London. She finds her the same devoted friend as ever; but a great change has at last occurred in her, for Miss Stackpole is going to give up her country. Again a flicker of comedy crosses the background of gloom. Henrietta, the comedienne, manages to lighten the tone in these last chapters. For her, the story does end as a comedy— in marriage. And the contrast between herself and the other confidante receives a final ironical twist in their reversed choices of countries. Madame Merle, who has always disdained "funny" America, will only "make a convenience" of it; but Henrietta will now be able to penetrate the "inner life" of England which heretofore has been closed to her. Isabel, briefly diverted, mentally criticizes this surprising step taken by the woman who had always represented an ideal to her. But Henrietta is not worried by having failed to measure up to her confider's romantic ideal. Instead she proves to be a realist of considerable dimensions, bright enough to change her prejudices when opportunity holds out a promise to her. Her inveterate optimism sounds the final note of the novel: " 'Look here, Mr. Goodwood . . . just you wait!' " (p. 482).

In keeping the confidantes separate, James was simplifying his treatment of each, and facilitating their separate influence on Isabel. A simultaneous action would only have defeated his purpose, for Madame Merle would, of necessity, have outshone Henrietta, and thus the "light *ficelle*" would have lost her role. Instead, James achieves the contrast of the two characters and roles by indirect reference and alternating shifts in scenes.

Henrietta's failure to save Isabel is compensated for by her own gratifying prospects. Besides Miss Hurter, she is the only confidante whose role terminates happily. Their function as comic figures explains this exemption from the customary frustration of the Jamesian confidante.

As for Serena Merle, her role as villainess in a tragedy destines her for a dark future. Her frustrations are more numerous than those of other confidantes: a loveless marriage; an episode in another man's life, from which she could emerge only as the loser; the sacrifice of her child for the sake of respectability; the failure to contract a brilliant, second marriage—all these are truly great disappointments. Ironically, pity is accorded to her only by her victim: " 'Poor woman—and Pansy who doesn't like her!' " (p. 445). The man for whom she has worked, plotted, and suffered, makes no secret of his being tired of her. Nothing, indeed, is spared her; and one is forced to admire the pride that can hold her head erect to the very end.

The difference in technical functions of "light *ficelle*" and "true agent" is consistently maintained throughout the novel. Henrietta watches Isabel from without; while Madame Merle shapes her fate from within. Both confidantes run the gamut of intimacy with, and estrangement from, their confider. But they differ in their tactics: the one is aggressive, the other suave. They differ also in their motives: the first is altruistic, the second selfish (for her child's sake). And finally they differ in their dramatic roles: Henrietta is only a foil for the more important rival confidante. The inadequacy of both women in their capacity of confidante is explained by their very characters. The American is too simple; whereas the subtle expatriate is too selfish and deep. Neither can help Isabel in her plight; even after her scene of remorse Madame Merle is incapable of begging pardon. When the confidantes fail, it is natural that the heroine's other friends should also fail to succor her. Much as Ralph and even Mrs. Touchett have tried, they are, for the most part, beyond the limits of Isabel's confidence.

The technical function of dramatizing exposition is not given to these two confidantes as exclusively as to those in the later novels. Madame Merle gives practically as much information about Osmond as Mrs. Tristram does about Claire de Cintré. In both novels, written in his early style, the author supplements this means of exposition by narration and subsidiary reporters; in *The Portrait* these reporters are old Mr. Touchett, Ralph, and the Countess Gemini. Henrietta supplies information about Mr. Goodwood and Mr. Bantling, both of minor interest. As for their eliciting information from the "center," this the confidantes do only to a limited extent; there is none of the complete recapitulation with which Strether, for instance, occupies himself in the presence of his confidante. Much of the interior analysis of Isabel's mind is carried on when she is alone, as in the famous Chapter 42.

Although Henrietta has been characterized as "simple" and Madame Merle as "subtle" and "deceitful," they are sisters in their human frailty. Miss Stackpole espouses a theory of matrimony that one hopes she will never practice on Mr. Bantling; and Madame Merle is sympathetically shown in her anguish of conscience and loss of what is dearest to her nature. Both are fully rounded characters. Their respective attitudes in regard to knowledge make their roles blend with the whole substance of the novel: Henrietta, with her prejudices, and Madame Merle with her power of knowledge, highlight in different ways their young confider, who has come to Europe to see and to learn.

Notes

1. Blackmur, p. 54. The following five references are to the Preface in this edition. (See Chapter 2 in this book.)
2. The parallels between Henrietta and Susan Stringham as confidantes have been pointed out by Ernest Sandeen, *"The Wings of the Dove* and *The Portrait of a Lady:* A Study of Henry James's Later Phase," *PMLA,* LXIX (December, 1954), 1060–1075. The author notes that Henrietta is a caricature. (See Chapter 16 in this book.)
3. *The Portrait of a Lady,* ed. Leon Edel (Boston: Houghton Mifflin Co., 1956), p. 79.
4. Her first appearance as "center" is in the scene with Mrs. Touchett (Chapter 20).
5. James's satire in this treatment of the emancipated woman was later made more explicit in *The Bostonians.*

6. James's early reflections on this point attribute a different motive to Madame Merle: " . . . Isabel . . . hesitates. Then Madame Merle, who wishes her to make a *coup de tête*, to leave Osmond, so that she may be away from Pansy, reveals to her her belief that it was Ralph who induced her [sic] father to leave her the £70,000. Isabel, then, violently affected and overcome, starts directly for England."(*Notebooks*, p. 17). (See Chapter 1 in this book.) In the novel, however, Isabel has already made arrangements to "go to England tonight." And Madame Merle recovers herself when she realizes that Isabel's motive is only Ralph's illness (p. 451). This would seem to justify my view that Madame Merle's intention is to glory in her knowledge, little else indeed being left her to glory in, although there still may be a latent desire to get rid of Isabel.

VII. The Total Novel

19 · The Portrait of a Lady

THIS IS the first of Henry James's books to sound with the ring of greatness, and in these remarks I intend to comment on some of the elements that let it ring. But first we had better put compactly what the novel is about. Isabel Archer is given the chance to do what she can with her life, thanks to her uncle's surprising bequest of some seventy thousand pounds. Everybody tampers with Isabel, and it is hard to say whether her cousin Ralph Touchett, who had arranged the bequest, or the Prince, Gilbert Osmond, who marries her because of it, tampers the more deeply. At any rate, the whole novel shows how people tamper with one another because of motives that pass like money between them. The story of the book is the story of Isabel's increasing awareness of the meaning of the relations between herself and her husband, her husband's ex-mistress Madame Merle, and the young girl Pansy Osmond (who passes as the child of the first Mrs. Osmond but is really Gilbert's daughter by Madame Merle). The money is at the center of these relations. But, surrounding these, there are also Isabel's relations with her three rejected lovers, Caspar Goodwood, Lord Warburton, and Ralph Touchett. Ralph dies, Warburton marries elsewhere; Goodwood, the ever returning signal, she finally understands, though she still rejects him, as the signal of love itself. Minor persons—Henrietta Stackpole, the Countess Gem-

From "Introduction," The Portrait of a Lady (New York, 1961), pp. 5–12. Copyright © 1961 by R. P. Blackmur and used with the permission of the publishers, Dell Publishing Co., Inc.

ini, and young Rosier—illuminate but are not part of either set
of relations, or of the devastations in which those relations result
(and in which, while we read the novel, we seem to live).

That we do not live by novels is plain enough. Novels,
rather, are sometimes ways of looking at failures and successes
—mainly failures—in human relations. Novels do not supply us
with morals but they show us with what morals have to do.
So it is with *The Portrait of a Lady*, where we see the American
Princess, Isabel Archer, brought slowly to recognize as much
as she can at the age of twenty-eight of the conditions of life.
Then, so far as the novel goes, she disappears into the ruins of
ancient Rome, which generalize for us all, and into the particular
ruins of her own marriage, which we will generalize for ourselves.
What will happen to her haunts us like a memory we cannot
quite re-enact. We have seen a bright-brash, conceited young
girl whose chief attractive power lay in her money, change into
a young woman who is luminous rather than bright, human
rather than brash, and whose conceit has turned to a suicidal
obstinacy. She still has her money but, if we can consent to
an exchange of this order, she is now worth her money. We have
seen her act with her money as an instrument of destruction,
and there is now the forward edge of a vision of money as an
instrument of freedom. This is the latent question about money
—and about morals, too—in James's novels: will they be instru-
ments of freedom or of destruction? As Henrietta Stackpole
says to Caspar Goodwood at the very end of the book: "Just
you wait!"

Miss Stackpole with her button eyes meant whatever one
wants her to mean; I should like her to have meant something
relating to the quality of human judgment as Isabel comes to
acquire and to ignore it. I hear Lord Warburton telling her
when she is quite fresh in England, "You judge only from the
outside—you don't care . . . you only care to amuse yourself"
—words which he spoke with a bitterness abrupt and inconsequent in his voice. But I hear more clearly still these words of
Madame Merle: "I judge more than I used to," she said to
Isabel, "but it seems to me one has earned the right. One can't
judge till one's forty; before that we're too eager, too hard, too
cruel, and in addition much too ignorant." Madame Merle has

more to say, which ends in this way: "I want to see what life makes of you. One thing's certain—it can't spoil you. It may pull you about horribly, but I defy it to break you up."

Madame Merle's own life, whatever the quality of her judgment, had not done so well by her. Her condition is such that she wishes to weep, to howl like a wolf, and she feels the pressure, in the company of Osmond, of "their *common* crimes." As she tells him, "You have made me as bad as yourself." But Madame Merle was false, and Isabel is given as by and large likely to be true. Madame Merle was enslaved by passions she no longer felt; Isabel, in the novel's scheme of things, should be liberated in the passion that as the book ends she has begun to feel, but which she must flee either in acceptance or renunciation—or in some peculiar state where the one doubles for the other: a shifting state, somehow not evasion, in which the sensibilities of James's heroes and heroines so often transpire. It is as well that we shall never know how Isabel might come to join her sensibility both in judgment and action. Literature is perhaps not capable of making such answers, except in the form of promises. Rather it brings us only to the threshold of discovery.

We are brought by pedagogy, by education, by training. We see Isabel change, and we see what Isabel sees as she changes and also something of what she cannot or will not or is not yet ready to see—and especially the things she has succeeded in not knowing. That is what pedagogy, education, training are like in the novel. It is for the reader to see under these heads what the heroine experienced in different degrees of aptness and response. (If experience were learned like the alphabet or the integers there would be no novels and life would be over very quickly; we should be thankful in both cases that we are such slow students. Just the same the alphabet and the integers are first helps.) In short, the novelist is offering her heroine the education suitable for her role.

The American Princess, whether Isabel Archer or another, always comes to us as innocent as possible, as innocent as the victim who reigns—yet, precisely because of that innocence, predatory to the fingernails upon all who come within her reach. She has, to begin with, only what she inherits. Doubtless she has been somewhere to school but she has never received any training for her job. In this respect she is not unlike another and once better known American production, nature's nobleman. But what will do quite well for one of nature's noblemen will not do at all for an American princess. The heiress to all the ages (James's own phrase) should at least know something about the age she lives in and perhaps what it has in common with the ages she inherits. It is not surprising that James's princesses, getting their training only on the job, come to bad ends, to abdication, death, or deep frustration. Yet the books these princesses inhabit constitute essays in training for active rule. It is a training they do not quite catch up with for themselves, although they often can apply it in looking at others. In Isabel's case, it sometimes seems she ought to have applied to herself the language of her mind in looking at others. Here, for example, is Isabel looking at her rightful lover, Caspar Goodwood, when he descends on her in Italy.

> Caspar Goodwood stood there—stood and received a moment, from head to foot, the bright, dry gaze with which she rather withheld than offered a greeting. Whether his sense of maturity had kept pace with Isabel's we shall perhaps presently ascertain; let me say meanwhile that to her critical glance he showed nothing of the injury of time. Straight, strong and hard, there was nothing in his appearance that spoke positively either of youth or of age; if he had neither innocence nor weakness, so he had no practical philosophy. His jaw showed the same voluntary cast as in earlier days; but a crisis like the present had in it of course something grim. He had the air of a man who had travelled hard; he said nothing at first, as if he had been out of breath. This gave Isabel time to make a reflexion: "Poor fellow, what great things he's capable of, and what a pity he should waste so dreadfully his splendid force! What a pity too that one can't satisfy everybody!"

As it turned out, it was Caspar Goodwood alone of her lovers whom she could neither deal with nor evade, unless by flight; this she was not ready to know, at that moment or when we leave her. For the present she thought she could deal with him merely by again rejecting him on the eve of her marriage to Gilbert Osmond—a marriage and a groom none of her friends approve, except perhaps Madame Merle who had arranged it all.

There are moments when the force of marriage—not love but
marriage—is greater than the force of the individuals who must
endure it. Isabel no doubt thought herself strengthened, when
merely bent or deflected, by that force. We know rather better
than Isabel and know partly because of one of her own insights
into Madame Merle which she had reached at about the time
she became engaged. Listening to that lady's long account of
herself during their trip to Greece and Egypt, Isabel got the
impression they came from different moral and social climes.
"She believed then that at bottom she had a different morality.
Of course the morality of civilized persons has always much in
common; but our young woman had a sense in her of values
gone wrong or, as they said in the shops, marked down."
Madame Merle was lady-in-waiting to this princess *incognita*
(James's phrase) and set up for her a court decadent beyond her
understanding and full of things and motives "of which it was
not advantageous to hear." We observe that at this point in her
education Isabel develops a deliberate deafness, as if deafness
were a special form of consciousness, nearly equivalent to what
she is learning to hear. I will not say this leaves her more vulnerable, but it certainly leaves her more exposed to fresh assaults
she could otherwise have avoided.

Innocence does not act, unless impaired by self-will and
self-deceit; that is to say innocence proceeds as a kind of infatuation without an object until it bursts or is punctured. Then,
since innocence is irrecoverable, there is, together with the dev-
astation, a necessary accommodation to be made, either a death
or a life, an abdication or an assumption—or, as we began by
saying, a renunciation or an acceptance. How long Isabel's
innocence lasted we do not exactly know. It is present in nearly
full force at the end of Chapter XXXV—more than half the
length of the novel—when on the suggestion that a little girl,
her step-daughter to be, be asked to leave the room, Isabel
responds: "Let her stay, please. . . . I would rather hear nothing
that Pansy may not." In the next chapter, three years later in
time, the innocence is virtually gone, but its consequences remain mingled with the many-troubled marriage in which we
find her. Self-will has been replaced with the effort to achieve a
will, and self-deceit has become the deceit of others. The public

and the private in her relations have now been reversed. Where so much of her that had been private was now forced into the public, what had been her public ease was now a matter of unremitting private concern. Where previously she had had to bring her life into existence, she had now to conceal the one that had come upon her. She had not only to face a civilized morality where her values were marked down, she had also to act by a morality whose values were not hers at all—as if there were a double morality with different degradations in each. She still expected too much for the one, and she had both the wrong illusions and the wrong disillusions for the other. Nothing was clear except that her husband "spoiled everything for her that he looked at"—an obscure form of intimacy she had certainly not been prepared for. She knew only, and this not too clearly, that without Madame Merle "these things need not have been." If Madame Merle had been the force from behind, little Pansy seemed now to be the only force to draw her on— as if where her own conceited innocence had failed her, the girl could succeed in her obedient naïveté and her naïve inner rebellion against the "base, ignoble world," which yet provided the standards and scope if not the springs of compulsive action.

Isabel's first and partial *éclaircissement* comes when after a walk with Pansy among the delicate winter flowers of the Roman Campagna, she "discovered" her husband and Madame Merle in the drawing-room. "The soundlessness of her step gave her time to take in the scene before she interrupted it. Madame Merle was there in her bonnet, and Gilbert Osmond was talking to her; for a minute they were unaware she had come in. Isabel had often seen that before, certainly; but what she had not seen, or at least had not noticed, was that their colloquy had for the moment converted itself into a sort of familiar silence, from which she instantly perceived that her entrance would startle them. . . . The thing made an image, lasting only a moment, like a sudden flicker of light. Their relative positions, their absorbed mutual gaze, struck her as something detected. But it was all over by the time she had fairly seen it."

It was all over so far as her consciousness went, but a larger form of it had entered what Freud calls the preconscious, thence to emerge from time to time—as it did that very night when she had lingered to all hours alone in her salon. It was dark in the big room. "But even then she stopped again in the middle of the room and stood there gazing at a remembered vision—that of her husband and Madame Merle unconsciously and familiarly associated." It is not conscious knowledge, or fresh knowledge, but the knowledge one did not know that one knew, or but dimly knew, that bursts upon one, an access of strength; and it bursts from inside where it has been nurtured with every unconscious skill. So it is with Isabel as she develops her judgment of her husband into action. The nurtured knowledge comes clear throughout, as it were, on the pages of fierce and eloquent polemic, those wonderful creative summaries of his character and sensibility, that are reported as a kind of constitution for her thoughts between the apparitions of the image of relations he has with Madame Merle, and into which we the readers can pour our own possibilities of coldness and egotism and greed, of worldly dilettantism without delight, of spiritual caddishness. It is the image that gives the meditations focus, and the meditations that give the image meaning.

What more is James telling us when he puts these sentences into his report of a discussion of Pansy's affairs between Isabel and Madame Merle? "More clearly than ever before Isabel heard a cold, mocking voice proceed from she knew not where, in the dim void that surrounded her, and declare that this bright, strong, definite worldly woman, this incarnation of the practical, the personal, the immediate, was a powerful agent in her destiny." A moment or two later, the *éclaircissement* was complete, except for the history and special treachery of what was illuminated. "She moved quickly indeed, and with reason, for a strange truth was filtering into her soul. Madame Merle's interest was identical with Osmond's: that was enough." The meaning of their history together, and with her, had become plain, though the history itself remained obscure and though it had been affecting her, almost absorbing her, all along.

The discovery that Pansy was daughter to Madame Merle and Osmond joined the history to the meaning. There were all sorts of things, as Osmond's sister Countess Gemini tells her, that Isabel had succeeded in not knowing, but which, as Isabel puts it, had nevertheless *occurred* to her. Now that these things had become available to knowledge as well as to experience, she could complete her judgment of Osmond. She could disobey him, leave him in Rome, and attend her cousin Ralph's death in England; and if she returned to Rome it was with another purpose than she had left it with, and with a new energy, greater in scope and intensity than before, though still with an object not altogether clear. At least she could now play her role if she could find it, and there is no place better than Rome to find a role for a princess without a proper domain. Rome is the city of Annunciation and Incarnation as well as ruins. Some such image awaits *éclaircissement* when we last see Isabel and enter her feelings. If she had renounced, it was for the sake of a later resumption, though it might be that at any given moment she might not know it—as if knowledge, for her, could never be quite *yet!* It is in souls like Isabel's, not invented by Henry James but seen by him in anguished clarity, that flight, as I said above, is the first form either of renunciation or acceptance, where the one may be taken as doubling for the other. We last see Isabel on the verge of such a flight—a flight that might have any and every meaning, whatever its subsequent history—a flight from the man whom she had at last known to be her rightful lover.

I will quote nothing of this; it belongs to the reader's own participation. I will quote instead a few fragments from the long, enlivening analogy to the story of Isabel Archer, the continuing image of Rome's ruins which sit, at any moment ready to rise, throughout that city's immediate life. The experience of cities is no longer intimate, and needs reminding. Here is Isabel, treading upon the daisies, which are like American daisies only in being endemic. "She had long before this taken old Rome into her confidence, for in a world of ruins the ruin of her happiness seemed a less unnatural catastrophe. She rested her weariness upon things that had crumbled for centuries, and yet still were upright. . . . She had become deeply, tenderly acquainted with Rome: it interfused and moderated her passion. But she had grown to think of it chiefly as the place where people had suffered." And again, from another page, one sentence about the Coliseum: "The great enclosure was half in shadow; the western sun brought out the pale red tone of the great blocks of travertine—the latent colour that is the only living element in the immense ruin." It is the latent colour of Isabel's vitality we know best as the book ends: a vitality which became, through the money her cousin had gotten for her, an instrument both of freedom and destruction. The money had indeed put wind in her sails, but whether it had made her rich enough to meet the requirements of her imagination is another matter. That there may be no such riches is perhaps what the look in the eyes of this portrait of a lady is saying.

20 · The Portrait of a Lady

To his brother William, in partial response to that brother's criticism of his fiction, Henry James confided on December 16, 1879, "I have determined that the novel I write this next year shall be 'big.' " [1] The most obvious implication of "big" here is "bigger"—bigger in dimensions, bigger in scope than any of his previous novels. Yet perhaps a clearer definition of the adjective may be got from a brief examination of Henry's comments on the large-scale productions of a novelist whom he then greatly admired, George Eliot. "*Romola* sins by excess of analysis; there is too much description and too little drama . . ."; hence a "big" novel may be analytical so long as its dramatic values are not subordinated. In *Middlemarch* James hoped for "an organized, molded, balanced composition, gratifying the reader with a sense of design and construction," but he found "a mere chain of episodes, broken into accidental lengths and unconscious of the influence of a plan." "The passion for the special case," he emphatically declared in an essay devoted to his fellow novelist's life, "is surely the basis of the story teller's art"; but he felt that George Eliot had swamped "the special case" by natural rather than systematic detail, by philosophy, by "the universe." So, too, *Middlemarch*, intended to present a picture of "an ardent young girl . . . framed for a larger moral life than circumstance often affords," becomes a detail in a panorama without compactness, rather than the focus, the central figure. Dorothea Brooke's

From *The Novels of Henry James* (New York, 1961), pp. 78–119. by permission of The Macmillan Company from *The Novels of Henry James* by Oscar Cargill. © 1961 Oscar Cargill.

unfortunate marriage to the "dry" and pedantic Casaubon has tragic overtones, but it lacks "the great dramatic *chiaroscuro*" which a steadily lighted center with a deliberately dulled background can give. Repeatedly James speaks with approval of the "moral" elevation of Eliot's novels, and he carefully defines "moral" as "the reaction of thought in the face of the human comedy." Excellent indeed as is the realism of Balzac, it is "a finer thing to unlock with as firm a hand as George Eliot some of the great chambers of human character." [2]

At the end of the seventies, then, James conceived a "big" novel as primarily the presentation of a "special case," a dramatic portrait of a carefully focused central figure, with every detail subordinated to that focus, the portrait itself to exhibit a luminous virtue in dark and tragic circumstances. The story of Isabel Archer is meant to meet fully and without excess these stringent limitations and ample prescriptions for the "big" novel.

II

Henry James tells us that he had completely possessed "the central image" for the *The Portrait of a Lady* [3] "for a long time" and that he harbored for fully as long a "pious desire" to place his "treasure right." The big advance in doing so came with the inspiration to make his heroine focal rather than contributory, which neither Shakespeare nor George Eliot, however deeply interested in their heroines, had done, and to center everything in her consciousness, particularly emphasizing her view of herself. After that he seemed "to have waked up one morning" in possession not merely of his other characters but also of their relations to Isabel Archer—the "concrete terms" of his plot.[4] The obvious affection of all his references to his heroine, together with his refusal in his prefatory recollection to retrace precisely how he became possessed of her image, has led to the natural conclusion that she was a person in the author's past and of consequence to him. The first apparently to proclaim her identity to the world was the novelist's nephew, who, in editing his father's letters, remarked in regard to Mary ("Minny") Temple, "Henry James drew two of his most appealing heroines from her image, Minny [sic] Theale in *Wings of the Dove* and Isabel Archer in *The Portrait of a Lady*." [5]

There are two initial difficulties in the way of accepting without hesitation the flat identification supplied by James's nephew: Isabel Archer seems quite a different person from Milly Theale,[6] and in *Notes of a Son and Brother* James seems to indicate only one full usage of his memory of Minny Temple: "she would have given anything to live—and the image of this, which was long to remain with me, appeared so of the essence of tragedy that I was *in the far-off aftertime* to seek to lay the ghost by wrapping it, *a particular occasion aiding*, in the beauty and dignity of art." [7] Do not the emphases on the time span and on the particular occasion point somewhat exclusively to Milly Theale as the character created from Henry James's recollection of his gallant invalid cousin, rather than to Isabel Archer?

Yet the view that Isabel Archer was based exclusively on the memory of Minny Temple has the support of the best informed of all Jamesian scholars, Leon Edel, who cites an unpublished letter to Grace Norton in reply to one of hers identifying the heroine with the deceased cousin. "You are both right and wrong about Minny Temple. I had her in mind and there is in the heroine a considerable infusion of my impression of her remarkable nature. But the thing is not a portrait. Poor Minny was essentially *incomplete* and I have attempted to make my young woman more rounded, more finished." Rejecting the idea of any considerable literary supplementation to the rounding out of the original, given figure, Edel adds, "This is quite true. Minny had died without ever going to Europe." The inference is that James "completed" the rounding of his cousin's image by the fictional adventures he gave his heroine in Europe.[8]

The letter to Grace Norton does not appear to me quite so conclusive as Edel judges it to be. James wrote it from Falmouth, England, on December 28, 1880, which means that, at best, Miss Norton had seen only the second installment of the serial in the *Atlantic*—not the full presentation of the heroine. Further, James's letter is a polite remonstrance at conclusions drawn at this stage. He owed a good deal to the Nortons, and he would hardly have intimated to Grace, any more than Melville did to Mrs. Hawthorne, that her guess was completely wrong, even if

it were. He would have taken recourse in "You are both right
and wrong. . . ." [9]

Opposed to the autobiographical theory of Isabel Archer's
creation is the contention that her portrait is copied from that
of Gwendolen Harleth in George Eliot's *Daniel Deronda*. In
one of the earliest reviews of *The Portrait of a Lady*, W. C.
Brownell indicated the possibility of an indebtedness to George
Eliot in pointing out that the relations of the Osmonds were
like those of the Lydgates in *Middlemarch*.[10] Joseph Warren
Beach, however, found a much more convincing parallel between George Eliot's drawing of Gwendolen Harleth and
Grandcourt in *Daniel Deronda* and James's portrayal of Isabel
Archer and Gilbert Osmond than *Middlemarch* provided.[11]
Cornelia Kelley, bringing into the discussion the "conversation
piece" that James had written by way of a review of *Daniel
Deronda* when that novel had completed its serial run, writes
with assurance, "From James's article more than from George
Eliot's novel, it is clear that Gwendolen Harleth was the prototype of Isabel Archer, for the points which James noted about
Gwendolen are the points which a critic must note about his
heroine. . . . Isabel's story, broadly looked at, is the same as
Gwendolen's. . . . Osmond's refined and distilled brutality is
like that of Grandcourt." She concedes, however, Brownell's
point, "Ralph's helpless devotion is related to that of Will
Ladislaw in *Middlemarch*." [12] The most detailed examination
of the indebtedness of James to *Daniel Deronda* for his characterization of Isabel and her husband is that of F. R. Leavis,[13]
who terms *The Portrait* a mere *variation* on the Gwendolen
Harleth-Grandcourt story: "Isabel Archer is Gwendolen Harleth
seen by a man. . . . Osmond so plainly is Grandcourt, hardly
disguised, that the general derivative relation of James's novel
to George Eliot's becomes quite unquestionable." [14] The Beach-
Kelley-Leavis case is a very strong one, but both Miss Kelley
and Leavis are a little too insistent that James's comprehension
of Gwendolen is summarized in a single speech by Theodora
in the "conversation piece" on *Daniel Deronda*:

> . . . Gwendolen is a perfect picture of youthfulness—its eager-
> ness, its presumption, its preoccupation with itself, its vanity

and silliness, its sense of its absoluteness. But she is extremely intelligent and clever, and therefore tragedy can have a hold on her.[15]

James, however, allows another character in the piece, Pulcheria, to take quite a different view of Gwendolen:

... when the author tries to invest her with interest she does so at the expense of consistency. She has made her at the outset too light, too flimsy. ... She [Gwendolen] was *personally* selfish ... an odious young woman, and one doesn't care what becomes of her. When her marriage turned out ill she would have become still more hard and positive; to make her soft and appealing is very bad logic.[16]

Obviously James meant neither of these commentators to be wholly right; Theodora sees her better than she actually is, and the comment describes a character closer to Isabel than is the original, who surely is as accurately described (that is, the Gwendolen of Books I–IV) by Pulcheria as by Theodora. Did James make no use of the idea of limitations suggested by George Eliot's first presentation of her heroine?

The truth would seem to be that Isabel Archer, though she is the most appealing of the lot, belongs, with Gwendolen Harleth, to a gallery of *limited* heroines, the great prototype of whom was the Emma of Jane Austen. George Eliot imposed such limitations at the outset on her heroine, in James's judgment, that to reinvest her with sympathy was impossible. To avoid this error became an initial creative problem for the novelist and took him beyond the suggestions of *Daniel Deronda* or the "conversation piece" related to it. After remarking that Isabel's "errors and delusions were frequently such as a biographer interested in preserving the dignity of his subject must shrink from specifying," James nevertheless gives, after the fashion of George Eliot,[17] a rather extended and acute summary of them in a long passage at the beginning of Chapter VI and concludes with:

Altogether, with her meagre knowledge, her inflated ideals, her confidence at once innocent and dogmatic, her temper at once exacting and indulgent, her mixture of curiosity and fastidiousness, of vivacity and indifference, her desire to look very well and to be if possible even better, her determination to see, to try, to know, her combination of the delicate, desultory, flame-like spirit and the eager and personal creature of conditions: she would be an easy victim of scientific criticism if she were not intended to awaken on the reader's part an impulse more tender and more purely expectant.

These are, in the main, American limitations, but there is such a characteristic bundle of them that Isabel loses all resemblance to Gwendolen, on the one hand, and to Minny Temple, on the other, that is, save as Minny possessed characteristic traits of American girlhood, of which James was by this time an acute observer. It is Isabel's independence—surely a most American trait—that is most often emphasized, observes Arnold Kettle, so much so, that, in his judgment, the theme of *The Portrait* "is the revelation of the inadequacy of Isabel's view of freedom." [18] Mrs. Touchett may point up the author's intention to make Isabel in a certain sense representative: "I found her in an old house in Albany . . . boring herself to death. . . . It occurred to me that it would be a kindness to take her about and introduce her to the world. She thinks she knows a great deal about it—like most American girls, but like most American girls she's ridiculously mistaken." [19] She was meant to be a fuller and more adequate person, despite her characteristic American limitations to offset Daisy Miller with the American public.

But along with her characteristic native faults, she had one idiosyncrasy not possessed by Gwendolen Harleth: although James draws her from the first as capable of deep sexual arousal, he also delineates her as cautious, theoretical, and inhibited; and the touch is satiric, as shown by this extract from the extended analysis of her character in Chapter VI:

. . . Of course, among her theories, this young lady was not without a collection of views on the subject of marriage. The first on the list was a conviction of the vulgarity of thinking too much of it. From lapsing into eagerness on this point she earnestly prayed she might be delivered; she held that a woman ought to be able to live to herself, in the absence of exceptional flimsiness, and that it was perfectly possible to be happy without the society of a more or less coarse minded person of another sex. The girl's prayer was sufficiently answered; something pure and proud that there was in her—something cold and dry an unappreciated suitor with a taste for analysis might have called it—had hitherto kept her from any great vanity of conjecture on the article of possible husbands. . . . Deep in her soul—it was the deepest thing there—lay the belief that if a certain light should dawn she could give herself completely; but this image, on the whole, was too formidable to be attractive. . . .

Isabel's formidable limitation suggests one of the least appealing of his early heroines—Mme de Mauves—but whereas James had presented that young woman's frigidity toward her erring husband and lover as a product largely of her convent training, here it is made intrinsic. But much closer to the time of the actual conception of his novel James in 1878 produced a romantic tale for *Scribner's*, a magazine for which he had a low regard but which paid him exceptionally well, entitled "Longstaff's Marriage," with a heroine, Diana Belfield, significantly named after the "queen and huntress, chaste and fair" in whom Isabel's limitation was made an impeccable virtue by the ancients. In Miss Belfield, however, it is no virtue; rejecting a proposal of marriage by a wealthy young consumptive who would confer on her his fortune, she suffers the revenge of her own nature when she tardily becomes inflamed for him and finds him recovered from his illness and no longer interested. Of Diana Belfield her creator writes:

> . . . she had had, in vulgar parlance, a hundred offers. To say that she had declined them is to say too little; she had really scorned them . . . it was not her suitors in themselves; it was simply the idea of marrying. She found it insupportable; a fact which completes her analogy to the mythic divinity to whom I have likened her. She was passionately single, fiercely virginal; and in the straight-glancing grey eye which provoked men to admire, there was a certain silvery ray which forbade them to hope.[20]

"Longstaff's Marriage" is certainly related in a generic way to *The Portrait of a Lady*, through the consumptive, hopeless lover, who suggests Ralph; through Diana's traveling companion, Miss Agatha Gosling, who has some of Henrietta's traits; and through the heroine herself, who not only has Isabel's marked idiosyncrasy but whose very name, Diana, obviously suggested the choice of "Archer" as the heroine's family name in *The Portrait*. [21]

But relating Isabel Archer and Diana Belfield does not establish their limiting trait as James's invention. I am aided in finding the most plausible source of this by Professor William Gibson, who, having noted the similarities of the names Goodwood and Boldwood, suggested to me that Thomas Hardy's *Far from the Madding Crowd* might be examined as a source for elements in *The Portrait of a Lady*. James had reviewed this novel unfavorably in the *Nation* on December 24, 1874, where he had characterized Bathsheba Everdene, the heroine, as "a young lady of the inconsequential, wilful, mettlesome type . . . the type which aims at giving one a very intimate sense of a young lady's *womanishness* . . . a flirt." [22] But Bathsheba is by no means consistently portrayed, and James could hardly have missed Hardy's summation of her attitude toward the other sex:

> Until she met Troy, Bathsheba had been proud of her position as a woman; it had been a glory to her to know that her lips had been touched by no man's on earth—that her waist had never been encircled by a lover's arm. . . . In those early days she had always nourished a secret contempt for girls who were the slaves of the first good-looking fellow who should choose to salute them. She had never taken kindly to the idea of marriage in the abstract. . . . In the turmoil of her anxiety for her lover she had agreed to marry him; but the perception that had accompanied her happiest hours on this account was rather that of self-sacrifice than of promotion and honour. Although she scarcely knew the divinity's name, Diana was the goddess whom Bathsheba instinctively adored. That she had never by word, look, or sign encouraged a man to approach her—that she had felt herself sufficient to herself, and had in the independence of her girlish heart fancied there was a certain degradation in renouncing the simplicity of a maiden existence to become the humbler half of an indifferent matrimonial whole— were facts now bitterly remembered. . . . [23]

That James drew on *Far from the Madding Crowd* is demonstrated not only because both heroines belong to the court of Diana and because the love-sick madness of Farmer Boldwood may have suggested the violence of Caspar Goodwood, but also because in the famous final scene when Isabel is passionately kissed by Goodwood the author thinks of the experience in Hardyesque terms of natural violence, actually imitating the description of a scene he had admired in his review. [24]

All of this goes merely to prove that Isabel Archer is a rich, synthesized figure about which the novelist had reflected a long time, gathering material from a variety of sources. With her faults she is hardly a memorial to anyone and had he had solely such a tribute to his dead cousin in mind he would not have written his father, "I am working with great ease, relish, and success" nor have enrolled himself among the "happy producers."[25] But this is far from saying that Isabel's portrait is devoid of autobiographical touches. "Another possible source of the living quality James was able to impart to Isabel Archer," Fred B. Millett writes, "is his bestowal on her of a considerable number of traits of his own younger self." Like himself, Isabel was thrice taken to Europe by her father before she was fourteen; she has James's own passion for experience, and she reacts, as he did, against "the detestable *American* Paris." Millett even cites a parallel passage for Isabel's drive with her stepdaughter into the Campagna from James's personal experience.[26] Into the conglomerate, it would be foolish to deny, James poured certainly some of his recollections of the young women whom he had known, including a few of those of Minny Temple.[27] Edel is certainly impressive in arguing that some of the feeling which Ralph betrays to Isabel in their final encounter is coined out of James's emotion over the death of his cousin.[28] In developing the affection of Pansy Osmond for Isabel, he may very well have recalled how the daughter of Frank Boott discovered a "quick affinity" for Minny Temple.[29] It is perhaps only in the scenes which involve the expression of the simplest and purest affection that James thought of his cousin. This seems capable of some demonstration, but to go further than this, in the face of the literary indebtedness, *which may not yet be fully explored*, is to indulge in pure conjecture.

III

Gilbert Osmond, who became Isabel's evil fate, cost the novelist far less reflection. One of the least acceptable theses about Osmond's creation is that of F. W. Dupee, who writes:

> Isabel herself . . . is clearly a tribute to the meaning of Minny Temple. . . . Among the men who surrounded her, two

could clearly have been related to James himself. Her cousin
Ralph Touchett . . . was perhaps James's idea of what he had
actually been to Minny Temple; while the terrible Osmond,
esthete and snob, on whose too refined nerves Isabel preys in
spite of herself, represented the kind of husband he fearfully
fancied he might have made had he actually married Minny.[30]

If the portrait of Isabel Archer is not "a tribute to the memory
of Minny Temple," Dupee's thesis has very shaky scaffolding
under it, indeed. He is apparently unaware that James has given
an account of some of the elements synthesized in the creation
of Gilbert Osmond which is at variance with his construction.
In *Notes of a Son and Brother*, James indicates that Frank
Boott, "an Italianate bereft American with a little moulded
daughter in the setting of a massive Tuscan residence was . . .
exactly what was required by a situation of my own . . . but he
had . . . not a grain of the non-essential in common with my
Gilbert Osmond." [31] All that is contemptible in Osmond, however, his calculated coldness, pride, and arrogance, may be found
in George Eliot's Henleigh Grandcourt. Osmond is a smaller
man than Grandcourt; the latter's wealth and Gwendolen's dependence make it more plausible that she marry and remain
with him; Lush gives him a vulgarity that Osmond does not
have; but Osmond's cold flesh makes him more repulsive than
is the arrogant Grandcourt. We are reminded of Chettam's cry
against Casaubon in *Middlemarch,* " 'Good God! It is horrible!
He is no better than a mummy!' " Frank Boott, Grandcourt,
and Casaubon (with the latter, aestheticism is substituted for
scholarship) provided the elements in the composition of the
"detestable" Osmond.

    Osmond is Henry James's most completely evil character.
Lyall H. Powers has found such characters supplemented and
symbolized by "those conventions and institutions whose nature
is dehumanizing" and, in the instance of Osmond, by the
Roman Catholic Church. He confesses to Isabel early in their
acquaintance to a commitment to propriety so extreme that she
does not take him seriously:

> "You say you don't know me, but when you do you'll dis-
> cover what a worship I have for propriety."

"You're not conventional?" Isabel gravely asked.

"I like the way you utter that word! No, I'm not conventional: I'm convention itself. . . ."

Osmond also confesses to Isabel that he has " 'envied the Pope of Rome—for the consideration he enjoys' "; and on her reminding him, " 'you ought indeed to be a Pope!' " Osmond admits, " 'Ah, I should have enjoyed that!' " Isabel returns again to the question, " 'You'd like to be Pope?' " and Osmond— " 'I should love it.' " Powers calls attention to the fact that it is in St. Peter's itself that Osmond "notably" resumes his pursuit of Isabel: "He now approached with all the forms—he appeared to have multiplied them on this occasion to suit the place." Once he is successful, he and his bride take up residence "in a high house in the very heart of Rome." That high house, the Palazzo Roccanera ("the Black Rock Palace"), Powers might have noted, carries in its title a possible sinister reinforcement of his theme.[33] Powers sees the use that Osmond makes of the convent in subduing Pansy a further symbolization of the resort to the dehumanizing process, for even a kindly remark by Mme Catherine, the mother superior, "seemed to represent the surrender of personality, the authority of the Church." [34] But we must avoid seeing sectarian allegory in all this, even though Isabel, in realizing the true nature of her husband, may use a familiar religious simile: "He took himself so seriously, it was something appalling. Under all his culture, his cleverness, his amenity, his egotism lay hidden like a serpent in a bank of flowers." To that end it will help us to remember Isabel's own extremism. James has ironically married fearful opposites— Isabel represents the ultimate of American idealism of her time and Osmond the ultimate of European orthodoxy in the same day. They are incompatible from the start, each deceived about the other because neither had any experience with the type of person the other was. Because Gilbert Osmond is wholly evil in his relation to Isabel his personal limitations are no reflection on his Church.[35] In fact, it should be noted that the most important representative of his Church in the novel, Mme Catherine, says that Pansy has had enough of the convent before Osmond himself relents in his punishment of her. It is not certain that she even approves of that punishment.

Nineteenth century fiction is full of faithful but unrequited lovers; hence one should not conclude as hastily as most Jamesian critics have that the admirable Ralph Touchett is none other than a self-portrait, barring physical differences. Yet the case is initially stronger for autobiographical elements in his composition than for any other in the novel. Putting aside his assumption that Isabel is Minny, Ernest Sandeen presents the fullest argument for semi-self-identification on the part of the novelist:

> Ralph Touchett is not literally an autobiographical character but he is closely related to his author. . . . Specifically what he wants to do is what James does for so many of his characters and for the same reason, i.e., Ralph wants to furnish Isabel with money so that she may be free to use her inner resources to the full. . . . The only good Ralph expects for himself, he says, is " 'that of having met the requirements of my imagination.' ". . . A practical purpose is served by Ralph's affliction. It eliminates him as a suitor of Isabel and therefore . . . what he does for her springs from disinterested motives. . . . Again an autobiographical parallel obtrudes. At the time when James might have regarded Mary Temple with the eyes of a lover, he was himself an invalid and therefore, he believed, not qualified as a suitor. He complained to William after Minny's death: "She never knew how sick and disordered a creature I was and I always felt that she knew me at my worst. . . ."[36]

In Roger Laurence in *Watch and Ward* James had created a character with considerable means willing to employ them to the heroine's improvement, and he repeated the idea, as we have seen, in "Longstaff's Marriage" with the added element of invalidism. One cannot quite ignore, however, the cousinship which George Sand made central in her novel, *Indiana*. Sir Ralph Brown, introverted and inept, is cousin, as well as the devoted protector and silent lover, of the frail and sickly heroine, Indiana. By concealing from her that Raymon de Ramière was the seducer of her maid and responsible for the latter's suicide and by warning her of the unexpected approach of her husband, the elderly Colonel Delmare, Ralph promotes the affair which she has with Raymon and, like Ralph Touchett, brings her much misfortune. Sand's novel bristles with suggestions James may have found usable in his *Portrait*. The naïveté of Indiana, her childhood in a distant and simple society, her unhappy marriage to an older man suggest Isabel's situation; transfer her illness to Sir Ralph, and he has many of the traits of Isabel's cousin: he even offers to share his wealth with Colonel Delmare when the latter loses his fortune. Most important, too, is the fact that Indiana, having deserted her husband, returns to him of her own free will.[37]

To look further, the hopelessly devoted adorer in the British novel ranges from Robert Martin to Will Ladislaw to Gabriel Oak, but devoted invalids are fewer. George Eliot provides, however, an arresting example of a devoted invalid lover in the hunchback Philip Wakem of *The Mill on the Floss*. Like Ralph Touchett, Philip brings disaster to the heroine through a well-meant act of kindness when he achieves the surrender of Dorlcote Mill, where Maggie and her brother Tom lose their lives, to the Tullivers. James grasped the irony of this, purged it of its elements of self-interest and sensationalism, gave it a larger moral ambiguity, and made it the fatal error in his novel. Mr. Wakem is not the banker Touchett, yet has the same affection for his son; and it is his property, as it is Touchett's, that is transferred at his son's behest. There is, connected with Maggie Tulliver's fate, the legend of a "ghostly boatman who haunts the Floss" which must have suggested to James the Gardencourt legend and the presence felt by Isabel the night of her cousin's death. Like Isabel in her last interview with Ralph, Maggie feels that Philip, in his last penetrating, analytical but tender letter, with its confession of illness and hint of death, understands her better than anyone else. Whatever autobiographical elements James superimposed, whatever he borrowed from the characterization of Will Ladislaw by way of detached artistic interest, concealed devotion, wit, and cousinship (they are all there), one cannot help but feel that James's germinal idea for the characterization of Ralph Touchett came from George Sand's portrayal of Sir Ralph and from George Eliot's limning and exploiting of Philip Wakem.[38]

One may suspect the same synthetic treatment accorded Isabel, Osmond, and Ralph with most of the other principals in *The Portrait*. We have noted a preliminary sketch for Henrietta Stackpole in Agatha Gosling of "Longstaff's Marriage";

Leon Edel sees her prototype in a young American female who came over to London just before James wrote his novel "armed with a letter from his brother, and Henry described her to William as the 'literary spinster, sailing-into-your-intimacy-American-hotel-piazza type.' She was a good girl but 'too adhesive, too interrogative, and too epistolary.' " The same authority declares: "The portrait of Lord Warburton was drawn from life. . . . Thus there might be a touch of Sir Charles Dilke in Warburton, as James saw him in the 1870's . . . , 'a very good fellow, and a specimen of a fortunate Englishman: born, without exceptional talents to a big property, a place in the world, and a political ambition'; or a bit of Sidney Holland, 'one of those manly, candid, reasonable, conscientious, athletic, good-looking Englishmen who only need a touch of genius or of something they haven't got to make one think that they are the flower of the human race.' "[39] Goodwood seems like Christopher Newman recast, but we should not too quickly conclude that this is the sum of him, for he has, as we have noted, some infusion of the violence of Farmer Boldwood. Further, he is quite the busiest man in James's fiction, traveling by the fastest boats and condensing his courtship into the briefest intervals. For models for Mme Merle, some of the grand unprincipled ladies of Balzac and Thackeray should be looked to, though James could readily have amplified the women of these authors from his own observation of society. Serena Merle's name had, however, a greater significance for Henry James, with his thorough familiarity with the affair between George Sand and Alfred de Musset, than it has, regrettably, for most of his modern readers: to him it suggested the ambiguous "white blackbird"—Madame Merle is very fair—of De Musset's once famous portrait, "Histoire d'un merle blanc." All in all, the characters of *The Portrait of a Lady* are composite figures, as one might expect them to be in a novel which is in a way a summary of all the novelist had learned in his apprenticeship.

In addition to borrowing suggestions for the characterizations from his predecessors, Henry James found in Edmond About's *Germaine* (1858) a hint for Mme Merle's exploitation of Isabel to provide for Pansy, the illegitimate child the former has had by Gilbert Osmond. Honorine Chermidy, unfaithful to her husband, a sea captain, during his absence from home, conceives the idea of marrying her lover, Don Diego, to the Countess Germaine, who, she is assured by Dr. Charles Le Bris, must inevitably die of tuberculosis, but may pose in the interim as the mother of Honorine's child. Germaine consents to the arrangement for the sake of her parents who are destitute but who will receive a generous income from the Don as a part of the agreement. Taken to Corfu by her husband (where Ralph also goes for his health), Germaine miraculously recovers and wins the love of the dowager Countess, the Don's mother; of the child (who prefers her to her own mother, just as Pansy prefers Isabel—often noted as one of James's best ironies); and of the Don himself. James altered this into Madame Merle's persuasion of Osmond to marry Isabel for her inheritance, both concealing from the girl their previous relationship.[40]

IV

Reinforced by the general approbation of his time,[41] James thought well of *The Portrait of a Lady*. When Robert Louis Stevenson, after praising *Roderick Hudson*, wrote James that he could not bear *The Portrait*, that it was "below" him, James expostulated, " 'Tis surely a graceful, ingenious, elaborate work —with too many pages, but with . . . an interesting subject, and a good deal of life and style."[42] James's Preface to the novel, especially important because of its fine tribute to Turgenev and because of certain dicta on the art of fiction, is not distinguished for unsparing self-analysis. James, however, noted that Henrietta Stackpole, for one who is not a "true agent" but only a "light *ficelle*," occupies too much space in the novel, that she has been "overtreated," and admits that he has been too conscious of his need to amuse his reader—"Henrietta must have been at that time a part of my wonderful notion of the lively."[43] This is surely a most self-indulgent observation, for Henrietta does effectively lighten without too much encumbering the story. If Bantling were not so much of a stock character, or if Henrietta had been even more susceptible to his charms, comic relief might have been had with more economy. To have assigned Henrietta the last word in the novel did more to overemphasize her importance than anything else; yet how else could James have closed his story? To end with the last scene between Isabel and Goodwood would have necessitated entering subjectively into Goodwood's despair, and James has hitherto viewed Goodwood wholly from the outside. To have assigned the final comment to Mrs. Touchett would have had the merit of giving the design a neat roundness, but that would have necessitated making her partisan to Goodwood, whereas her prejudice for Warburton is more in keeping with her character; furthermore, how could she act the role of consoler without appearing plagued by conscience, which indubitably she was not? All in all, James seems to have had Henrietta's final role forced upon him.

In his *Notebooks*, while *The Portrait* was appearing serially, James examines two other possible limitations which were to occur to later critics: "a want of action in the earlier part" and a failure to see "the heroine to the end of her situation."[44] Joseph Warren Beach goes beyond James himself in commenting on the earlier part of the novel:

> . . . Nearly the whole first volume is taken up with material which would have been excluded from the more distinctive work of the later years. The episode of Lord Warburton and his proposal, the death of Mr. Touchett and his bequest to Isabel, are two major blocks of material which would have been treated briefly and referentially as part of the antecedent facts of the story. . . . When he has once got her launched on this earlier career, he stops for the length of more than two chapters to bring up to date her history as a girl and that of her cousin Ralph. And this is not done, as would have been done after 1896, by reminiscence and dialogue as an integral part of the narrative of present experience.[45]

There is no denying the facts in this stricture, if it be a stricture, but it should be pointed out that the difference of aim in *The Portrait* and, say, *The Ambassadors* has something to do with the difference in structure of the two novels—it is not a mere matter of gauging their comparative artistic economy. With the most distinguished work of his major period behind him, James himself still expressed deep satisfaction with the form of this novel; it had for him the character of a "literary monument":

> Such is the aspect that today *The Portrait* wears for me: a structure reared with an "architectural" competence, as Turgenieff

would have said, that makes it, to the author's own sense, the
most proportioned of his productions after *The Ambassadors*—
which was to follow it so many years later and which has, no
doubt, a superior roundness. On one thing I was determined;
that, though I should have to pile brick for the creation of an
interest, I would leave no pretext for saying that anything was
out of line, scale, or perspective. I would build large. . . .[46]

"With this judgment of James's, anyone who is at all responsive
to the beauty of the structural element in fiction must, I think,
agree," writes Fred B. Millett, who also points out that the
novel falls "into three almost equal parts, like the three acts
of a play, followed by an epilogue." The first part (Chapters
I-XIX) carries through to the death of Daniel Touchett; part
two (Chapters XX-XXXV) includes Isabel's involvement with Osmond through the machinations of Madame Merle and her
defense of her choice to Goodwood; part three (Chapters XXXVI-
LII) reveals the consequences of this choice and Isabel's defiance
of her husband in her visit to her dying cousin—"a scene adroitly
placed so as to constitute the climax, not only of the third act,
but of the whole novel"; and the epilogue (Chapters LIII-LVI)
covers Isabel's departure from Gardencourt and return to Osmond, with its own climactic scene in Goodwood's passionate
appeal.[47] Millett notes another structural excellence in the
parallel James creates between the first and second halves of
the novel in duplicating Isabel's quest for a husband by Pansy's:
"It is not the least of James's ironies that the convent-bred, so-
cially inexperienced young girl manifests a reliability of judgment in this matter that Isabel unfortunately lacked."[48] And,
of course, little Ned Rosier, who is willing to sacrifice his precious
bibelots for Pansy, is introduced to balance off the cold esthete
Gilbert Osmond, who will not give up anything for Isabel. If
we grant that it is quite as legitimate in a novel to give a sense
of amplitude and of leisurely accretion as one of the strictest
means and of concentration, Beach's comment on the structure
of *The Portrait* has no particular force save as it emphasizes
James's change of aim in his career as a novelist.

    Accepting Professor Millett's analysis of the structure of
the novel does not commit us to accept his location of the climax of the narrative in the scene in which Isabel receives her

husband's ultimatum.[49] The Countess Gemini's revelation and Isabel's visit to the convent, both with mounting tension and each within what Millett designates as the third part, come after that. In terms of portraiture, which we must hold to as James's primary aim, the convent episode has the best claim to the designation besides being one of the best dramatic confrontations the novelist ever conceived. Through the reverence Isabel has paid Mme Merle, the latter has come to stand for the "lady" of the younger woman's aim; disillusioned now about Mme Merle's motives in all that concerns herself, Isabel must still measure herself in terms of self-possession and human dignity against this other woman—the confrontation is imperative to the portraiture. Determined to see Pansy before leaving Rome, Isabel goes to the convent where she encounters her former friend whose visit to her unrecognized and unrecognizing daughter has doubtless disturbed her composure and, divining instantly from Isabel's bearing that she now knows her duplicity, Madame Merle loses her perfect poise. But by the effort of her will she regains composure only to lose it again when Isabel senses her advantage in silence, reducing the "cleverest" woman in the world to the "meanest" before quietly announcing her intention to go to England without her husband. Madame Merle chooses to remain while Isabel goes in to visit Pansy—a visit in which she finds the girl, spirit-broken and willing perfectly to obey Osmond, upset by her previous visitor, whom she frankly declares that she does not like. Isabel's announced intent to go to England produces such consternation in Pansy who must now face her father alone that Isabel pledges to return to her—a momentous commitment to be measured later. Madame Merle has waited purposefully Isabel's return to the anteroom and puts to her a strange question with a stranger smile: " 'Are you very fond of your cousin?' " On Isabel's affirmation, Mme Merle reveals that it was Ralph who had imparted " 'that extra lustre which was required to make you a brilliant match,' "—he had given her the money that had made her interesting to Osmond. Diabolically playing her last card for her former lover (who no longer has any interest in her) and desiring to turn Isabel against Ralph, she adds triumphantly, " 'At bottom, you have him to thank.' " Isabel withstands the shock of this with a superb retort that shows a

social competence beyond anything she has hitherto exhibited:
" 'I believed it was you I had to thank.' " The women part as
mortal enemies, Isabel surviving a poisonous attack meant wholly
to frustrate her. Her mastery in this situation leaves her "free"
to choose her destiny—and she goes straight to Ralph as she had
planned. Madame Merle, unloved and repudiated, is to return
to America. There remains only in the epilogue the test of Isabel's moral maturity, furnishing another climax, as Professor
Millet remarks.

Supporting the structure of the novel is the superb pattern
of the prose, a prose reworked for precision, economy, and vividness, between periodical and book publication, and again, for
the New York edition.[50] Though in the revision of his earlier
novels James had worked in the extended or expanding metaphor, *The Portrait of a Lady* would appear to be the first novel
in which he employed this device—though not with the magical
skill he later exhibited—from the start. Studying the images related to connoisseurship, aestheticism, and art, Miss Adeline R.
Tintner has come to the conclusion that it is in *The Portrait*
that James first took a clear-cut position against "art for art's
sake," against pure connoisseurship and aestheticism. The evil
is partly exposed in little Rosier's sharing with Gilbert Osmond
the view that Pansy is an *objet d'art:* he thought of her " 'in
amorous meditation a good deal as he might have thought of
a Dresden-china shepherdess,' and the struggle to possess Pansy
is a struggle for a piece of Kleinkunst." She is subtly related to
her mother when Mme Merle, speaking of herself, tells Isabel
that she is a good deal like a chipped and cracked pot that has
been cleverly mended. Later she identifies herself with one of
her bits of china that Osmond is handling: "Please be careful
of that precious cup,' " she begs.[51]

> "It already has a small crack," said Osmond, dryly, as he put it
> down. . . . After he had left her, Madame Merle went and lifted
> from the mantel-shelf the attenuated coffee-cup in which he
> had mentioned the existence of a crack; but she looked at it
> rather abstractedly. "Have I been so vile all for nothing?" she
> murmured to herself.

In this very area of sensibility, Miss Dorothy Van Ghent
makes a very rewarding observation on the growth of Isabel's

appreciation, a matter of developing the "inward eye" through "errors and illuminations." Thus, when Isabel views the pictures in the Touchett gallery, she sees only "vague squares of rich colour." Miss Van Ghent contrasts this with Isabel's contemplation of Rome after she has learned of the part Serena Merle has played in her marriage; now deep and tender acquaintance with the city makes her appreciate it "chiefly as a place where people have suffered."[52] Robert L. Gale notes the images of keys and bolts as continuously employed in the novel and attaches to them a Freudian significance.[53] Among the several classes of extended metaphor cited by Lotus Snow are military images applied to Isabel's early conduct and Caspar's later behavior, key images (already noted), and those of drifting and sailing, in appropriate contexts.[54] One of the most startling "discoveries" about the novel is that, in revising for the New York edition, James was allegedly influenced by his friend Henry Adams' concepts of sexual inertia and force. William Bysshe Stein, the author of this theory, sees it as recognition on James's part that he had dealt with the same limitations in American women in *The Portrait* that Adams was to deal with much later.[55] The idea is appealing, but cannot be conclusively demonstrated, since these images exist from the earliest version and may have been merely reinforced and extended in the last revision, without a thought of Adams.

v

The substance of *The Portrait* is, on certain grounds, much more open to twentieth century criticism than is its architecture. Leon Edel has ably summarized the animadversions of a number of critics on this score: "At moments the story verges on melodrama when it isn't pure fairy-tale: a rich uncle, a poor niece, an ugly sick cousin who worships her from a distance, three suitors, an heiress, and finally her betrayal by a couple of her cosmopolite compatriots into a marriage as sinister as the backdrop of a Brontë novel: of such time-worn threads is this book woven." "And yet to say this," Edel adds, "is to offer a gross caricature of a warm and human work."[56] If these elements relate *The Portrait* to the novels of Dickens, Thackeray, and George Eliot and seem to put it in the category of the Victorian

novel, they are of such little consequence in the total impression
which the book makes that they seem severed strands with the
past. The thought and artistic effort of the author are not entangled in them. Whereas George Eliot must stop for moral-
izing and exegesis, James threads his theme through his story
without ever resorting to explicit statement and makes his heroine known to us by the very extraordinary company she keeps.
Isabel engages our attention because of her wonderful yet naïve
aspiration for complete freedom—

> "I always want to know the things one shouldn't do."
> "So as to do them?" asked her aunt.
> "So as to choose," said Isabel.

In an exchange between herself and Mme Merle on the
limits of the self, Isabel is thought by Philip Rahv to be uttering pure Emersonianism, and there is a convincing similarity
between her declaration and the Yankee prophet's. Thus Isabel:

> "I don't know whether I succeed in expressing myself, but
> I know that nothing else expresses me. Nothing that belongs to
> me is the measure of me; on the contrary, it's a limit, a barrier,
> and a perfectly arbitrary one."

Emerson, in "The Transcendentalist," had written:

> You think me a child of my circumstances. Let any
> thoughts of mine be different from what they are, the difference
> will transform my condition and economy. . . . You call it the
> power of circumstance, but it is the power of me.[57]

Rahv does not note that, on the afternoon when her aunt discovers her in Albany, Isabel is reading "a history of German
Thought," but the fact adds, of course, to his suggestion that she
has imbibed too deeply of Transcendentalism. However, the
revelation is, after all, but one aspect of her fresh individualism,
and tells us more about Henry James's skepticism in regard to
radical Yankee idealism, than it does about Isabel, whose attitudes are a product of her nature, her father's indulgence, and
her total inexperience, as well as of her reading. She is no Yankee
shilling, but an American gold piece, perhaps too freshly minted,
but symbolic of the emancipated women of the whole youthful
nation nevertheless. It is the obverse side of this eagle-stamped
coin, it is an excess of naïve self-confidence that is Isabel's tragic

flaw which leads to her downfall in a society of whose ruthlessness she had no more comprehension than Desdemona had of the motivation of Iago. She is a successful candidate for more sympathy than Desdemona simply because James accomplishes the miracle of keeping her always to the fore; his art does not surrender to Victorian or pre-Victorian conventions. Isabel is a very tentative modern young woman presented in a critical modern way.

The variety of conjecture as to Isabel's motives in returning to her husband and as to her future raise the question whether, if James did not see his heroine "to the end of her situation," he might not have given more positive hints as to what that end might be.[58] Carl Van Doren writes, "Something in the intricate, never quite penetrable fiber of the heroine sends her in the end back to her husband for the sake of her stepdaughter, thinking, it seems, that she thereby encounters her destiny more nobly than in any previous chapter of it. The conclusion, on various grounds, does not satisfy, but it consistently enough rounds out Isabel's chronicle."[59] Ford Madox Ford sees the ending as a product of the "New England . . . virus": "There [for] the self-conscious, self-bridling New England heroine ensues a lifetime of yearning misery at the hands of a possibly exaggerated, but still quite possible, pair of selfish scoundrels, so that Providence fails of its mission."[60] Following out Ford's idea, Michael Swan holds,

> It is her destiny . . . to settle in New England and to reject the life which has brought her such bitter experience. To our amazement she affronts her destiny and returns to her husband. Because she has been made aware "what people most know and suffer," she renounces a possible happiness; she will not be happy with Osmond, but he has brought her knowledge and experience, and these it was necessary for her to possess. . . . No explanation of this strange action can entirely satisfy. It is better . . . to accept James's suggestion that in her special case the action was inevitable. . . . After the book is laid down . . . we begin to question its greatness as a true history of life.[61]

"Isabel returns," says Joseph Warren Beach,

> because her pride requires that she shall carry through what she has undertaken. . . . Osmond himself had expressed it for her in

their last talk before her departure for England. He had reminded her of their inescapable nearness to one another, as husband and wife. It might be a disagreeable proximity, but it was
of their own deliberate making: "I think," says Osmond, "we
should accept the consequences of our actions, and what I value
most in life is the honor of the thing." These words "were not
a command, they constituted a kind of appeal; and, though she
felt that any expression of respect on his part could only be a
refinement of egotism, they represented something transcendent
and absolute, like the sign of the cross or the flag of one's
country."[62]

The late F. O. Matthiessen, citing *The Notebooks*, defends
the verisimilitude of the ending of the novel; James had written
that the obvious criticism of his novel would be that he had "not
seen the heroine to the end of her situation—that I had left her
en l'air"; then James had continued, "This is both true and
false. The *whole* of anything is never told; you can only take
what groups together. It is complete in itself—and the rest may
be taken up or not, later."[63] Matthiessen brings into the discussion a letter from William James to Henry, as early as 1868,
on a story with a similar "open" ending, containing William's
remark that this has "a deep justification in nature," after which
Matthiessen buttresses his own approval of the ending with a
quotation from the Preface to *Roderick Hudson*: "Really, universally, relations stop nowhere, and the exquisite problem of
the artist is eternally but to draw, by a geometry of his own, the
circle within which they shall happily *appear* to do so." For
Matthiessen, the circle *does appear* complete and satisfactory in
The Portrait.

Isabel's link with humanity, if not through sin [as in Hawthorne]
—unless her willful spirit counts as such—is through her acceptance of suffering. . . . Isabel lays the most scrupulous emphasis
upon the sacredness of her promise. . . . She is a firm granddaughter of the Puritans, not in her thought but in her moral
integrity. In portraying her . . . James was also writing an essay
on the interplay of free will and determinism. Isabel's own view
is that she was "perfectly free," that she married Osmond of her
most deliberate choice, and that . . . one must accept the consequences of one's acts. . . . James knew how little she was free.
. . . He knew . . . how little experienced she was in mature social
behavior. He had shown that she was completely mistaken in
believing that "the world lay before her—she could do whatever

she chose." But James also knew the meaning and value of renunciation. . . . Through Isabel Archer he gave one of his fullest
and freshest expressions of inner reliance in the face of adversity.[64]

But after arguing so confidently and persuasively about Isabel's
austerity, Matthiessen feebly surmises as to what lies ahead in
her relation with Osmond, "It may be that, as Isabel herself
conjectures, he may finally 'take her money and let her go.' It
may be that once she has found a husband for Pansy, she will
feel that she no longer has to remain in Rome."[65] But if we
accept Matthiessen's argument that Isabel demonstrates her
"moral integrity" in returning to Osmond, it becomes an equally
strong argument that she will remain with him. Her hope that
Osmond will "take her money and let her go" is a hope without
foundation, as Isabel herself knows; above everything else, Osmond has stressed appearances; this was the motive which impelled him to assume charge of Pansy and separate her from
her mother—he will hardly be bought off. And of course, Isabel
will not find a husband for Pansy; Osmond will attempt that.
If compassion is a motive in hurrying Isabel back to Rome—
and it is, though a minor one—compassion is likely to keep her
there; for Osmond will not satisfy his little daughter's heart and
she will need the lasting comfort her stepmother can give.

After finding three reasons for Isabel's return to her husband—her promise to Pansy, the preservation of appearances,
and an "excessive pride that will not permit her to let the world
see that she has made a horrible mistake,"—Fred B. Millett accepts Matthiessen's reasoning (though he makes a more forceful statement of it) and adds: "But perhaps James's most explicit pronouncement on Isabel Archer's ultimate fate is put in
the mouth of her dying cousin, the most concerned and responsible observer of her unhappiness: 'I don't believe such a generous mistake as yours can hurt you for more than a little.'
With this insight, the attentive follower of Isabel Archer's 'affronting her destiny' can hardly disagree."[66] But Ralph had believed that Isabel's large inheritance would do her no harm,
and this last unsupported wish of his is merely in character; furthermore, it is ambiguous; possibly divining Isabel's resolution,
Ralph may be saying simply that she will have the fortitude to

rise above the pain of her situation—it can hurt her only a little while.

There is, however, a much more explicit passage about Isabel's future than that which Professor Millett has noted. It occurs during that famous reverie when Isabel deduces the relationship of Mme Merle to Osmond; she is thinking about the mutual residence of her husband and herself:

> She could live it over again, the incredulous terror with which she had taken the measure of her dwelling. Between those four walls she had lived ever since; they *were to surround her for the rest of her life*. . . .[67]

It must be recognized that at the end of *The Portrait* Henry James presents the very sort of marital situation which his father, one of the notable opponents of divorce in his day, would still have thought provided sufficient grounds for legal separation.[68] In his *Notebooks* the novelist says that the reader "must get the sense of Isabel's exquisitely miserable revulsion. Three years have passed—time enough for it to have taken place. His [Osmond's] worldliness, his deep snobbishness, his want of generosity, etc.; his hatred of her when he finds that she judges him, that she morally protests at so much that surrounds her. The uncleanness of the air; the Countess Gemini's lovers, etc."[69] Yet despite this intolerable situation, Isabel makes no attempt to leave it even at the direct urging of Henrietta: "Why don't you leave him?" When Isabel says she cannot, Henrietta challenges her with false pride:

> ". . . You won't confess you've made a mistake. You're too proud."
>
> "I don't know whether I'm too proud. But I can't publish my mistake. I don't think that's decent. I would much rather die."
>
> "You won't think so always," said Henrietta.
>
> "I don't know what great unhappiness might bring me to; but it seems to me I shall always be ashamed. One must accept one's deeds. I married him before all the world; I was perfectly free; it was impossible to do anything more deliberate. . . ."
>
> Henrietta gave a rich laugh. "Don't you think you're rather too considerate?"
>
> "It's not of him that I'm considerate—it's of myself!" Isabel answered.[70]

Despite the fact that Isabel does not acknowledge the charge that it is her pride that keeps her from leaving Osmond, it would seem from this passage that pride is an ingredient in her failure to escape her bondage. Yet shortly after this she calls on her cousin Ralph who, very ill, is about to leave Rome in the care of Henrietta and Caspar Goodwood whom Isabel has all but assigned to him. "I ought to go with you," she says. When Ralph suggests that her husband would object, Isabel, after an empty interchange, confesses that she is afraid. "Afraid of your husband?" Ralph asks. "Afraid of myself!" she replies. Here is quite a different explanation for Isabel's acceptance of her situation than she has given to Henrietta, and James must mean for us to note the difference. What had Isabel to fear in herself unless it were her own nature? Both Lord Warburton and Caspar Goodwood penetrate her unhappiness; each is willing to be the agent of her release; yet with an almost desperate urgency she sends them from her—because she fears them? Or because she fears her weakness in their presence? Yet having left Osmond to be with her dying cousin at Gardencourt, she does not grasp at the opportunity to escape her husband. "It is all over then between you?" Ralph inquires. "Oh, no; I don't think anything's over," Isabel replies. "Are you going back to him?" Ralph gasped. "I don't know—I can't tell. . . . I don't want to think—I needn't think," is the only satisfaction Ralph gets. After this she sees Warburton and realizes he has accepted his fate; then comes the violent scene with Goodwood. "Turn straight to *me*," the direct American urges. "Why should you go back—why should you go through that ghastly form?" "To get away from *you!*" she answers. But Goodwood persists in his effort at persuasion, "I never knew *you* afraid!" But apparently she is afraid, for though she acknowledges to herself that it would be "a kind of rapture" to feel herself "sink and sink," she again repels him and, after his kiss, flees from him to return to her husband. "She had not known where to turn; but she knew now. There was a very straight path."[71]

VI

That Caspar Goodwood's passionate embrace is the compulsive force in deciding Isabel to go straight back to Rome and to Gilbert Osmond necessitates our most careful examination of the final scene in the novel. Common sense, as represented by the advice of Henrietta Stackpole and Ralph Touchett, are against her decision; Ralph had even talked frankly with Caspar Goodwood to induce him to "save" Isabel. We must see that somehow Goodwood fails in this mission. May it not lie partially in the nature of the appeal which Goodwood makes to her as well as in the physical violence he resorts to? Speaking with great feeling, he declares:

> "Why shouldn't we be happy—when it's here before us, when it's so easy? . . . What have you to care about? You've no children. . . . You've nothing to consider. You must save what you can of your life; you mustn't lose it all simply because you've lost a part. . . . You took the great step in coming away; the next is nothing; it's the natural one. I swear, as I stand here, that a woman deliberately made to suffer is justified by anything in life—in going down into the streets if that will help her! . . . We can do absolutely as we please; to whom under the sun do we owe anything? . . . The world's all before us—and the world's very big."[72]

What is this but an offer of complete freedom and a restoration of independence to Isabel—a very typically indulgent American offer to an American woman, backed by Goodwood's considerable means. Isabel is momentarily swayed; "she gave a long murmur, like a creature in pain; it was as if he were pressing something that hurt her. 'The world's very small,' she said at random." Goodwood is not aware that she and he have uttered almost these same views on the world before—and on a very vital occasion to each—but the memory comes back to Isabel clearly. When she had dismissed Caspar and sent him back to America, declaring she too much prized her liberty to have him around, Caspar had gloomily expressed his fear of losing sight of her in the world:

> "I don't know," she had answered rather grandly. "The world . . . comes to strike one as rather small."
> "It's a sight too big for *me!*" Caspar exclaimed with a simplicity our young lady might have found touching if her face had not been set against concessions.

The association of the words has a terrible import for Isabel; she realizes that Caspar is offering her the very independence, the very liberty, which has cost her so much. " 'Do me the greatest kindness of all,' she panted. 'I beseech you to go away.' " Instead of obeying, he tries to break down physically her resistance and for the first time in her life she experiences the temptation that yielding to the other sex affords. She resists.

She resists because all that she has learned about the folly of complete feminine liberty rushes in on her. Ralph Touchett, with the quixotism characteristic of American men and the unselfishness peculiar to himself, had wondrously extended her independence through the bequest he had persuaded his father to make her—with the result that she had freely and against counsel gone straight into the arms of Gilbert Osmond. Moreover, her association with the Touchetts has brought her another spectacle of the frustration and emptiness of complete liberty— the barren spectacle of her aunt. Mrs. Touchett provides the ultimate illustration of complete freedom in marriage such as Caspar Goodwood offers.[73] It is from such a freedom as she had had herself before her marriage and that her aunt offers her an example of, that she flees. Besides the prospect of an empty independence like her aunt's (Caspar is a busier businessman than the banker Touchett ever was), keeping the forms of her duty to her husband and her promise to Pansy, with all it entails, seems to Isabel to afford a more meaningful life. " 'Certain obligations were involved in the very fact of marriage,' she had thought, 'and were quite independent of the quantity of enjoyment extracted from it.' " Duty has meaning for Isabel—this is the lesson she has derived from her experience—and sheer liberty has none. As against the brief enjoyment of Caspar's snatched embraces, a life with, but apart from, Gilbert Osmond appeals more to her ascetic nature than the American kind of mockery of marriage.[74]

Matthiessen makes one observation on this final scene which he does not fully follow up. Reflecting on the effect of Caspar Goodwood's passionate embrace, he writes, "That conveys James's awareness of how Isabel, in spite of her marriage, has remained essentially virginal, and how her resistance and flight from Caspar are partly fear of sexual possession. But the fierce attraction she also feels in this passage would inevitably operate likewise for a girl of her temperament, in making her do what she conceived to be her duty, and sending her back to her husband."[75] Quoting Gide's stricture, "They [James's heroines] are only winged busts; all the weight of the flesh is absent, all the shaggy, tangled undergrowth, all the wild darkness," Dupee writes, "And James himself seems to acknowledge the limitation, when, at the peril of retroactively compromising his portrait of Isabel, he shows her fleeing from Goodwood's kiss. With all his wider experience, James is more Puritan—if not simply less human—than Hawthorne, for whom, in *The Scarlet Letter*, the color of adultery is also the color of life-blood and of roses."[76] Nothing could be more mistaken than Dupee's hasty romantic impression in this instance; on the other hand, nothing could be much closer to the scent of truth than Matthiessen's suggestion.

As we have seen, James drew from the start a heroine capable of deep sexual arousal, but cautious also, and inhibited. "Deep in her soul—it was the deepest thing there—lay the belief that if a certain light should dawn she could give herself completely; but this image on the whole was too formidable to be attractive. . . ." Bookish and without passional experience, she had married Osmond out of illusion, but even though she had given him a child,[77] he had never really touched the core of her nature—it needed Goodwood's kiss to do that, and Matthiessen is right in testifying to its effectiveness in revealing the virginal nature of the heroine; indeed, when the handicap of Victorian reticence is remembered, no brief episode ever revealed more, for is not the "whole shaggy, tangled undergrowth," the abhorrent darkness of her private life instantly laid bare? To the attentive reader it has already been disclosed that her relations with her husband are no longer intimate in his insistence that she knock before entering his room and in her cry, "We don't live decently together!"[78] Yet it is to this fleshless existence that Isabel elects to return more or less as Mme de Cintré had sought the convent, rather than to surrender to the pleasure that union with Goodwood holds out. This is central, whatever other factors enter in. But to assume that the heroine has the novelist's approval in her dramatic return is to assume much too much. Here, the first use James made of some of the essential material of *The Portrait* in "Longstaff's Marriage" is very helpful: Diana is punished by violent sexual desire for coldly treating the appeal of a dying man. James was no Puritan—eight years earlier he had censured George Eliot for making Lydgate so sexless—but he certainly understood the ascetic temperament, the dreadful limitations of which he presents as boldly as the conventions of his day allowed. The difficulty readers have had with Isabel's actions comes largely from the mistaken assumption that James presented her as an ideal type—a notion fostered largely by the dubious assumption that she is drawn wholly from his cousin, Minny Temple. To see her correctly, we have to see her as in the tradition of the limited heroine. She is the most subtly drawn figure, and the most complex, in that tradition.[79]

VII

To the general acclamation of the character drawing in *The Portrait* there have been scattered dissents. To Rebecca West, Isabel's conduct is "inconsistent" and "suggestive of the nincompoop, clearly proceeding from a brain whose ethical world was but chaos." But the chief count against Isabel appears to be her return to Osmond, proving her "not the very paragon of ladies but merely ladylike." As militant a feminist as Miss West hardly brings to so complex a decision as Isabel's the depth of sensibility to render a fair verdict; and she negates her own criticism by writing, "Yet for all the poor quality of the motives which furnish Isabel's moral stuffing, *The Portrait of a Lady* is entirely successful in giving one the sense of having met somebody far too radiantly good for this world."[80] Quinn has a low opinion of Isabel's intelligence because she selects Gilbert Osmond after refusing "real men" like Caspar Goodwood and Lord Warburton and remaining blind to "the tender chivalry of Ralph Touchett."[81] James, of course, wished one to see Isabel's immaturity, but not to count that against her. After all, Isabel was wooed not merely by Osmond, but by Mme Merle whom this stricture does not take into account. Dupee carefully distinguishes the characterization of Osmond from the role assigned him in the plot which makes him "still the stock conspirator in melodrama." On the other side, Osmond is "a notable study in modern perversity," and Dupee furnishes an excellent summary of the development of his nature.[82] The same critic puts his finger fairly on the least satisfactory characterization in the novel, that of Caspar Goodwood: "Something of Christopher Newman, only stiffer and grimmer, he is not adequately developed; and the plot, which requires that he be jockeyed in and out of Isabel's life like a wooden Indian on wheels, succeeds only in making him look superfluous."[83] Citing Henrietta Stackpole as prime example, Beach mildly observes that the characters of *The Portrait* "exhibit some of the variety and picturesqueness proper to . . . a Victorian novel. . . . Even Mme Merle is occasionally given a touch that suggests Thackeray more than James." But then Beach adds, "She is perhaps the most perfect creation in the book, and her line is by no means any sort of vividness. Her line is the most perfect suavity of manner, the most impeccable of self-effacing good taste."[84] The Countess Gemini, Mr. Touchett, and Ralph have some of the vividness which Beach finds Victorian, but how little Beach wishes made of his point can be seen in his declaration concerning Ralph: "He is a figure beautifully conceived and executed."[85] Pansy has been called "exquisite, . . . one of the best of the portraits of children in which James's genius shines clearest."[86] Certainly it is in this novel that Henry James first achieves complete mastery of the "set" portrait, one of the best examples of which is that of Isabel's aunt; it should be noted that the description is in terms of her mind and conduct and not in those of her appearance:

> Mrs. Touchett might do a great deal of good, but she never pleased. This way of her own, of which she was so fond, was not intrinsically offensive—it was just unmistakably distinguished from the ways of others. The edges of her conduct were so very clear-cut that for susceptible persons it sometimes had a knife-like effect. The fine hardness came out in her deportment during the first hours of her return from America, under circumstances in which it might have seemed that her first act would have been to exchange greetings with her husband and son. Mrs. Touchett, for reasons she deemed excellent, always retired on such occasions into impenetrable seclusion, postponing the more sentimental ceremony until she had repaired the disorder of dress with a completeness which had the less reason to be of high importance as neither beauty nor vanity were concerned in it. She was a plain-faced old woman, without graces and with-

out any great elegance, but with an extreme respect for her own
motives. She was usually prepared to explain these—when explanation was asked as a favor; in such case they proved totally
different from those that had been attributed to her. She was
virtually separated from her husband, but she appeared to perceive nothing irregular in the situation. It had become clear, at
an early stage of their community, that they should never desire
the same thing at the same moment, and this appearance had
prompted her to rescue disagreement from the vulgar realm of
accident. She did what she could to erect it into a law—a much
more edifying aspect of it—by going to live in Florence, where
she bought a house and established herself; and by leaving her
husband to take care of the English branch of his bank. This arrangement greatly pleased her; it was so felicitously definite. . . .

All in all, the artistry of James in presenting his people has
stood up well under critical scrutiny—with the sole exception,
perhaps, of the characterization of Goodwood, in the drawing of
whom James was hampered by the prudery of the time. If variety
and vividness are traits of the characterization, balance and proportion are also traits, for none of the characters outshines the
central figure or usurps her interest.

James's triumph in keeping Isabel to the fore is achieved
by centering much of the story in her consciousness. "Without
her sense of them [her adventures], without her sense *for* them,
. . . they are next to nothing at all; but isn't the beauty and difficulty just in showing their mystic conversion by that sense into
the stuff . . . of 'story'?"[87] James cites two triumphant instances
of "conversion": the first when Isabel finds Mme Merle, absorbed and serene, a stranger playing the piano in Gardencourt,
and has a sense that her destiny is to be tied to this woman; and
the second, Isabel's meditative vigil, when she is "under the
spell of recognitions on which she finds the last sharpness suddenly to wait." The former instance seems to him to "produce
the maximum intensity with the minimum of strain," and the
latter, designed to "have all the vivacity of incident and all the
economy of picture," and "to throw the action further forward
than 'twenty incidents' might have done."[88] But some material
resisted conversion, and the reader knows more about her situation than she does. He knows, for example, more about Ralph's
devotion than she knows. And there are episodes in which she is
not a participant, between Ralph and his uncle, Ralph and his

aunt, Henrietta and the Countess Gemini, Ralph and Goodwood. The final scene between Osmond and Mme Merle is out
of her focus; James yielded to an impulse to include this for its
drama, but its chief accomplishment being the revelation of Osmond's ingratitude toward his one-time mistress, the drama
should have been sacrificed for integrity in point of view and
the substance of the revelation brought to Isabel indirectly.

Joseph Warren Beach is the only commentator who has
much concerned himself with James's "pictorial preoccupation"
in his novels. Whereas George Eliot conceives her material in
terms of a moral thesis, James conceives his as the subject of a
picture. We should not forget this, Beach contends, nor "the
inveterately esthetic bias of the author."[89] If *The Portrait of a
Lady* were properly approached, then, we should consider its
relative effectiveness as a picture over against other methods of
presenting a heroine. Beach does something in this direction in
considering the *chiaroscuro* effect achieved by James in placing
his heroines Isabel Archer and Milly Theale in menacing surroundings and company. "The secret of this effectiveness lies
more in the background than in the main foreground subject.
As much art went to the creation of Mme Merle and Gilbert
Osmond as to that of Isabel."[90] We might add that the thought
of Isabel shining out forever in tragic splendor is enhanced by
her lodgment with her husband. Thought of as a developing
portrait,[91] Isabel's growth, or better, *definition*, is rendered
sharper by her successive suitors and admirers: less distinguished
at first by her relation to Goodwood, a fellow American, her
delineation becomes substantial through the attentions of Lord
Warburton and is highlighted by her marriage to Osmond. As
all moving objects need their motion clarified by relatively sta-
tionary things, so Isabel's growth, and especially the reader's
sense of it, is established by the human markers the novelist
has posted on her way.[92] No antecedent novelist had used his
characters in such a completely contributory way. There is not
an accidental relationship or a badly proportioned one in *The
Portrait of a Lady*. Judged on purely aesthetic grounds, the book
is possibly matchless. James had realized his aim to create a
truly "big" novel.

Notes

1. Ralph Barton Perry, *The Thought and Character of William James* (2 vols., Boston, 1935), I, 380. George A. Finch, *The Development of the Fiction of Henry James from 1879 to 1886* diss. abridge., (New York, 1949), pp. 11–15.

2. See especially "The Life of George Eliot" and "Daniel Deronda: A Conversation," *Partial Portraits* (New York, 1888), pp. 35–62, 63–93; and "George Eliot's *Middlemarch*," ed. Leon Edel, *Nineteenth-Century Fiction*, VIII (Dec., 1953), 161–170; also Henry James, *The Future of the Novel*, ed. Leon Edel (New York, 1956), pp. 80–89. One must understand that these views of Eliot are obtained through the lenses of Turgenev, of whom Constantius, the only "professional" in the "Conversation" on *Deronda*, says, "Turgenieff is my man." Something about style might be added, for James found Eliot sometimes "loose" and "baggy."

3. When James began writing the novel at the Hotel de l'Arno in Florence in the spring of 1880, it was not *de novo*, he tells us, but "I took up, and worked over, an old beginning, made long before." *The Notebooks of Henry James*, ed. F. O. Matthiessen and Kenneth B. Murdock (New York, 1947), p. 29. (See Chapter 1 in this book.) In his "Preface," relying on a faulty memory, James says that *The Portrait* was "begun in Florence, during the three months spent there in the spring of 1879." *The Art of the Novel*, ed. R. P. Blackmur (New York, 1934), p. 40. (See Chapter 2 in this book.) In the summing up of the last six years of his life, which he made on the fresh pages of "notebook 11" in Boston, on Nov. 25, 1881, he makes it clear that he worked very intensely at the novel for over a year, rewriting every part of it as he progressed. *Notebooks*, pp. 29–31. His labors were not concluded until the summer of 1881, months after the book had begun to appear serially, almost simultaneously in England and America (*Macmillan's Magazine*, Oct., 1880—Nov., 1881; *Atlantic*, Nov., 1880–Dec., 1881), LeRoy Phillips, *A Bibliography of the Writings of Henry James* (New York, 1930), p. 21. Leon Edel thinks that by 1878 he had conceived the outline of his story." "Introduction," *The Portrait of a Lady* (Boston, 1956), p. xvi. See also pp. vi–vii. There is an observation for the sociologist in the preference of Americans for "Lady" in titles (*The Lady of the Aroostock, The Lady or the Tiger, My Lady Pocohontas, The Lady of Fort St. John, A Lady of Rome*) and the British preference for "Woman" (*The Woman in White, A Woman of No Importance, The Woman Thou Gavest Me*, etc.). With the exception of the final exchange between Caspar and Isabel, where I quote the New York edition, I follow the text of the first American edition.

4. *The Art of the Novel*, pp. 42–53.

5. *The Letters of William James*, ed. by his son Henry James (2 vols., Boston, 1920), I, 36. This view is accepted by C. Hartley Grattan, *The Three Jameses* (New York, 1932), p. 295, by Graham Greene, "Introduction," *The Portrait of a Lady* (2 vols., London, 1947), I, xi–x, and, on other evidence, by Ernest Sandeen, "*The Wings of the Dove* and *The Portrait of a Lady*," *PMLA*, LXIX (Dec., 1954), 1060–1075, (See Chapter 16 in this book.) and by Edel, "Introd.," pp. xiv–xvii. F. W. Dupee turns the

identification into grist for a psychological thesis about James himself. *Henry James*, AML (New York, 1951), pp. 113–126.

6. What has Milly of Isabel's self-assurance?—to cite only one trait. Their physical differences are marked: Isabel is "willowy" ("ponderably light and probably tall"); her hair is "dark, even to blackness"; and her eyes are "light grey" (p. 38). She is called "beautiful" (p. 14). Milly Theale is "the slim, constantly pale, delicately haggard, . . . agreeably angular young person . . . whose hair was somehow exceptionally red even for the real thing" (I 95). Minny Temple was "erectly slight and so more than needful, so transparently, fair" (*Notes of a Son and Brother* [New York, 1914], p. 437). Neither she nor Milly Theale is specifically "beautiful." James noted in Minny "the handsome largeish teeth that made her mouth almost the main fact of her face" (p. 469); Milly had "rather too much forehead, too much nose, and too much mouth" (I, 118) —a detail lacking in the portrait of Isabel.

7. *Notes of a Son and Brother*, p. 479. (Italics mine.)

8. Edel, "Intro.," *Portrait*, pp. xiv–xv.

9. With characteristic generosity, albeit at his own cost, Leon Edel has supplied me with the date and place of this letter and the context in which the quoted passage appears. Grace Norton became acquainted with Mary Temple when the latter visited her Cambridge relatives in Quincy Street late in 1869, though there is no record of such a meeting. See Edel, *HJ: The Untried Years* (Philadelphia, 1953), pp. 316–317. Henry was in Europe.

10. *Nation*, XXXIV (Feb. 2, 1882), 102–103. It would seem likely that the resemblance of Gwendolen and Isabel provoked Howells' comment on the common analytical methods of James and George Eliot in "Henry James, Jr." (*Century*, XXV [Nov., 1882], 25–29), though he does not compare the heroines.

11. *The Method of Henry James* (London, 1918), pp. 35 ff. (See Chapter 7 in this book.)

12. *Early Development of Henry James* (Urbana, 1930), pp. 293–295. (See Chapter 8 in this book.) Yet in Gwendolen's sense that she deprived Deronda of an inheritance, there is a hint for money connection of Isabel and Ralph. Oliver Elton is content to say that Osmond "is of the race of Grandcourt in *Deronda*." *Modern Studies* (London, 1907), p. 247.

13. *The Great Tradition* (New York, 1950), pp. 79–125.

14. Leavis, pp. 86, 113.

15. "*Daniel Deronda:* A Conversation," *Partial Portraits* (New York, 1911), pp. 88–89. In addition to this speech (p. 86), Leavis reprints the entire piece as an appendix in *Great Tradition* (pp. 249–266), apparently unaware that Miss Kelley had seen the importance of the "conversation piece" before him and had anticipated his argument for James's indebtednesses; Miss Kelley notes a resemblance between Isabel and Mme de Mauves (See Chapter 8 in this book.) which singularly enough occurs to Leavis also (p. 15).

16. *Partial Portraits*, p. 88.

17. Compare the presentation of Isabel (though James reserves it for this later chapter) with that of Dorothea and that of Gwendolen at the outset, respectively, of *Middlemarch* and *Daniel Deronda*. Both writers owe much to Mme Sand's methods here; James appears to be

further influenced by Sainte-Beuve's sympathetic dissection of famous women—Sévigné, Roland, De Staël, for example.

18. *An Introduction to the English Novel* (2 vols., London, 1953), II, 22. This *is* the theme. (See Chapter 10 in this book).

19. Edel thinks that the list of Isabel's shortcomings (given above) "could have been applied with equal force to Minny" (Intro.," *Portrait*, p. xv). But this is far from saying that they could have been applied *exclusively* to her.

20. "Longstaff's Marriage," *Scribner's Monthly*, XVI (Aug., 1878), 537.

21. These things are differently but brilliantly pointed out by Edel (*HJ: The Untried Years*, pp. 327–330), who singularly enough in his "Introduction" to *The Portrait* (p. xvii) drops the whole connection and suggests her descent from the heroines of "Poor Richard" and *Watch and Ward*—a far less palatable idea to me.

22. XIX, 423–424. Despite its unfairness, this is one of James's very important reviews, for in it he proclaims against long or three-volume novels and proposes some modern Aristotelian views to keep them strictly to 200 pages. He reversed himself in writing *The Portrait of a Lady*. He was lucky that no one apparently threw this review at him when his own book appeared in England in three volumes! See Phillips, *Bibliography*, p. 21.

23. *Far from the Madding Crowd* (New York, 1895), pp. 322–323.

24. "His kiss was like white lightning; when it was dark again she was free" (p. 519). "Then there came a third flash. . . . A poplar in the immediate foreground was like an ink stroke on burnished tin. Then the picture vanished leaving a darkness so intense that Gabriel worked entirely by feeling with his hands" (*Nation*, XIX, 424). See both passages and also Hardy's account of Bathsheba's first kiss from Sergeant Troy (*Madding Crowd*, pp. 217–218).

25. Edel, Intro., *Portrait*, p. vi.

26. "Intro.," *The Portrait of a Lady*, ML (New York, 1951), pp. xxv–xxviii. Millett makes these observations after a declaration that James "was, to a degree, using as his model his brilliant but short-lived cousin Minny Temple."

27. There may be even something of "Clover" Hooper (Mrs. Henry Adams), for James linked the two girls: "Clover Hooper has it—intellectual grace—Minny Temple has it—moral spontaneity." *The Letters of Henry James*, ed. Percy Lubbock (2 vols., New York, 1920), I, 26. Or see John Hay to Henry Adams, ". . . that bright intrepid spirit, that keen, fine intellect, that social charm which . . . made hundreds of people love her." W. R. Thayer, *The Life and Letters of John Hay* (2 vols., New York, 1915), II, 60.

28. Especially the play upon the word "adored" in the revision of the novel and in *Notes of a Son and Brother*. Edel, "Intro.," *Portrait*, p. xv.

29. *Notes of a Son and Brother*, pp. 480–482. It is not to be passed over that the name Henrietta appears in this context of Bootts and Temples (p. 483).

30. *Henry James*, pp. 114–115. In "Who Was Gilbert Osmond?" *Modern Fiction Studies*, IV (Summer, 1958), 127–135, R. W. Stallman

tries to show that Henry B. Brewster was the model for Osmond; in the same periodical Leon Edel proves that James did not meet Brewster until long after the novel was published (*M.F.S.*, VI [Summer, 1960], 164).

31. *Notes of a Son and Brother*, p. 482.

32. (New York, 1926), p. 53. "Gilbert Osmond . . . cold as a fishmonger's slab." Graham Greene, "Introduction," *The Portrait of a Lady* (New York, 1948), p. x.

33. *Ròcca néro* could read "dark fortress or citadel." See A. De R. Lysle, *The Latest Modern Italian-English & English-Italian Dictionary* (Turin, 1939); P. Petòcchi, *Novo Dizionario Universale della Lingua Italiana* (2 vols., Milan, 1924); and Carlo Battist and Giovanni Alessio, *Dizionario Etimologico Italiano* (5 vols., Florence, 1957). James's play upon *Ròcca* (rock) may be an allusion to the Church founded by Peter upon a rock. A recent G.I. informs my friend, Professor Robert Clements, that *Roccanera* has the sense of a prison like Alcatraz in the south of Italy; this may be because *néro* came to be synonymous with Fascist; *néro* suggested "blackshirt."

34. "*The Portrait of a Lady*: 'The Eternal Mystery of Things,'" *Nineteenth-Century Fiction*, XIV (Sept., 1959), 143–155.

35. James does not appear to have been hostile to the Roman Catholic Church. See Robert M. Slabey, "Henry James and 'The Most Impressive Convention in All History,'" *American Literature*, XXX (Mar., 1958), 89–102.

36. "*The Wings of the Dove* and *The Portrait of a Lady*: A Study of Henry James's Later Phase," *PMLA*, LXIX (Dec., 1954), 1060–1064. (See Chapter 16 in this book.) One cannot wholly dismiss the passage between Ralph Touchett and his father over whether cousins should marry as having no personal reference so far as Henry James and his cousin are involved.

37. *Indiana* (Paris, 1869).

38. *The Writings of George Eliot* (Boston, 1908), Vols. V–VI. The early careers of Maggie and Philip should, of course, be ignored. But see especially VI, 235–245, 293, 356–360. I find no argument for the identification of Ralph with James himself really persuasive beyond the passage mentioned in note 36 and the deathbed scene, and even here the charity of Philip Wakem's letter interposes. Physically, Ralph more closely resembles William James, ill at the time of Minny's death and also an admirer, than he does Henry. Isabel is (unimportantly) the name of the aunt in *The Mill on the Floss*.

39. Edel, "Intro.," *Portrait*, p. xiii. Miss Kelley also notes the resemblance of Henrietta to Miranda Hope (p. 295). (See Chapter 8 in this book.)

40. Edmond About, *Germaine*, tr., Mary L. Booth (Boston, 1860). For a long time I supposed this plot device borrowed from *Monsieur Alphonse* by Alexandre Dumas, *fils*. The novel and the play have many points in common; James knew both and may have used both, though I am now inclined to think that he relied solely on *Germaine* or upon the stage version of that novel by A. P. Dennery and H. J. Crémieux (Paris, 1858). "Dennery" is, of course, "d'Ennery," with whose work James was familiar. *Notebooks*, p. 100.

41. Lyon Richardson, *Henry James* AWS (New York, 1941), p. xxxviii,

n. 85, lists the following favorable reviews: *Nation*, Feb. 2, 1881, pp. 102–103 [sic]. (See Chapter 4 in this book.) *Literary World*, Dec., 17, 1881, pp. 473–474; *The Californian*, Jan., 1882, pp. 86–87; and *Harper's*, Feb., 1882, p. 474. Private opinion did not always tally with the reviews: "Came *Portrait of a Lady*, which the author kindly sent me. It's very nice, and charming things in it, but I'm ageing fast and prefer what Sir Walter called the 'big bow-wow style.' I shall suggest to Mr. James to name his next novel 'Ann Eliza.' It's not that he 'bites off more than he can chaw,' . . . but he chaws more than he bites off." *Letters of Mrs. Henry Adams*, ed. Ward Thoron (Boston, 1936), p. 306. "I frankly own that I broke down on *The Portrait of a Lady*, but some of my friends, of whose judgment I think highly, admire it warmly, and find it deeply interesting." *Letters of Henry Adams 1858–1891*, ed. W. C. Ford (Boston, 1930), p. 333. "It's too fine flavored for me." J.J.C., June 18, 1882. M. A. De Wolfe Howe, *John Jay Chapman and His Letters* (Boston 1937), p. 29.

42. *The Letters of H.J.*, I, 132–133.

43. *The Art of the Novel*, pp. 54–55, 57–58.

44. *The Notebooks*, pp. 15–18. (See Chapter 1 in this book.)

45. *The Method of H.J.*, pp. 205–206. (See Chapter 7 in this book.)

46. *The Art of the Novel*, p. 52.

47. "Intro.," *Portrait*, pp. xx–xxiv. However meritorious this analysis of structure is, the analogy with the drama is unfortunate, for the theater did not directly influence James in regard to form until later; here he is interested in the analogy of portraiture in art and fiction. See below. The tripart division of the material of the novel was influenced possibly by the British practice of printing long novels in three volumes.

48. "Intro.," *Portrait*, pp. xiii–xiv.

49. In *The Notebooks* James writes of Caspar's passionate outbreak and of what follows: "She is greatly moved, she feels the full force of his devotion—to which she has never done justice; but she refuses. She starts again for Italy *which is the climax and termination* of the story" (pp. 17–18; italics mine).

50. Sydney J. Krause, "James's Revisions of the Style of *The Portrait of a Lady*," *American Literature*, XXX (Mar., 1958), 67–88.

51. "The Spoils of Henry James," *PMLA*, LXI (Mar., 1946), 242–244.

52. "On *The Portrait of a Lady*," *Interpretations of American Literature*, ed. Charles Feidelson, Jr., and Paul Brodtkorb, Jr. (New York, 1959), pp. 249–250.

53. "Freudian Imagery in James's Fiction," *The American Imago*, XI (Summer, 1954), 182–183. Miss Van Ghent cites the same images as those of "doors" (pp. 257–258).

54. "The Disconcerting Poetry of Mary Temple," *The New England Quarterly*, XXXI (Sept., 1958), 315–323. Also for the military imagery, Alexander Holder-Barell, *The Development of Imagery and its Functional Significance in Henry James's Novels* (Bern, 1959), pp. 26–27, 71–72.

55. "*The Portrait of a Lady: Vis Inertiae*," *Western Humanities Review*, XIII (Spring, 1959), 177–190). (See Chapter 15, in this book.)

56. "Intro.," *Portrait*, p. ix.

57. *Image and Idea* (Norfolk, Conn., 1957), pp. 62–70. (See Chapter 13 in this book.) See also Kettle's excellent full discussion of the theme of *The Portrait* in the essay already alluded to (See Chapter 10 in this book.)

58. Not all conjectures betray the insight and assurance of the follow-

ing: "It is also significant that in *The Portrait of a Lady* an analogous situation [to that in *The Wings of the Dove!*] (a virtuous American girl married to a fortune hunter) is resolved into a conventional happy ending with a divorce and rescue by an American business man." H. R. Hays, "Henry James, the Satirist," *Hound & Horn*, VIII (Apr.–June, 1934), 518.

59. *The American Novel* (New York, 1921), pp. 201–202.

60. *Henry James* (London, 1918), p. 142.

61. *Henry James* (London, 1952), p. 50.

62. *Method of H.J.*, p. 138. (See Chapter 7 in this book.) Pelham Edgar finds Isabel's motive to be "a kind of spiritual pride" but contends that the ending is inartistic: "We are cheated of our desire to see an abundant nature expand, and we are not permitted to witness in exchange for this extinguished hope her recovery of strength through suffering." *Henry James, Man and Author* (London, 1927), p. 251. David Daiches, on the other hand, sees Isabel's return as an adequate exhibition of her strength: "Isabel Archer, having made the initial—though cumulative—moral error, which results in her unhappy marriage, justifies and redeems herself morally (though not physically) by her decision to return to her husband and abide by her earlier ideal of marriage in spite of the fact that her husband for his part does not represent the ideal." "Sensibility and Technique," *Kenyon Review*, V (Autumn, 1943), 573–574.

63. *Henry James: The Major Phase* (New York, 1944), p. 181. Matthiessen cites *The Notebooks*, p. 18. (See Chapter 9 in this book.)

64. *H.J.: The Major Phase*, pp. 182–186.

65. *Ibid.*, pp. 185–186.

66. "Intro.," *Portrait*, pp. xxxiv–xxxv.

67. P. 375 (italics mine). Osmond's house, when Isabel first sees it, looks "as if, once you were in it, it would not be easy to get out" (I, 321).

68. The father declared himself for "such a law of divorce as might permit everyone to whom marriage was hateful or intolerable to leave its ranks as soon as possible, and so to close them up to its undefiled lovers alone." *Love, Marriage and Divorce, and the Sovereignty of the Individual. A Discussion Between Henry James, Horace Greeley, and Stephen Pearl Andrews, etc.* (Boston, 1889). We should look, then, for reasons peculiar to Isabel Archer herself for her return.

69. *The Notebooks*, pp. 15, 17. (See Chapter 1 in this book.)

70. *The Portrait*, pp. 427–428.

71. Pp. 441, 506–507, 517–519. Note how *fear* is underlined in this last scene. "You've frightened me," Isabel tells Goodwood before he says a word; and after his first speech, "She couldn't have told you whether it was because she was afraid, . . . she listen[ed] to him as she had never listened before."

72. James's final revision of Goodwood's appeal is most important for understanding Isabel's flight; earlier versions obscure to a degree her reasons, unless one follows the main theme and comes to a realization of how barren Isabel regards her aunt's independence in marriage.

73. William Bysshe Stein's most important contribution to the study of *The Portrait of a Lady*, in my judgment, is in relating Isabel's early independence to the freedom of her aunt in marriage (see note 55 above). I would stress Isabel's close observation of the emptiness of Mrs. Touchett's life after Ralph's death, which Stein does not. I cannot quite accept his

conclusion, but his observation of the parallels between the two women is surely vital.

74. Her pragmatic action is a working out of the injunction, "He who loses his life shall find it" (Van Ghent, p. 245; Powers, pp. 143–155) only if we accept the injunction with all these qualifications; then it has validity. But see also C. B. Cox, "Henry James and Stoicism," *Essays and Studies*, VIII (English Assoc., London, 1955), 76–88.

75. *H.J.: The Major Phase*, pp. 179–180. (See Chapter 9 in this book.)

76. *Henry James*, p. 125.

77. One of the weaknesses of the book is James's neglect of the death of Isabel's child in the context of her emotional relation to Gilbert Osmond. James provided her with a child to counterbalance the effect of Merle's being a mother—though an unnatural one. Osmond could not have been adequate at the time of the child's death, and this would have haunted Isabel and appeared indirectly even in her cautious self-revelations. H. G. Finn and Howard C. Key in "Henry James and Gestation," *College English*, XXI (Dec., 1959), 173–175, present some speculations about the time scheme for Isabel's marriage, pregnancy, and the death of her child in relation to other events in the novel. They have been shown unfounded by Jack E. Wallace, "Isabel and the Ironies" and John C. Broderick, "'H.J. and Gestation': A Reply," *Col. Eng.*, XXI (May, 1960), 497–499.

78. P. 472. Also: "They were strangely married, at all events, and it was a horrible life" (p. 379).

79. May I suggest that there is an element of irony in James's title for the novel? Isabel reacts from Goodwood's undisguised passion (and it is important here to keep the sex madness of Hardy's Farmer Boldwood in mind) as James's father would have had her react. (See the whole passage in the original *Discussion* cited in note 68 above, beginning with "Speculative free love" and running to "I hold just as clearly that it is fatal to all mankind—*much more, then, to womanhood*— to make such indulgence [of natural appetite] an end of action." The criticism of Eliot is found in the reprint of the review of George Eliot's *Middlemarch* in *Nineteenth-Century Fiction*, VIII (Dec., 1953), 166. Like many another artist son, James is rebelling against his father. James Hafley finds that *The Portrait of a Lady*, like Poe's "The Oval Portrait," is inimical to life and that this is so because James is not treating her as a human being but as the subject of his art. "Malice in Wonderland," *Arizona Quarterly*, XV (Spring, 1959), 5–12. This is an overemphasis on the title, but there is possibly a very faint truth in the observation.

80. *Henry James* (New York, 1916), pp. 69–70. "If Mr. Henry James, who knows the theory of fiction so much better than Hawthorne, fails to make *The Portrait of a Lady* as great a book as *The Marble Faun*, it amply proves, not that romance is superior to realism, . . . but simply that Nathaniel Hawthorne is a better story-writer than H.J." Bliss Perry, *A Study of Prose Fiction* (Boston, 1904), p. 231.

81. *American Fiction* (New York, 1936), p. 288.

82. *Henry James*, pp. 118–121. Philip Rahv, "The Heiress of All the Ages," *Partisan Review*, X, 241, likewise notes, "Osmond still retains some of the features of the old-fashioned villain. . . ." (See Chapter 13 in this book.)

83. Dupee, p. 115. Horace Scudder lays the "dissatisfaction" of the reader with the final scene to "his dislike of Goodwood, the jack-in-the-box of the story, whose unyielding nature seems somehow outside of the events." *Atlantic*, XLIX (Jan., 1882), 128.

84. *The Method of H.J.*, p. 206. (See Chapter 7 in this book.)

85. *Ibid.*, p. 211.

86. A. F. Bruce Clark, "Henry James," *The University Magazine*, XVIII (Feb., 1919), 54.

87. *The Art of the Novel*, p. 56.

88. *Ibid.*, p. 57. Pelham Edgar (p. 255) greatly admires Isabel's last scene with Ralph. I feel the scene would have been better had it closed with Ralph's last utterance. I admit, however, that when Isabel calls him *"my brother"* she reveals something about her nature.

89. *The Method of H.J.*, pp. 24, 38–39.

90. *Ibid.*, p. 35.

91. A sequence of titles—*The Portrait of a Lady* (1881), *Portraits of Places* (1883), and *Partial Portraits* (1888)—shows how much James was working under the pictorial-analytical influence of Turgenev and Sainte-Beuve at this time.

92. None more important, of course, than her cousin Ralph Touchett, who, if he is the source of her ruin, perfectly idolizes and evaluates her. E. M. Snell sees a curious pairing: "Isabel Archer is betrayed, significantly enough, by an Italianate-American, paired off, for contrast, against Ralph Touchett, the Anglo-American. The one is corrupt; the other frustrate; these two fates in the Jamesian annals exhaust the possibilities for the Europeanized American. The curse of frustration can, of course, be mitigated by the exercise of bravery and understanding. Touchett has these qualities, and Isabel's fate will, as indicated [how?], be like his; she will make the best of a bad situation, a *best* that will principally involve attitude, only incidentally location." *The Modern Fables of Henry James* (Cambridge, Mass., 1935), p. 63, n. 50.

With *Watch and Ward, Roderick Hudson, The American,* and *The Portrait of a Lady* I have endeavored to show how much the work of Henry James was a synthetic creation, an equal product of his observation and his reading, particularly of Old World writers. If I needed to justify this process—and perhaps I do, for there is still a type of American reader who believes that a writer, if at all good, is pure genius and never learns anything from a predecessor, least of all a European—I have only to cite a letter to T. S. Perry, of Sept. 20, 1867, in which James rejoices in being an American writer because of the privilege to "pick and choose and . . . claim our property whenever we find it." The American character of the creation will be the infusion of "our moral consciousness, our unprecedented spiritual lightness and vigor." *The Selected Letters of H.J.*, ed. Leon Edel (New York, 1955), p. 23.

STUDIES OF THE PORTRAIT OF A LADY:
A SELECTED BIBLIOGRAPHY*

ABEL, DARREL. American Literature (New York: Barron's Educational Series, 1963), III, pp. 256–69.

*ALLEN, WALTER. The English Novel: A Short Critical History (London: Phoenix House, 1954), pp. 253–56; (New York: Dutton Paperbacks, 1957), pp. 314–18.

ANDERSON, QUENTIN. The American Henry James (New Brunswick: Rutgers University Press, 1957), pp. 183–98.

————. "Introduction," The Portrait of a Lady. (New York: Washington Square Press, 1963), pp. v–xiii.

*BEACH, JOSEPH WARREN. The Method of Henry James (New Haven: Yale University Press, 1918), pp. 205–11; (Rev. ed.; Philadelphia: Albert Saifer, 1954), pp. 205–11.

*BLACKMUR, R. P. "Introduction," The Portrait of a Lady (New York: Dell, 1961), pp. 5–12.

BLEHL, VINCENT F., S. J. "Freedom and Commitment in James's The Portrait of a Lady," Personalist, XLII (Summer, 1961), pp. 368–81.

BOWDEN, EDWIN T. "The Mighty Individual," The Dungeon of the Heart (New York: Macmillan, 1961), pp. 89–102.

————. The Themes of Henry James (New Haven: Yale University Press, 1956), pp. 54–60.

BROWN, E. K. "Two Formulas for Fiction: Henry James and H. G. Wells," College English, VIII (October, 1946), 7–17.

* In order to give this bibliography a self-contained completeness, the essays reprinted in this volume are also included, an asterisk marking those here collected.

298   A SELECTED BIBLIOGRAPHY

---

*BROWNELL, WILLIAM C. "James's *The Portrait of a Lady*," *Nation*, XXXIV (February 2, 1882), 102–103.

CANBY, HENRY SEIDEL. *Turn West, Turn East: Mark Twain and Henry James* (Boston: Houghton Mifflin Co., 1951), pp. 153–60.

CARGILL, OSCAR. "Afterword," *The Portrait of a Lady* (New York: Signet, 1964), pp. 547–56.

*———. "The Portrait of a Lady," *The Novels of Henry James* (New York: Macmillan, 1961), pp. 78–119; "*The Portrait of a Lady:* A Critical Reappraisal," *Modern Fiction Studies*, III (Spring, 1957), pp. 11–32 (an earlier, briefer version).

*CHASE, RICHARD. "The Lesson of the Master," *The American Novel and Its Tradition* (Garden City: Doubleday Anchor Books, 1957), pp. 117–37.

COX, C. B. "Henry James and the Arts of Personal Relationships," *The Free Spirit* (New York: Oxford University Press, 1963), pp. 42–46.

CREWS, FREDERICK C. *The Tragedy of Manners: Moral Drama in the Later Novels of Henry James* (New Haven: Yale University Press, 1957), pp. 13–19.

DAICHES, DAVID. "Sensibility and Technique: Preface to a Critique," *Kenyon Review*, V (Autumn, 1943), pp. 569–79.

DOVE, JOHN ROLAND. "Tragic Consciousness in Isabel Archer," *Studies in American Literature*, Louisiana State University Studies, Humanities Series, No. 8, eds. Waldo McNeir and Leo B. Levy (Baton Rouge: Louisiana State University Press, 1960), pp. 78–94.

DUPEE, F. W. *Henry James* (Rev. ed.; Garden City: Doubleday Anchor Books, 1956), pp. 97–106.

EDEL, LEON. *Henry James: The Conquest of London: 1870–1881* (New York: Lippincott, 1962), pp. 417–36.

———. "Introduction," *The Portrait of a Lady* (Rev. ed.; Boston: Houghton Mifflin Co., 1963), pp. v–xx.

———. "Who Was Gilbert Osmond?" *Modern Fiction Studies*, VI (Summer, 1960), p. 164.

EDGAR, PELHAM. *Henry James, Man and Author* (Boston: Houghton Mifflin Co., 1927), pp. 245–55.

FALK, ROBERT. *The Victorian Mode in American Fiction* (East Lansing: Michigan State University Press, 1965), pp. 142–46.

FLINN, G. H., and HOWARD C. KEY. "Henry James and Gestation," *College English*, XXI (December, 1959), pp. 173–75; see also Jack E. Wallace, "Isabel and the Ironies," (May, 1960), p. 497; John C. Broderick, pp. 497–99; and Howard C. Key, pp. 499–500.

*FOLEY, RICHARD N. *"The Portrait of a Lady," Criticism in American Periodicals of the Works of Henry James from 1866 to 1916* (Washington: Catholic University of America Press, 1944), pp. 26–30.

FRIEND, JOSEPH H. "The Structure of *The Portrait of a Lady*." *Nineteenth-Century Fiction*, XX (June, 1965), pp. 85–95.

GALE, ROBERT L. *The Caught Image: Figurative Language in the Fiction of Henry James* (Chapel Hill: University of North Carolina Press, 1964), *passim*.

————. *Plots and Characters in the Fiction of Henry James* (Hamden, Conn.: Archon Books, 1965), pp. 60–62.

*GASS, WILLIAM H. "The High Brutality of Good Intentions," *Accent*, XVIII (Winter, 1958), pp. 65–70.

GEISMAR, MAXWELL. *Henry James and the Jacobites* (Boston: Houghton Mifflin Co., 1962), pp. 39–47.

GRATTAN, C. HARTLEY. *The Three Jameses* (Rev. ed.; New York: New York University Press, 1962), pp. 303–09.

GREENE, GRAHAM. "The Portrait of a Lady," *The Lost Childhood and Other Essays* (New York: Viking, 1952), pp. 40–44.

GRENANDER, M. E., BEVERLY J. RAHN, and FRANCINE VALVO. "The Time-Scheme in *The Portrait of a Lady*," *American Literature*, XXXII (May, 1960), pp. 127–35.

HAFLEY, JAMES. "Malice in Wonderland," *Arizona Quarterly*, XV (Spring, 1959), pp. 5–12.

HOLDER-BARELL, ALEXANDER. *The Development of Imagery and its Functional Significance in Henry James's Novels.* (Berne: Francke Verlag, 1959), pp. 57, 63, 66–67, 71–72, 90–91, 101–102, 106–108, 124–25, 129–30, 140–41.

HOLLAND, LAURENCE BEDWELL. *The Expense of Vision: Essays on the Craft of Henry James* (New York: Princeton University Press, 1964), pp. 3–54.

*JAMES, HENRY. *The Notebooks of Henry James*, eds. F. O. Matthiessen, and Kenneth B. Murdock (New York: Oxford University Press, 1947), pp. 15–18.

*———. "Preface," *The Novels and Tales of Henry James* (New York: Charles Scribner's Sons, 1908), III; *The Art of the Novel*, ed. by R. P. Blackmur (New York: Charles Scribner's Sons, 1934), pp. 40–58.

JEFFERSON, D. W. *Henry James and the Modern Reader* (New York: St. Martin's Press, 1964), pp. 108–13, 133–36; *Henry James* (New York: Grove, 1961), pp. 36–43.

*KELLEY, CORNELIA P. *The Early Development of Henry James.* University of Illinois Studies in Language and Literature, No. XV (Urbana: University of Illinois Press, 1930), pp. 284–300; Rev. ed., "Introduction" by Lyon S. Richardson (Urbana, 1965).

KENNEY, BLAIR GATES. "The Two Isabeles: A Study in Distortion," *Victorian Newsletter*, No. 25 (Spring, 1964), pp. 15–17.

*KETTLE, ARNOLD. *An Introduction to the English Novel*, (London: Hutchinson House, 1953, II 13–34.

KRAUSE, SYDNEY J. "James's Revisions of the Style of *The Portrait of a Lady*," *American Literature*, XXX (March, 1958), 76–88.

KROOK, DOROTHEA. *The Ordeal of Consciousness in Henry James* (Cambridge: Cambridge University Press, 1962), pp. 26–61, 357–69.

LEAVIS, F. R. *The Great Tradition: George Eliot, Henry James, Joseph Conrad* (London: George Stewart, 1949), pp. 85–94, 109–15, 146–53; (Garden City: Doubleday Anchor Books, 1954), pp. 155–87.

———. "*The Portrait of a Lady* Reprinted," *Scrutiny*, XV (Summer, 1948), pp. 235–41.

LEAVIS, Q. D. "A Note on Literary Indebtedness: Dickens, George Eliot, Henry James," *Hudson Review*, VIII (Autumn, 1955), pp. 423–28.

LEBOWITZ, NAOMI. *The Imagination of Loving: Henry James's Legacy to the Novel* (Detroit: Wayne State University Press, 1965), pp. 64–86 and *passim*.

LERNER, DANIEL. "The Influence of Turgenev on Henry James," *Slavonic Yearbook*, XX (December, 1941), pp. 28–54.

LEVINE, GEORGE. "Isabel, Gwendolen, and Dorothea," *ELH*, XXX (September, 1963), pp. 244–57.

LEVY, LEO B. *Versions of Melodrama: A Study of the Fiction and Drama of Henry James, 1865–1897* (Berkeley: University of California Press, 1957), pp. 40–52.

LILJEGREN, STEN BODVAR. *American and European in the Works of Henry James* (Lund: Lund Universities Arsskrift, 1920), pp. 17–35.

MARCELL, DAVID W. "High Ideals and Catchpenny Realities in Henry James's *The Portrait of a Lady*," *Essays in Modern American Literature*, ed. by Richard E. Langford (Deland, Fla.; Stetson University Press, 1963), pp. 26–34.

MATTHIESSEN, F. O. "James and the Plastic Arts," *Kenyon Review*, V (*Autumn,* 1943), pp. 538–40.

*———. "The Painter's Sponge and Varnish Bottle," *Henry James: The Major Phase* (New York: Oxford University Press, 1944), pp. 152–86.

MC ELDERRY, BRUCE R., JR. *Henry James* (New York: Twayne, 1965), pp. 58–63.

MC INTYRE, CLARA. "The Later Manner of Henry James," *PMLA*, XXVII (1912), pp. 361–64.

MILLETT, FRED B. "Introduction," *The Portrait of a Lady* (New York: Modern Library, 1951), pp. v–xxxv.

MILLS, A. R. "*The Portrait of a Lady* and Dr. Leavis," *Essays in Criticism*, XIV (October, 1964), pp. 380–387.

MONTEIRO, GEORGE. "John Hay's Review of *The Portrait of a Lady*," *Books at Brown*, XIX (1963), pp. 95–104; reprinted in *Henry James and John Hay: The Record of A Friendship* (Providence: Brown University Press, 1965), pp. 65–76.

MONTGOMERY, MARION. "The Flaw in the Portrait: Henry James vs. Isabel Archer," *University of Kansas City Review*, XXVI (March, 1960), pp. 215–20.

MOODY, A. D. "Henry James's Portrait of an Ideal," *The Melbourne Critical Review*, IV (1961), pp. 77–92.

*MURRAY, DONALD M. "The Critical Reception of Henry James in English Periodicals, 1875–1916," (Unpublished Dissertation, New York University, 1951), pp. 45–49.

OFFEN, SUSAN. "Isabel Archer: An Analysis of Her Fate," *Hunter College Studies*, No. 2 (1964), pp. 41–50.

PATTERSON, REBECCA. "Two Portraits of a Lady," *Midwest Quarterly*, I (Summer, 1960), pp. 343–61.

POIRIER, RICHARD. *The Comic Sense of Henry James: A Study of the Early Novels* (New York: Oxford University Press, 1960), pp. 183–246.

———. "The Portrait of a Lady," *The American Novel*, ed. by Wallace Stegner (New York: Basic Books, 1965), pp. 47–60.

POWERS, LYALL H. "*The Portrait of a Lady*: The Eternal Mystery of Things," *Nineteenth-Century Fiction*, XIV (September, 1959), pp. 143–55.

*RAHV, PHILIP. "The Heiress of All the Ages," *Image and Idea: Fourteen Essays on Literary Themes* (Rev. ed.; New York: New Directions, 1957), pp. 51–76.

RODENBECK, JOHN. "The Bolted Door in James's *The Portrait of a Lady*," *Modern Fiction Studies*, X (Winter, 1964–65), pp. 330–40.

SACKVILLE-WEST, EDWARD. *Inclinations* (London: Secker and Warburg, 1949), pp. 42–71.

*SANDEEN, ERNEST. "*The Wings of the Dove* and *The Portrait of a Lady*: A Study of Henry James's Later Phase," *PMLA*, LXIX (December, 1954), pp. 1060–75.

*SHARP, SISTER M. CORONA, O.S.U. *The Confidante in Henry James: Evolution and Moral Value of a Fictive Character* (South Bend: Notre Dame University Press, 1963), pp. 67–96.

SMITH, THOMAS F. "Balance in Henry James's *The Portrait of a Lady*," *Four Quarters*, XIII (May, 1964), 11–16.

SNOW, LOTUS. "The Disconcerting Poetry of Mary Temple: A Comparison of the Imagery of *The Portrait of a Lady* and *The Wings of the Dove*," *New England Quarterly*, XXXI (September, 1958), pp. 312–39.

STALLMAN, R. W. "The Houses That James Built—*The Portrait of a Lady*," *The Houses That James Built and Other Literary Studies* (East Lansing: Michigan State University Press, 1961), pp. 1–33; *Texas Quarterly*, I (Winter, 1958), 176–96 [earlier, briefer version].

———. "Who Was Gilbert Osmond?" *Modern Fiction Studies*, IV (Summer, 1958), pp. 127–35. [See Edel, above, for rebuttal].

*STEIN, WILLIAM BYSSHE. "*The Portrait of a Lady*: Vis Inertiae," *Western Humanities Review*, XIII (Spring, 1959), pp. 177–90.

STEWART, J. I. M. *Eight Modern Writers* (New York: Oxford Univ. Press, 1963), pp. 87–92.

SWAN, MICHAEL. *Henry James* (London: Arthur Barker, 1952), pp. 48–51.

TANNER, TONY. "The Fearful Self: Henry James's *The Portrait of a Lady*," *Critical Quarterly*, VII (Autumn, 1965), pp. 205–19.

*VAN GHENT, DOROTHY. *The English Novel: Form and Function* (New York: Rinehart, 1953), pp. 211–28, 428–39; (New York: Harper Torchbooks, 1961), pp. 211–28.

WARD, JOSEPH A. *The Imagination of Disaster: Evil in the Fiction of Henry James* (Lincoln: University of Nebraska Press, 1961), pp. 44–55.

WEGELIN, CHRISTOF. *The Image of Europe in Henry James* (Dallas: Southern Methodist University Press, 1958), pp. 63–78.

WEST, REBECCA. *Henry James* (London: Nisbet, 1916), pp. 70ff.

WILLIAM, PAUL O. "James' *The Portrait of a Lady*," *Explicator*, XXII (March, 1964), item 7.

For continuing studies of *The Portrait of a Lady*, see the annual bibliographies (May issues) of *PMLA*, the quarterly issues of *American Literature*, and the monthly issues of *Abstracts of English Studies*.

DATE DUE